Communication, technology and society

# Communication, technology and society

Lelia Green

SAGE Publications

London • Thousand Oaks • New Delhi

For my uncles and aunts:
Philip and Gail, Colin and Jackie, Richard and Anne,
David and Carol, and Edith;
and in memory of Ted, Kay and Tom, and Lucinda.
There's nothing quite like the extended family. Thank you all.

Copyright © Lelia Green 2001

First published in 2002 by
Allen & Unwin
83 Alexander Street
Crows Nest NSW 2065
Australia

SAGE Publications Ltd
6 Bonhill Street
London EC2A 4PU

SAGE Publications Inc
2455 Teller Road
Thousand Oaks, California 91320

SAGE Publications India Pvt Ltd
32, M-Block Market
Greater Kailash—I
New Delhi 110 048

**British Library Cataloguing in Publication data**

A catalogue record for this book is available from the British Library
ISBN 0-7619-4708-6 (hbk)
ISBN 0-7619-4709-4 (pbk)

**Library of Congress catalog record available**

Set in Bembo 11.5/13 pt by Midland Typesetters, Maryborough, Victoria
Printed by South Wind Productions, Singapore
10 9 8 7 6 5 4 3 2 1

# CONTENTS

The mythology of technology • Is technology neutral?
Mythology and gun control • Technology's relationship to
power and privilege • The method and the mythology of the
electric light bulb • The ABC of technological advantage
• Progress—for whom? • Being postmodern • The challenge
of change • Conclusion

Piecing together an understanding of technoculture • The
social control of the telephone • Discourse analysis and
the social biography of things • The expectation and experience of technology use • The theories of adoption and
diffusion • High and low involvement in technology adoption
• Adopter characteristics • Factors which affect product
diffusion • Interpersonal influence • Opinion leaders
• VALS (Values and lifestyles segmentation) • Conclusion

What is a 'domesticated technology'? • Integrating
technology into the household • Imagining community
• Boundary markers • Technology as a boundary-breaker
• Power and consumption • Maslow's hierarchy of needs
• Applying Maslow's theory to online behaviour • Household

telecommunications: the language of debate • A global
information infrastructure • Regulation and national identity
• Regulating freedoms of speech and communication
• Undermining government: media and communications
underground • Regulating the access and dissemination of
information • Moral panics • Conclusion

# FIGURES AND TABLES

## FIGURES

## TABLES

# ACKNOWLEDGMENTS

No significant milestone in my life is achieved without the love and support of an army of friends and helpers. I'd like to acknowledge: Judy Allan, Claire Andrews, Judy Clayden, Paddy Green, Sue Jarvis, Linda Jaunzems, Julie Johnson, Heather McLean and Elizabeth Weiss, without whose help this book would not exist as it does; Matt Allen, Julie Atkinson, Maureen Baker, Trevor Barr, Sue Bessell-Browne, Fay Campbell, Jeanette Connolly, Emma Cotter, Steve Doyle, Lynne Frolich, Rod Giblett, Paul Godfrey, Robert Jaunzems, Alan McKee, Russell Miller, Tom O'Regan, Marge Perry, Emma Portwood, Debbie Rodan, Debbie Sadique, Mim Smith-Blaber and Peter White for their help along the way; my first ever Virtual Communities/Technoculture class, with thanks for all they taught me: Eddy Ata, Alison Bugno, Zoe Byrne, Russell Carman, Jessica Hayes, Katie James, Adam Koutsoukos, Lee McDonald, Shonay Mitkus, Sarah Morgan, Marian Palandri, Rebecca Richardson, Stacey Thorne, Steven Wayman, Masafumi Yokota; the Australian and New Zealand Communication Association and the journal editorial teams for the *Australian Journal of Communication* and *Media International Australia incorporating Culture and Policy*, especially Helen Molnar, Ros Petelin, John Sinclair, Graeme Turner and Helen Wilson; Jenny Benjamin, Carmel Elwell, Liz Ferrier, Nadine Henley, Rachel Hutson, Gabrielle O'Ryan, Joan Smith, Pam Steenbergen and Sue Turnbull for talking books with me; my children, Carmen and Benedict Guinery, for being wonderful (most of the time).

This book was made possible by a grant of Academic Study Leave through the Faculty of Communications, Health and Science, Edith

Cowan University; and by the support of my Dean, Pat Garnett, Head of School, Robyn Quin and Brian Shoesmith.

I am grateful to the following authors and publishers for work included in this book:

Figure 1.2, The photographer, R. C. James; Figure 2.1, Morgan Stanley Technology Research, first published in W. F. Arens, 1999, *Contemporary Advertising*, 7th edn, Irwin/McGraw Hill, Boston, p. 513; Figure 2.2, McGraw Hill Publishers, first published in D. Hawkins, C. Neal, P. Quester and R. Best, 1994, *Consumer Behaviour: Implications for Marketing Strategies*, Richard D. Irwin, Sydney, p. 414; Figure 2.3, McGraw Hill Publishers, adapted from a figure first published in D. Hawkins, C. Neal, P. Quester and R. Best, 1994, *Consumer Behaviour: Implications for Marketing Strategies*, Richard D. Irwin, Sydney, p. 417; Figure 2.4, Prentice Hall Australia, first published in L. Schiffman, D. Bednall, J. Watson and L. Kanuk, 1997, *Consumer Behaviour*, Prentice Hall, Sydney, p. 485; Figure 2.6, Stamford Research Institute International, first published in D. Hawkins, C. Neal, P. Quester and R. Best, 1994, *Consumer Behaviour: Implications for Marketing Strategies*, Richard D. Irwin, Sydney, p. 350; Figure 5.3, Tomito Tetsuro and MIT Press, first published in T. Tetsuro, 1980, 'The new electronic media and their place in the information market of the future', in *Newspapers and Democracy: International Essays on a Changing Medium*, ed. A. Smith, MIT Press, Mass., p. 54; Figure 5.4, Barry Jones, Oxford University Press and Australian Bureau of Statistics, adapted from a figure published in B. Jones, 1995, *Sleepers, Wake! Technology and the Future of Work*, 4th edn, Oxford University Press, Melbourne, p. 58; Figures 5.5 and 5.6, Spyros Makridakis, update of graphs published in S. Makridakis, 1995, 'The forthcoming information revolution: Its impacts on society and firms', *Futures*, vol. 27, no. 8, October, pp. 799–822, cited in G. Hearn, T. Mandeville and D. Anthony, 1998, *The Communication Superhighway: Social and Economic Change in the Digital Age*, Allen & Unwin, Sydney, pp. 4, 5; Figure 10.1, Georgia Technology Research Corporation, www.cc.gatech.edu/gvu/user_surveys; Figure 12.1, Barry Jones, Oxford University Press and Australian Bureau of Statistics, adapted from a figure published in B. Jones, 1995, *Sleepers, Wake! Technology and the Future of Work*, 4th edn, Oxford University Press, Melbourne, p. 134; Figure 12.2, Maureen Baker adapted from information in M. Baker, 2001, *Families, Labour and Love*, Allen & Unwin, Sydney, table 7.2.

Table 2.1, McGraw Hill Publishers, adapted from information published
in D. Hawkins, C. Neal, P. Quester and R. Best, 1994, *Consumer Behaviour: Implications for Marketing Strategies*, Richard D. Irwin, Sydney,
pp. 414–16; Table 4.2, Oxford University Press, first published in
B. Jones, 1995, *Sleepers, Wake! Technology and the Future of Work*, 4th edn,
Oxford University Press, Melbourne, p. 33, after Y. Masuda, 1972, *Social
Impact of Computerization: An Application of the Pattern Model for Industrial
Society*, Kodansha, Tokyo; Table 5.1, NUA Internet Surveys at www.nua.
net/surveys/how_many_online/index.htm, and adapted from a table
published in T. Barr, 2000, *newmedia.com.au*, Allen & Unwin, Sydney,
p. 122; Table 11.1, Rob Kitchin and Angus Kennedy, adapted from
material first published in R. Kitchin, 1998, *Cyberspace: The World in the
Wires*, John Wiley & Sons Ltd, Chichester, p. 7 and A. Kennedy, 1999,
*The Internet: The Rough Guide 2000*, Rough Guides Ltd, London, p. 458.

| | |
|---|---|
| | is a construct or product of the individual or group that creates the understanding, and all knowledge is subjective. |
| **CSO:** | Community Service Obligation: an obligation (e.g., upon a corporation or utility) to provide a community service, even where this may not be profitable |
| **cultural studies:** | the study of culture, sub-cultures, popular culture, etc., often using ethnographic tools and post-structuralist, and/or postmodern discourses |
| **customer service:** | presumes that the consumer is rich enough to be a customer. Citizenship is not sufficient—wealth is also required (*see* public interest). |
| **cyber:** | commonly used as a prefix to indicate 'pertaining to the digital or virtual'—thus cyberspace, a digital construction of space; and cyborg, a meld of digital/organic (often conceived of as actually-living machines) |
| **cybersex:** | sexual behaviour involving online interaction |
| **cyberspace:** | term coined by William Gibson to refer to the cyber-world created by the convergence of IT/computers, digital media and telecommunications |
| **determinism:** | the notion that something is so powerful that it is beyond human control, e.g., in technological determinism |
| **digitisation:** | the rendering of information in digital form. In analogue phone services, the sound is modulated at the mouthpiece, retaining the pattern of sound waves until it is converted back into waves at the earpiece of the listener. Digitised sound is encoded algorithmically, using on/off states, and allows compacting of the signal with consequent benefits in terms of carriage capacity, cost, and varied and flexible delivery channels. |

**discourse:** given that understanding depends upon the construction of meaning, a discourse frames the parameters within which meaning is shared with other/s—it involves the concept of communication. Feminism, for example, assumes that gender is a political as well as social construction and that to be feminine is to struggle with dominant masculine and patriarchal discourses. There is choice as to discourse/s employed (e.g., feminist, ecological, Christian), and several discourses can be used simultaneously. Once inside it, a discourse is unassailable—it is not possible to dismantle the discursive paradigm from within that discourse.

**DNA:** dioxyribonucleic acid (a nucleic acid) which, plus protein molecules, makes up chromosomes

**DVD:** digital video disk

**EFF:** Electronic Frontier Foundation: www.eff.org

**effects research:** a branch of audience/readership research which attempts to describe and quantify media effects, such as the effect of violent television images upon children, or of pornography upon sex offenders. (There is a tendency to assume that there is an effect; *see* construction of meaning.)

**electronic and microelectronic:** applied to microchip technologies where the electrical circuits have been progressively miniaturised to allow quantum leaps in available processing capacity while minimising physical size; often used to indicate some element of in-built digital control

**email:** electronic mail, the use of computers in LANs or the Internet to communicate privately (between individuals) or semi-publicly

**ethnography:** the study of patterns of living of a series of individuals, or of a group of people. Tends to provide large amounts of data, which are affected by the presence of the observer/researcher, and which reflect their priorities. Often associated with postmodern discourses.

**fourth estate:** this refers to the media and/or journalists in the media, acknowledging their political importance. The three estates which made up the estates-general in France at the time of the French Revolution were: nobility (first estate), clergy (second estate) and commoners (third estate); hence journalists constituted the fourth estate.

**gender:** a social construction with political implications, justified by biological difference. Conceptualisations of biological difference are also social constructions (*see* discourse).

**genre:** an identifiable form (or discourse) which allows texts to be categorised according to whether they conform to an appropriate genre paradigm, e.g., detective fiction includes clues; romances have a happy ending. A text need not be written, or be a media product; it can be any human/social construct—a life or a city. To view such entities as texts, however, a reader would normally subscribe to a cultural studies-type discourse, and use appropriate discursive practices.

**global/isation:** the notion that a networked world is interconnected—rather than divided—by ICTs, and that the whole is greater than the sum of the parts

**global village:** the idea that better communications reduce the relevance of physical distance and allow participants to network as if they contribute to a shared community

**GVU:** graphics, visualisation, usability

**hardwired:** machines that are permanently interconnected are 'hardwired', as opposed to

|  | stand-alone machines that connect to a network with a modem |
| **hegemony:** | a concept which describes the encircling/engulfing power of dominant discourses (capitalism, patriarchy, technological determinism, etc.) to set the frameworks, or paradigms, within which meaning is constructed |
| **HIV:** | human immunodeficiency virus |
| **http:** | hypertext transfer protocol—protocol that allows pages of text held on servers accessible via the web to be accessed by remote computers |
| **ICT, ICTs:** | information and communication technologies |
| **imagined community** | a term coined by Benedict Anderson whereby people imagine/conceive of the nation to which they belong as a community |
| **imperialism/ colonialism:** | associated with the domination by one culture or country (the colonial power) of other countries or cultures (the colonies). Involves the enrichment of the imperial power by the impoverishment of the oppressed. |
| **information:** | central point on the chaos–data–information–wisdom–knowledge continuum. According to the semantic (= 'meaning') definition, information is organised data with the capacity to inform. Classic information theory sees information as data; it needs to be measurable, but doesn't need to be understood. |
| **information rich/poor:** | as the knowledge explosion accelerates, those with access to the information produced—the information rich—become richer. At the same time, the information gap widens between the information rich and poor. |
| **information society:** | a description of nations whose economies are based upon information. Conceived |

broadly, the information economy includes libraries, education, law, administration, media, etc. Information societies are sometimes referred to as post-industrial societies, because the industrial base is no longer judged to be the prime determinant of wealth. These societies are characterised by wide ICT use and by a knowledge explosion.

**intelligent communications:** this has artificial intelligence built into the communications system, monitoring flow and quality of information communicated, making sure it reaches its destination in the correct form, e.g., ISDN

**interactive:** the capacity of a communication medium to be altered by, or to have its products altered by, the actions of a user or audience. A technology which requires input from a user to work effectively, e.g., voice messaging.

**interface:** the material/system which both joins and separates two different entities—hardware and software, machine and organism

**Internet:** the interconnected, global network of computers including the World Wide Web, email and proprietary networks

**Intranet:** a network that connects a restricted number of member computers, e.g., in a workplace or organisation. A LAN.

**IP:** Internet protocol that defines how packets of information get from place to place; also, intellectual property

**IRC:** Internet relay chat. Synchronous (= same time) chat over the Internet using text and/or images and sound. Sometimes called simply 'chat'.

**ISDN:** integrated, switched digital network (an intelligent system). ISDN pathways utilise a variety of communications media, e.g., satellite and/or fibre optics.

| | |
|---|---|
| **ISP:** | Internet Service Provider—an organisation that sells access to the Internet |
| **IT:** | information technology, e.g., computer |
| **Kbps:** | kilobits per second |
| **LAN:** | a local area network |
| **liberalisation:** | used to indicate that the commercial market-place will play a bigger part in regulating goods and services, e.g., in telecommunications |
| **listserver:** | A server-based list of email recipients, usually accessed by a single key term. Thus my email package sends an email to 220+ people when I write 'anzca' in the send-to line. (ANZCA refers to the Australian and New Zealand Communication Association.) |
| **LMAO:** | chat for 'laugh my ass off' |
| **LOL:** | chat for 'laugh out loud' |
| **Mbps:** | megabits per second |
| **merkin:** | female pubic wig, used in burlesque shows as a defence against the accusation that women were unclothed; and in early theatre by boys/men acting female parts |
| **mixed economy broadcasting:** | this indicates that major sectors of the media environment are funded differently, e.g., commercial, public service (funded through taxes) and community (funded through sponsorship and subscription) |
| **modems:** | *mod*ulator-*dem*odulators, used to transfer digital data between computers using analogue phone lines |
| **MOO:** | multiple object-oriented—virtual environment created and altered by the participants who assign meanings and values to 'objects' which can be stored in a database for future use (subset of MUD) |
| **moral panic:** | when a society or mainstream group reacts to a change in the environment as if it 'threatens life as we know it' |
| **MSP:** | minimum service provision—a service so central to the society that  regulators work |

|                                     | to make it universally available (sometimes USP, universal service provision), e.g., telephone, television, mail |
|-------------------------------------|---------------------------------------------------------------------|
| **MUD:**                            | multiple-user domain—textual virtual environment with built-in features described to users as they enter the 'room' |
| **multimedia:**                     | the use of interactive multiple media components which respond to inputs, e.g., a computer programme through which a user can trigger text, graphics, pictures and sound |
| **myths:**                          | shared understandings which inform a cultural group as to their nature and unity—for example, in the creation of national identity. Stories, fictions, narratives and legends frequently serve mythic ends. |
| **narrative theory:**               | readers bring to an event or experience a sense of before and after required to understand the story or myth |
| **national identity/ies:**          | more than flags, anthems and coinage, national identity is constructed through a sense of 'imagined community' and rests upon shared narratives and myths |
| **Net:**                            | the totality of networks—email, proprietary (e.g., AOL), www, etc.; contraction of 'Internet' |
| **Netizen:**                        | a citizen of the Net—someone who sees themselves as part of the Net community |
| **newbie:**                         | a newcomer to the Net, or to a room, group or discussion area |
| **nouveau information poor:**       | people who lose access to ICTs as a result of sudden poverty or change in life circumstances, e.g., unemployment, divorce |
| **nouveau information riche:**      | people who get sudden access to ICTs, e.g., through promotion, becoming a student |
| **NWICO:**                          | New World Information and Communication Order, a political movement involving Third World countries |
| **objectivity:**                    | *see* construction of meaning |
| **online community:**               | 'virtual' community that exists solely as a result of online interaction |

**opinion leader:**    someone whose opinions are sought by others in the context of personal decision-making

**paradigm:**    the framework of understandings within which discourses are constructed and communicated. Analysing a paradigm can be the first step to resisting or subverting the hegemonic power of an elite whose interests that paradigm serves. Paradigms can be analysed using, for example, discourse analysis.

**pomo:**    postmodern

**post-colonial:**    *see* imperialism/colonialism. Post-coloniality involves living with the effects of colonisation.

**post-industrial:**    *see* information society

**postmodern/ism:**    a philosophy which sees life characterised by the random, the fragmented, the contradictory and the shifting. Postmodernism denies the possibility of 'truth', 'objectivity' and 'certainty' (including about the pomo).

**premodern:**    peasant, pre-industrial society

**privatisation:**    the passing into private ownership, usually by share float, of publicly (government) owned industries

**profiling:**    the use of information to create a data-based identikit of an individual or group

**public interest:**    requires consideration of wider social costs and benefits than company profitability or government efficiency.

**public service:**    whereas 'public service' privileges the needs of the public regardless of their financial status, customer service considers the needs of people rich enough to be customers. The introduction of user-pays changes a public service into customer service.

**reader:**    one who reads, but also the active power of the person constructing meaning and interpreting a text

**RL:**    real life (as opposed to VL)

| | |
|---|---|
| **sci-fi:** | science fiction—often used to explore social and moral technocultural issues |
| **social determinism:** | sees technology as expressing the priorities of the social elites which create or utilise the technology (*see* determinism) |
| **sovereignty:** | (mythic) idea that a nation is independent, and in control of its own future |
| **stories:** | social constructs which explore or explain some element of life, often serving a mythic purpose |
| **technological determinism:** | technology constructed as being outside social control, determining future social development and direction |
| **technological/technical dynamism:** | acceleration of technological change; the merging of new technologies to form novel products and resources as in 'convergence' |
| **telecommunications:** | communications at a distance, usually implying cable, satellite, broadcasting spectrum, fibre optics, etc. |
| **text:** | *see* genre |
| **TNC:** | transnational corporation (part of the cause and effect of globalisation) |
| **UK:** | United Kingdom |
| **UNESCO:** | United Nations Educational, Scientific and Cultural Organisation |
| **universal service:** | *see* MSP |
| **URL:** | uniform resource locator—the addressing system for the WWW |
| **user-pays:** | *see* public service |
| **VALS, VALS2:** | values and lifestyles segmentation—a proprietary market segmentation and analysis tool owned by Stamford Research Institute International |
| **VCR:** | videocassette recorder |
| **VL:** | virtual life (as opposed to RL) |
| **VR:** | virtual reality |
| **WWW:** | the World Wide Web—the section of the Internet where information and opinion are accessible through a search engine and a URL |

# INTRODUCTION

The challenge with writing a book on communication, technology and society—apart from the fact that it takes us on a journey from alphabet to cybersex—is where to start, rather than what to say. The task brings issues of technology and culture into focus, but it also affects policy matters and the structure of society. Our lives are articulated around one or more of these themes, yet so little attention is paid to the cross-over points which illuminate the ways in which the whole is greater than the sum of the parts. This, then, is the rationale for the book—to celebrate and interrogate the powerful and dynamic ways in which our societies and our lives interweave themes of:

- culture with society, technology and policy;
- society with technology, policy and culture;
- technology with policy, culture and society; and
- policy with culture, society and technology.

In addressing technology, society, policy and culture as a way of investigating technoculture and technocultures, my aim is to examine the raw materials with which we construct our sense of ourselves, and of the communities in which we live and to which we feel connected. A specific objective is to explore the digital age, and the meanings of space, time and the virtually real. The book ultimately focuses upon the technoculture of cyberculture and the Internet, and one effect of this is to centre-stage the world of digital communications. These arenas concern a still-emerging human experience—we're in the process of making sense of what we're learning. Further, as we learn more about the digitally connected world, we also learn more about ourselves.

The dynamism that fuels the development of digital technologies is outstripping the ability of researchers and investigators to keep up with the pace of change. Some of the research we'd most love to have has yet to be started, let alone completed. Detailed ethnographic audience studies—such as those that (coincidentally) marked 50 years of television—have yet to investigate in depth the multi-faceted ways in which Internet technoculture interacts with our daily lives. In the absence of ready-packaged answers, these chapters set out to explore relevant questions by using existing research that illuminates the major topic. Such research might analyse broadcasting, or other societies, or a historical technological moment with implications for culture, like the domestication of electricity. For some questions, the research means going back to the origins of language, and to the way in which the brain evolves physiologically within an individual's lifetime. Elsewhere there may be an emphasis on marketing theory: how technological innovations spread in our society. Nonetheless, the studies and under-standings discussed in this book have helped form our sense of the mediated world in which we live, and are currently forming our expectations of contemporary technoculture and our interactions with it.

One of the critical issues raised by technoculture is that of com-munity, and what we mean by society and connectedness when we have choices which include the digital and the analogue, the virtual and the real. A variety of case studies across time, space and culture have been chosen to illustrate elements of the technocultural debate. In talking about society and technology, however, it is difficult to avoid using the shorthand developed over the decades to refer to the First (or the industrialised, or the developed or the western) World. It is possible to talk about information societies, or knowledge economies, or post-industrial nations—but the implications are the same. All these terms lump the wealthy nations together and position the poorer nations as 'lacking'. Further, there is nothing uniformly 'western' about all richer countries. Rich countries include Australia and Japan, although these nations might be more conventionally seen from the vantage point of the Anglo-American English-language hegemony as 'South' or 'East'.

Given the opportunity, the Third (or developing, or newly industri-alised, or pre-digital) World tends to refer to itself as the South. Citizens of Southern countries also point to their (usual) status as post-colonial nations, since the seeds of their current poverty were often sown in their exploitation as colonies of former colonial powers. Indeed, the notion of the First World is nearly synonymous with that of 'the formerly colonial' world. These concerns are more than semantic, and they are flagged here to acknowledge the difficulties faced in discussing them. Nonetheless, most readers of this book will be of the First World, so I have used western terms to refer to the developed nations of the globe.

A discussion of technoculture which involves axes of society, technology, policy and culture necessarily also covers issues such as the 'neutrality' of technology, the public interest, popular culture, regulation, gender, modernism and postmodernism and the nature of the information society. Mediated communications are so important to information societies that more than just the technology changes whenever new communication technologies are introduced. There is a cycle operating here: cultures create new communication technologies, which become integrated as technocultures, which themselves fuel further technological innovation.

All changes in communications patterns have complex social and cultural ramifications, and eventuate from complex social and technological forces. One role of policy and regulation is to attempt to minimise 'negative' change while maximising the positive benefits. At the same time, the uncertainty concerning new media, and their impact upon existing social structures, has—over time—precipitated a succession of moral panics, which are also discussed here. Established commercial media are not noted for their generosity to competitors, and it is unsurprising that many of the moral panics circulating about pornography on the Net, Internet stalking, Web addiction, hate sites, etc. are promulgated in the older media forms.

In terms of multiple-user domains (MUDs), virtual communities and interactive sites, the Internet can be conceptualised as a location for individuals to produce a kind of folk technoculture, embedded within the lives of people who create and consume it. The Internet provides the tantalising possibility of a partial rebuttal to the concerns of cultural purists who lament the fact that much popular culture is mass-produced by media interests to circulate at a profit, displacing more locally based folk culture. As well as being a site for popular technoculture, the Internet is a subject of popular culture. Hopefully the ideas and cases contained within this book will serve to enrich and challenge future interactions with film, television, magazines, the Internet and other cultural products which address our nature as human beings and our lives as we experience them in our technocultural societies—past, present and elsewhere.

Technoculture as a term is frequently used in a woolly manner to refer to technologies implicated in western cultures, and to constructions of culture that incorporate technological aspects. An opportunity to convey a specific meaning is lost in this everyday usage. Arguably, the concept of technoculture should be reserved for communications technologies used in the mediated construction of culture. To be technocultural, the technology concerned must facilitate cultural communication across space and/or time and should, in some way, raise issues of place. Since culture is a construction involving communication, and more than one person, technoculture involves the communication of cultural material in technological contexts—which is to say, other than the face-to-face. If this definition were to be adopted, future discussions of technoculture would indicate reference to a technology that allows the construction of culture across space and/or time.

A reading of *Technoculture*, the Penley and Ross (1991) edited collection, indicates that the term 'technoculture' has evolved to mean something different from that hinted at in their critical text. 'Like most of the contributors to this volume', they write,

> we, as editors, are conscientiously aligned with the technology-as-social-control school of thought and reject the post-industrialist fantasy of technical sweetness and light . . . Technoculture, as we conceive it, is located as much in the work of everyday fantasies and actions as at the level of corporate or military decision-making . . . *Technoculture* [their book] is presented in the knowledge that the odds are firmly stacked against the efforts of those committed to creating technological counter cultures (Penley & Ross 1991, p. xiii).

Their collection then examines a range of cultural sites: female reproduction, AIDS treatments, heterosexual women's written fantasies about *Star Trek* characters Captain Kirk and Mr Spock in a homosexual relationship, a Japanese erotic computer game and Bob Geldof/Live Aid/popular music.

The corporate–military complex is absent from Penley and Ross' book, but opposition to these power elites is implicit in the book's contents. Their edited collection addresses instances where technology and culture have been harnessed to challenge and resist the status quo: an implicit assertion that technoculture is a term usually associated with the actions of technological/power/cultural elites. The volume serves as a celebration that such a power-driven construction of technoculture is undermined in a variety of everyday and unexpected cultural contexts. Some of Penley and Ross' examples still resonate strongly today—particularly the 'dissident use' of video cameras (designed for surveillance) to monitor the actions of surveillance and law enforcement organisations. On the whole, however, it is difficult to recognise Penley and Ross' 1991 definition of technoculture as referring to the same subjects and issues associated with the term today.

Franklyn argues:

> Like democracy, technology is a multifaceted entity. It includes activities as well as a body of knowledge, structures as well as the act of structuring. Our language itself is poorly suited to describe the complexity of technological interactions. The interconnectedness of many of these processes, the fact that they are so complexly interrelated, defies our normal push-me-pull-you, cause and consequence metaphors. How does one speak about something that is both fish and water, means as well as end? That's why I think it is better to examine limited settings where one puts technology in context, because context is what matters most (Franklyn 1999, pp. 14–15).

The creation and circulation of culture is the essential context within which technoculture operates.

Culture itself is generally accepted as a social construction, not a 'given' (Game 1991). Anything and everything human can be constructed as a cultural text—a life, a car, music, the stock exchange—and we write our culture as a collection of such texts. The implication is that the creation of culture is an ongoing process involving individuals in communicative exchanges of appropriation, opposition and negotiation. There is no certainty (or reality) apart from what we choose to see as such. In contrast, technology seems scientific, and certain—bound by laws of physics, and cause and effect. Nonetheless, technology has been a contested concept since at least the 1960s when Marshall McLuhan used it as a description of written language.

We tend not to think of language as technological, since the term 'technology' is more frequently applied to innovative 'high-tech' technologies (Wajcman 1991, p. 144). Unlike high-tech technology, language is everywhere, discussed at length and easy to get to use. Given this, Dale Spender (1995) and others have argued that language has been used as a technology of domination. Female illiteracy was used for centuries as a means of locking women out of power and decision-making, analogous to the way in which the medieval Church used ecclesiastical Latin to maintain a stranglehold upon the affairs of state, and to oppress the vernacular. Thus, in the early 1990s, Spender challenged women to become cyber-literate; to help construct cyberspace as a place where women would want to be.

James Carey's 'ritual view' of communication (Carey 1989) suggests that it is communication—including use of the technology of language—that creates culture, and perpetuates its existence. So is it possible to see culture as necessarily related to technology, and technology as intrinsically dependent upon culture? While it is hard to conceive of a technological innovation that is not grounded in the lived culture of the innovator, it is possible that the technological could represent an innovation within an individual life, shared with no one, but useful in the specific life-context of the innovator. In terms of absolute difference, therefore, the cultural is a necessarily shared construction—because it involves communication—whereas the technological need not be.

While McLuhan argues that the written alphabet operates as a technology, MacKenzie and Wajcman (1999 [1985]), and probably Beniger (1986) would debate whether it was the technology of language which led to a new cultural repertoire, or changes in the cultural repertoire which led to the invention of alphabetic language. Leaving aside the social determinism of the technology of language and/or the technological determination of the language of society, if something as cultural as language can be termed 'technological', are we suggesting that all culture can be reframed as technology, and as technocultural?

What is technoculture? Can electricity be constructed as an example of a technoculture, or a swimsuit, or a cottage garden? An apartment block, a batik company and synchronised swimming could all have technocultural elements. These examples may be more or less reliant upon technological innovations in building, or in fabric painting, or cultural innovations in music, movement and in using plants for recreation and display. The balance between the techno/cultural might be constructed as more towards the technological in the case of electricity, for example, and more towards the cultural in the case of synchronised swimming. Such ubiquitousness creates imprecision, however.

Timothy Druckrey posits a progressive societal shift from 'industrial culture to media culture to information culture to technoculture' (1994, p. 6). This book argues against such a progression: technoculture is not a time-bound social interval, but a communication context. If we decline to use 'technoculture' to mean 'all technologies created through human culture', and instead reserve it exclusively for 'tools of mediated communication through which cultural material is created and circulated', then its usefulness increases. Thus the fridge, the car and electricity would not be technocultural (although they might enable technocultural exchanges), but written language, the phone, the book, films, television and the Internet would be.

The Internet, for example, is undoubtedly high-tech: it is so involved with directing the future (Wajcman 1991, p. 144) that it is difficult to find discussions of the Internet that are not themselves future-oriented. Internet culture is not a virtual culture but a real culture operating in virtual space, created through ritual communication in the context of Internet interactivity. Such a culture is necessarily technological; such a technology is necessarily cultural. In Kitchin's (1998) terms, the Internet is the 'world in the wires'—even where there is not a wire in sight and where no world is visible. Both Franklyn's fish and water are implicit, but absent.

There are no indigenous peoples inhabiting the Internet, so there is no complicating evidence of an Internet culture with pre-modern face-to-face communication—a culturally 'spoken' word before the technologically 'written' language. Internet culture is always mediated culture. Further, no Internet culture can be unproblematically imagined as 'looming out of an immemorial past', to use Benedict Anderson's (1991 [1983]) description of the nation. The Internet is a settler culture—with time, space and place all reconceptualised and reconstructed to fit within the cyberspatial context (although we could argue about an evolutionary trajectory of culture on the Internet which starts with the Nerdgeek and moves towards a more inclusive present).

If Morley and Robins' (1995, p. 128) argument is accepted—that 'place' should be seen as 'spaces of interaction'—then the Internet's space of interaction is the place central to the cultural project of ritual communication. Cyberspace offers unparallelled global opportunities for interactivity, and the lack of bounded areas make it no less real a place than the Roman Forum or the American Senate, and no less real a space than the human mind. Cyberspace is accessed by the terminal, screen and keyboard used by individual cybertravellers. The communication and the cultural creation which characterise cyberspace occur more in the minds of individual participants than on any server—even as culture is written, literally, in front of a participant's eyes.

Donna Haraway argues that: 'Late twentieth-century machines have made thoroughly ambiguous the difference between natural and artificial, mind and body, self-developing and externally designed, and many other distinctions that used to apply to organisms and machines' (1991, p. 152). The screen at the edge of cyberspace—the point at which the hardware, the software and the individual interact—also screens the individual from the contents of cyberspace, and from its other users. This is, arguably, the specific cyborg juncture for everyday twenty-first century (western) life. Here the emotion, the psychology and the culture of humans (as organisms) are translated into digital cyber communication for the construction of culture and understanding through interactivity in a virtual, not material, domain.

If we assume that the Internet can be constructed as fully techno-cultural, since it is a culture that exists only through communication in conjunction with technology, what can we identify as the technocultural antecedents that set the scene for cyberspace? Technologically, the high-tech is preceded by the (now) low-tech, and by the ex-tech, superseded eons ago (arguably written language might fit into this category). 'Family trees' of technological offspring might place the Internet and digital technologies at the farthermost reaches of the outermost leaves, and position the telegraph in the roots, and the telephone at the juncture of the trunk and the branches. Television sits in the upper canopy, *en route* to the Internet. If the Internet is an example of the merging of technology, communication and culture in a contemporary technoculture, then the telegraph, the telephone and television may offer examples of a trajectory to this end-point—stepping stones along the way. These older technologies have all been used in the construction of culture, as part of Carey's (1989) conception of ritual communication.

Some technocultural tools—the telegraph, the computer, the digital phone—can be used remotely to program machinery and technological processes. These activities constitute the creation of communications channels operating without a direct human presence, remotely controlling the environment, allowing processes of technological integration and convergence to proliferate. This is not a cultural exchange, however. It does not create or circulate culture as part of a ritual view of communication. Such non-cultural usage of technology is not technocultural as such, but part of the progress of cultural activity using technological means. Technologies affect processes; technocultural tools affect perceptions.

In western societies, communities tend no longer to be based purely (or at all) upon geographical proximity and daily face-to-face contact. Dispersed social and cultural systems rely upon mediated communications for their existence and their strength. As well as using mediated communication to create and circulate culture, technocultures operate to negate the effects of space or time. In the case of the telegraph and telephone, this happens by allowing instantaneous communication across distance. With writing, printing, music and similar arts and sciences, technocultures make the ephemeral lasting by fixing a communication in a concrete place—as a photo, book or CD.

Further, the car and the plane, although not technocultural themselves, can be constructed as technoculturally relevant insofar as they permit different perceptions of the time and space that separate people. A journey that once took four weeks by sea may now take 20 hours. These perceptions of distance and separation can help make continuing cultural connections (and the use of technocultures to this end) seem more vivid and sustainable. When the 'ritual' communication occurs at the end of a journey of reunion, however, it is not technocultural but face-to-face.

This book argues that technoculture is too useful a word, and too useful a term, to be used indiscriminately (see also Green 2001). The term has the capacity to refer specifically to technologies that facilitate and mediate the communication through which culture is constructed. According to this definition, written language is a technology, and it is also technocultural. Spoken language, however, is not technocultural unless it is preserved in some way (e.g., tape-recorded) for transmission across time, or transported in some way (e.g., phone) for transmission across space. In both of these time/space instances, the technocultural element of the communication has the effect of impacting upon the user's sense of place, cognitively connecting the recipient (and the sender) to a different location, 'place'.

Changed perceptions are reflected in different cognitive processes and conceptual contexts. Human encounters in cyberspace impact upon people's ways of relating to others, reflecting new experiences and expertise gleaned from this technocultural environment. Cyberspace may be the quintessential example of high-tech technoculture in contemporary society, but it is only one of a number of examples, and will be superseded in time.

We bring the past with us into the present and the future, and if we feel disempowered at the prospect of 'the future', then we are effectively silencing our own voice and allowing other voices and perspectives to be heard more clearly. The discussions in this book are not the only possible ones, but they are among the many discussions we should be having about communication, technology and society. Hopefully this book will help stimulate debate and encourage conversants to contribute to the wider exploration of hopes and fears, options and opportunities as they are played out in technology and policy debates of the future—and in the choices we make concerning our cultures and our societies.

# 1

## WHAT FUELS TECHNOLOGY CHANGE?

### THE MYTHOLOGY OF TECHNOLOGY

Technology has a central role in all human culture and society. Whether the domestication of fire or the depictions of complex hunting rituals that adorn the caves at Lascaux, France, the beginnings of significant technologies tend to be mythologised. This is as true of the light bulb and the computer as it is of the Trojan horse of the ancient Greeks. The mythologising of technology means that we tell stories about how technologies started and the people who invented them. Such myths may have a foundation in fact, but their role is to celebrate these developments as important in our lives. They are created and sustained within our popular culture.

You will be aware of the story of Archimedes in the bathtub shouting 'Eureka!'—he had realised that a mass, immersed in water, displaces its own volume. In other words, he got into a full bath of water and it overflowed . . . Eureka! Archimedes suddenly understood that if he collected the water that overflowed his bath, he would be able to measure the precise volume of his body, even though it was irregular in shape. Similar tales are told of Thomas Edison and his work to perfect a filament for the electric light bulb. Edison's scientific method was one of 'trial and error'. He tried hundreds of potential filaments before he eventually found the right materials to deliver the properties he knew he needed. The specifications of the ideal filament, however, had been worked out long before the trial and error began, and that (intuitive and) deductive process will be discussed shortly. It is the Eureka moment that is mythologised, however, so our culture associates progress with individual inventors and moments of understanding and discovery.

What is rarely included in these myths of scientific and technological advancement is a sense of the *social environment* in which the discoveries are made. It is as if the advances happen in a vacuum, as if Newton were the first person to be hit on the head by a falling apple. Newton's flash of insight into the principle of gravity had more to do with the time and culture in which he was working than with him being bopped by a piece of fruit. The issue of gravity was on his intellectual agenda—just as issues of global warming, HIV/AIDS, cancer and globalisation are on ours.

Leonardo da Vinci is another thinker whose work has been mythologised extensively. Da Vinci's scientific work included an exploration, in principle, of the physics behind flight, the bicycle and the submarine— inventions which were not to be realised until hundreds of years later. For these inventions to be adopted, the cultural environment had to support the development of da Vinci's ideas, and nurture them to the point where they could become integrated into everyday life. The environment in Renaissance Italy acknowledged da Vinci's genius but chose to concentrate on the support and development of several of his other projects. Why are some ideas championed and developed while others languish for centuries—or never see the light of day?

Twenty years ago—and it may partly have been as a result of the feminist revolution in intellectual thought—the mythology of technology development and adoption was reconsidered. Donald MacKenzie and Judy Wajcman (1999 [1985]) collected together a number of case studies of different technologies and used them to argue that the vital ingredient determining which technologies are adopted, and which languish, is the *social circumstance*. This term 'social' includes economics, politics and existing infrastructure. MacKenzie and Wajcman's point is that it is wrong to see any given 'technology' as something that is as inevitable as the law of gravity. There was no necessity that computers would exist, or that—once existing—they would be connected into an Internet, or used to administer the taxation system. The reasons why things develop as they do are not technological reasons, they are social reasons.

The old way of looking at things was one of *technological determinism*. This perspective argued that it was the features of the technology that determined its use, and the role of a progressive society was to adapt to (and benefit from) technological change. The new way of looking at technology is *social determinism*. This suggests that society is responsible for the development and deployment of particular technologies. The technocultures in which we participate reflect the choices of elites in our societies, the people who have most say in how we plan for the future and how we allocate our resources.

## IS TECHNOLOGY NEUTRAL? MYTHOLOGY AND GUN CONTROL

At times when technology was perceived as being outside society, it made sense to talk about technology as neutral. It was as if technological progress and development were inevitable. No one could stop technological development, and no one could be blamed for the way it progressed. This viewpoint can be summed up in terms of the perspective that 'guns are neutral, it's up to us how we use them'. Such a perspective ignores the development of the whole military–industrial complex, and the incentive to create weapons that can kill at a distance. A case study of a 'mindless massacre' will help illustrate the debate about the neutrality of technology.

In 1996, madman Martin Bryant murdered 35 people in the Port Arthur massacre in Tasmania, Australia—and ignited international debates about guns and human fallibility. In Australia, the disaster led to much stricter gun controls (Stockwell 1997) as part of the nation's reaction to the horror of the events. In the United States, the same event has been taken by some to show that there should be more guns in society. Had gun ownership been more pervasive in Australia, the argument runs, then Bryant might have been shot before the death toll spiralled. (As it was—and it happens rarely in such cases—Bryant was captured alive.)

The different ways of looking at such events—arguing on the one hand that guns cost lives, and on the other that guns save lives—polarise people and communities. They represent differences of perspective and of belief, underlining the fact that our beliefs are formed and expressed through our social interactions with other people and the world around us. So which perspective is 'right'? Do guns cost lives, or do they save them? My personal belief is that guns cost lives, but that's not relevant to the discussion here. What is relevant is the social dimension to why we hold the beliefs we do about technology and technological artefacts (such as guns), and what it means to live in the twenty-first century in terms of our experience of 'being postmodern' (see below).

Sadly, the carnage of Port Arthur was not an isolated incident, and Stockwell has suggested that Bryant himself may have been influenced by 'the intense media coverage of the Dunblane massacre [in Scotland, of a group of primary school children and their teacher] in the weeks before the incident and earlier stories about the easy availability of high-powered guns in Tasmania' (1997, p. 56). In Scotland and the rest of the United Kingdom—as in Australia—the shooting tragedies prompted a reconsideration of the neutrality of guns as a technology. Guns are designed to target, kill and maim (whether for food, sport, defence or murder). In terms of life and death, there is nothing intrinsically neutral about guns. In terms of 'good' or 'bad' outcomes, it is a mechanical matter of who shoots first, or who shoots more accurately, rather than a 'moral' outcome of the 'good' person being protected by the technology.

In the United States, the recurring instances in 1998–99 of school children shooting classmates traumatised the nation, but no clear consensus on gun control has emerged as a result. On the contrary, US society has become increasingly divided over the issue. As repeated tragedies have strengthened the anti-gun lobby, so they have also galvanised the NRA—the powerful National Rifle Association (www.nra.org/ [April 2000])—to organise in defence of the Second Amendment: 'the right to bear arms'.

In March 2000, the NRA sparked an international semi-incident by linking crime in Australia to tougher gun laws following Martin Bryant's rampage at Port Arthur. This is the report on the NRA website:

> Rather than acknowledging one man's insanity, opportunistic gun control activists and scared politicians, rushed to blame 'loose gun laws' . . . In a March 22, 2000, letter, Australia's Attorney General Daryl Williams raised objections to an NRA video (www.nralive.com/gunban/gunban.cfm) . . . Williams said NRA was using 'misleading' statistics to make its case against gun control. He also claimed 'the national firearms agreement has succeeded in removing more than 640,000 dangerous weapons from circulation in the community' . . . The video shows real people protesting their loss of liberty and loss of the right to self-defense. Those people are Australians. And the statistics presented in the NRA video were reported in real newspapers—Australian newspapers. Attorney General Williams

should look closer to home if he truly objects to 'misleading' the public policy debate. In fact, he should look directly at the anti-gun group Gun Control Australia (GCA). When the Sporting Shooters Ass'n of Australia (SSAA) recently ran a TV campaign that promoted the shooting sports as activities for the whole family, GCA spokesman Randy Marshall said: 'People should not be fooled by pretty images of family life enjoying shooting—shooting is about practising to kill—that's why guns are manufactured. Every person who joins SSAA helps destroy the gun laws which protect Australians'.

Gun control is self-evidently a complex issue with social, cultural, technology and policy ramifications. I use the gun control debate here to illustrate that it is possible for different societies and different people in those societies to hold opposite beliefs about the nature of the technology: 'neutral', 'good' or 'bad'. The beliefs held by an individual about guns and gun control say more about that person and how they see the world than they do about the technology of the gun itself. To argue that any technology is neutral is to ignore the social and cultural circumstances in which that technology was developed, and the policy and regulatory regimes under which that technology is deployed. Neither technology nor culture is neutral—both reflect people and society, the power of different social groups and the outcomes of competing priorities.

## TECHNOLOGY'S RELATIONSHIP TO POWER AND PRIVILEGE

MacKenzie and Wajcman's (1999) argument is that a technology is only neutral insofar as no one knows what the technology is used for, and insofar as it is never used. Effectively, guns would only be neutral at the level of a sculpture, in a society where there was no knowledge of their function or their genesis. Naturally, no such society exists. Once knowledge comes into play, technology is implicated in social processes, and there is nothing neutral about society. Differences of gender, wealth, power and education—to say nothing of the First World/Third World divide—all determine that knowledge is political. Where knowledge is associated with power—such as with new technologies—it is vigorously protected. Copyright, patents and intellectual property rights, along with industrial espionage, arms embargoes and lists of prohibited technological exports, are all elements which indicate that those who develop technology and enjoy the advantages of technological ascendancy are loath to forfeit the benefits of these advantages. For them, technological advance means increased power and privilege.

Technology advance is often the result of years of investment, research and development. The laws of patents, copyright and intellectual property exist to protect that investment and ensure that developers have some prospect of recovering their venture capital. If technology were neutral, and if it offered no specific benefits to its developers, then it is hard to see why individuals and corporations would continue to develop it in the ways they currently do.

The knowledge of how to create and enhance technology, and of how to use technology, is *socially bound knowledge*. Each society operates to determine who will acquire this knowledge, and in which circumstances. In most western societies, access to knowledge is granted through a combination of education, application and ability. At one level, this appears to be access through merit. Increasingly, however, education and access to knowledge closely reflect indicators of social and economic advantage within society. Knowledge is no more neutral than technology.

Thus MacKenzie and Wajcman (1999) argue that even if the physical object of a technology were neutral, as soon as this was combined with knowledge of what the technology was used for and/or how it worked, it would be implicated in patterns of privilege and exclusivity. These patterns are further emphasised when a newly developed (hi-tech) technology is actually used. Users of such a technology are a specialised subset of those who have knowledge about the technology. Issues of access, power and gender determine who uses a technology and in which circumstances, even more than knowledge does. MacKenzie and Wajcman's argument is that there is no useful sense in which technology is neutral. Their argument that 'the social determination of technology' makes much more sense than 'the technological determination of society' is now generally accepted. These general principles—that technologies express the priorities of those who champion them—will be explored by reference to the specific case study of Edison's electric bulb. The social elite most evident in the development of electricity for domestic power and light is that of corporate capital—excluding those elements of corporate capital backing the development of domestic gas!

## THE METHOD AND THE MYTHOLOGY OF THE ELECTRIC LIGHT BULB

Thomas Hughes' study of Thomas Edison and the electric light is one of the examples included in MacKenzie and Wajcman's collection (Hughes 1999, pp. 50–63). Edison's name is remembered in the screw fitting for electric bulbs—ES, or Edison Screw. Edison was passionate about developing a system for the household delivery of electricity which, at that point, was not established as a domestic power source and was well behind gas, which had been developed for domestic consumption. Hughes calls Edison an 'inventor-entrepreneur', not because Edison developed electric light to make a profit (although he did do that) but because Edison's drive was to do more than invent electric light—it was to develop a coherent system for the delivery of electric light and power.

In the mythology of technological advance, inventors are generally portrayed as inspired geniuses. This was not Edison's viewpoint. It was he who, speaking from experience, coined the saying that invention 'is 99 per cent perspiration and 1 per cent inspiration'. Hughes argues that Edison's search for the elusive filament material for his incandescent light was conditioned as much by economics as by science:

> Wanting to reduce the current in order to lower conductor losses, [Edison] realized that he could compensate and maintain the level of energy transfer to the lamps by raising the voltage proportionately [energy transfer = current (Amps) 2 volts]. Then he brought Ohm's Law into play (resistance = voltage divided by current). It was the eureka moment, for he realized that by increasing the resistance of the incandescent lamp filament he raised the voltage in relationship to the current . . . Hence his time-consuming search for a high resistance filament—but the notable invention was the logical deduction; the filament was a hunt-and-try affair (Hughes 1999, p. 59).

The moment Edison realised the need for the highly resistant filament was the moment at which his vision for an electrical power and lighting system became potentially realisable. The mythology of technological advance, however, sees the ultimate achievement as being made on the day that the ideal material for the incandescent filament was actually discovered. Further, the myth (helped by Hollywood) identifies Edison as the individual carrying out the research at the moment of discovery.

Yet Edison was far from acting alone. He headed up his own research laboratories and led a team of 'electricians, mechanics and scientists and cooperated with associates concerned about the financial, political and business problems affecting the technological system' (Hughes 1999, p. 52).

What is clear from Hughes' account is that the intuitive genius which led to the development of electric power only resulted in an operational technology through the systematic labour of a number of people over a number of years—aspects of invention underplayed in mythological retellings. Further, Edison was not scared of sharing his idea at the concept stage, and went public with the vision in 1878—some years before the system was developed. The mythology is that good ideas should only be made public once they have been proven, otherwise they might be stolen and developed by others. The reality is that the electric light system envisioned by Edison required huge amounts of financial investment, and was itself a triumph of public relations. Without the public relations, the money to fund the research and development would not have been forthcoming. Edison's genius included being able to sell his idea to a corporate elite who invested their money in his research laboratories. This corporate investment enabled Edison to run his research laboratories, needed for the painstaking hunt-and-try research and development which eventually resulted in the electric bulb and domestic electricity.

My purpose in discussing Edison's invention of the electric light is to illustrate that social processes determine technology for social purposes. There was nothing technologically inevitable about the way in which the domestication of electricity developed. Economic opportunism was the driving force behind the technological developments, and the domestication of electric light and power was shaped socially first, and technologically second.

If technology were entirely neutral, and the result only of scientific progress, then there would be no point in debating it. It would be as amenable to debate and regulation as the law of gravity. Technologically determinist sayings such as 'You can't stop progress', 'You can't turn back the clock', and 'The runaway juggernaut of technology' all imply that we are unable to control technology. They suggest that we are as powerless against technological progress as the Danish King Canute was against nature, when he put an end to the sycophantic flattery of his courtiers by demonstrating that—King though he was—he was incapable of stopping the tide from coming in.

Helpless/hopeless perspectives become a self-fulfilling prophecy.

People who assume that technology advance and adoption are beyond social control apply few checks and balances. Areas where the uncontrollability of technology *is* challenged—for example, in terms of genetically modified (GM) food, human embryo experimentation and performance-enhancing drugs—confirm that social controls (and social sanctions) are possibilities. Around the world, genetically modified crops are regulated by labelling and other legislation, by consumer concern, by direct action (e.g., by Greenpeace) and by the growth of market niches for organic and non-GM foods. Research ethics committees and legislation control the artificial creation of, and experimentation upon, human embryos. Performance-enhancing drugs are often banned by national law, and are regulated in competitive sport by international sporting bodies. Regulation is underlined by random tests of athletes' urine and other biological markers, and through the banning of athletes found guilty of artificially enhancing performance.

The perspective of the social determination of technology leaves open the possibility that people can make a difference to their technological future if they are interested and get involved.

## THE ABC OF TECHNOLOGICAL ADVANTAGE

When we discuss the social determination of technology, it is easy to imply that this is a democratic, inclusive way to develop technology. Such a perception is generally erroneous, however, since some visions of the future are more inclusive than others. The visions which tend to attract funding, anticipation and active commitment from the social elites who have power in western society are those visions which offer these elites the greatest benefits. In fact, it is arguable that population-wide 'progress' is only ever an accidental spin-off of some powerful group's self-interest. Technology is developed as a result of specific choices made by influential power brokers representing a limited rage of social elites. These can be summed up as the A, B and C of social power:

- A = armed forces
- B = bureaucracy
- C = corporate power.

Even where there are other elements (such as academia) which may appear to be hot-housing technological change, the funding which supports those institutions tends to be attributable to one or more of the A, B and C power blocs. Thus technology, as it develops, represents the priorities of the elites which sponsor it, rather than representing the society as a whole. (The Internet has been heralded as a potentially liberating and democratic technology, but such benefits can only occur after the Internet user has access to the technology, and the skills and resources to use it. Initially, these restrictions made Internet use an elite activity.)

The empowerment of A, B and C through technological change is not a necessary situation. It is possible to democratise technology development and choice; but it is not in the interests of A, B or C to do so. Politically and economically A, B and C gain advantage from powering technological research and development according to their own priorities, and for their own benefit. In this they are supported by free market philosophies which enshrine the principle that 's/he who pays the piper calls the tune'.

As well as identifying the power elites in a society by investigating which groups benefit from the technologies that are produced, we can judge the priorities of a society's social elites from the technologies developed. Affordable, renewable energy and an efficient public transport system say different things about a society than do power stations (conventional or nuclear) and high rates of prestige car ownership. The way in which domestic electricity was trialled and developed, for example, indicates that the environment was not high on Edison's list of priorities (even if he was unaware of global warming at the time). Current searches for solar, wind and wave power systems indicate that we do care about the environment. Nonetheless, comparatively few people seem prepared to pay more to have their electricity generated in greener ways.

Historically, the A, B and C elites use their advantages to build their power in national contexts. With the advent of globalisation, these elites also build power internationally. The technologies they develop and sponsor affect their own society, but they also have effects in the societies to which the technology 'transfers'. In particular, it is more than the technology which is transferred. The creation of a computer centre in a transnational corporation's (TNC) head office in a Third World country, for example, involves the virtual creation of a First World environment dislocated from its immediate geographical/social context. This is because a computer centre requires reliable 24-hour power, a dust-free work space, competent operators with First World levels of education and competitive rates of pay, and tight security. The technological umbilical cord may end in a Third World country but it remains firmly attached to the western industrial placenta.

It is as if the technology, in international technology adoption, works as the genetic material (DNA) of the social elites that create it. Technology, transplanted into a new location, necessarily replicates certain of its operational conditions without regard for the social, political and cultural context of the country to which it is transferred. It also transplants elements of the A, B and C social elites from the First World into whichever society adopts the technology concerned. Like a baby cuckoo in a nest, it is possible to construct First World technology as depleting the resources of the Third World to the continuing benefit of the techno-corporate powerbrokers located elsewhere.

Shareholders of TNCs have been major financial beneficiaries of technological progress. Economist Dick Bryan observes that 'Communications technology relates to our understanding of TNCs in two ways: communications technology is central to the internal organisation of TNCs; and the companies which produce communications technology are themselves often TNCs' (1994, p. 146). The growth of financial markets, media corporations and other late twentieth century conglomerates means that almost all big players in free-market economies have some offshore presence and rely upon communication technologies.

Electronic communication across frontiers becomes both easy and necessary in the global environment. For those with technological competence and technology access, political borders become essentially irrelevant to information flow. Further, where bottlenecks occur in the communication process, these act as a spur for the refinement and incorporation of technological solutions to overcome the logjam, conferring further political advantage. Global social change is increasingly both a cause and effect of technological change in information and communications contexts.

Ramifications of such a situation are political as well as technological. If poverty-stricken countries use their best land to grow crops for export, to meet interest repayments on international debts acquired as part of a communications modernisation program, then there may well be insufficient food to feed their people, and poor people in that country starve. Within affluent western cultures it may be that, as the rich get richer, the welfare state kicks in to offer a social safety net to the poor. But this is a wealthy-country phenomenon. There is no safety net for the poor in the developing world. In these circumstances, technology is so far from neutral that it comes with a life-or-death price tag. As with gun control, however, some argue that it is only through modernisation that food, water, health care and education will eventually be delivered to the world's poor. In the meantime, a lucrative contract for a western communications giant can represent long-term debt for a Third World nation.

## PROGRESS—FOR WHOM?

Progress in one area is often bought at the expense of impoverishment elsewhere. This is not a new phenomenon—futurist Ian Miles described its operation in the mid-1980s:

> It is clear that the so-called 'developed' nations are far from being in a state of timeless perfection, and that the alluring models of material progress they offer the rest of the world are seriously flawed. It is likewise evident that the term 'developing nations' is inappropriate to many of the countries to which it was so readily applied in the recent past. In many respects, the Third World seems to be importing most of the social problems of the industrial countries, but failing to acquire much of their material affluence. Increasingly, attention has been drawn to the linkages between material prosperity in one world region and poverty in another; and those between the emphasis on satisfaction (and unlimited extension) of material needs and the discounting of more social relations, political and non-material aspects of well-being. Across and within countries the world displays an inequitable and lop-sided pattern of development and repression of human potentialities. It is maldeveloped (Miles 1985, p. 10).

Social and equitable definitions of progress continue to be sought, and contemporary futurists ask whether, in anticipating the future, we are attempting to foresee it, to manage it or to create it. The philosophical distinctions between these perspectives provide very different rationales for our actions when we wish to influence the future. According to futurist Graham May (2000), attempts to foresee, or predict, the future—for example, by extrapolating trends—presuppose that in some very particular ways the future already exists and/or is closely related to the forces evident in the present and the past. May further suggests that managing the present with the future in mind accepts that present actions and decisions influence the future, and that the future does not exist and is capable of being influenced by our choices. The creation of the future—through techniques such as 'creative visioning'—works on the basis that once situations that do not exist have been imagined, they can be brought into existence. These three approaches, separately and in parallel, offer ways of negotiating the uncertainty and essential unpredictability of the future. In the meantime, however, while the future is being revealed, the question generally begged by the concept of progress, both now and for the future, is 'progress—maybe—but for whom?'

Approaches to technology and technology transfer, which draw upon the past as a way of defining 'progress' for the future, may have a distinguished academic pedigree but they are not the only way of looking at these issues. Such models offer what might be termed a very 'modern' way of viewing technology development. Postmodern perspectives are one way to explore alternative and fruitful ideas.

## BEING POSTMODERN

Current notions of progress are clearly contradictory. The sense of things getting better and better—with greater prosperity, choice, education and opportunity—travel in tandem with local and global evidence of incredible disparity between the unbelievably rich and the death-rattlingly poor, and with evidence of growing rates of depression and suicide in the western world. A postmodern notion of progress sees no contradiction between celebrating new car registrations, or a rise in building permissions, at the same time as worrying about the depleted ozone layer or global warming. The 'progress' from agricultural, to industrial, to information society (to be outlined in Chapter 4) may have been technologically and materially beneficial for the First World, but a price has been paid, although it is likely that we will never know exactly what it was.

Postmodernism offers a way of holding the paradoxes and contradictions we experience in our daily lives in creative tension, recognising truths which may appear to cancel each other out. Guns can be good in some situations, bad in others, but this doesn't make them 'neutral'. Opponents of postmodern perspectives (there is nothing unitary about postmodernism) claim that the postmodern doesn't exist, and that the phenomenon dubbed 'postmodern' is a new phase of the modern: 'late modernism' or 'late capitalism'. Postmodernists retort that the controversy about the status of the philosophy proves its usefulness. They go on to argue that the postmodern condition is one of uncertainty and internal contradiction, and it is not entirely relevant whether postmodernism 'really' exists. Notions such as 'right', 'wrong', 'truth' and 'objectivity' become positional statements. What is right/wrong/true and objective depends upon who is speaking and in which circumstances.

This apologia for postmodernism can quite legitimately attract derision. If there is no truth or certainty, what is the point of trying to understand anything, or say anything? Technologists, philosophers, lecturers, students—we might as well all pack our bags and go home. Not so, claim postmodernists. Truth may be relative, but it is still relevant and anyway, who said that the postmodern can't exist side by side with modernism and the premodern? Postmodernists aren't claiming that they're right, or that the modern is wrong—that wouldn't be postmodern—the best they can claim for postmodernism is that 'the postmodern *is*'. But postmodernism is more than happy to accept that postmodernism *is* postmodern in a very fractured, partial, surface and contradictory way.

Paradoxically, there are signs of optimism in the postmodern chaos. For centuries, up to the start of the modern era (some put this at the invention of printing, others at the French Revolution), there was no positive notion of 'progress'. On the contrary, the world was deemed to have been created in perfection and to have been steadily deteriorating ever since, mainly due to the twin activities of a fallen mankind and the Devil. It was generally assumed that things would go from bad to worse to the point where the world ended and Judgement sorted the sheep from the goats, damning some and sending the chosen to Paradise. Compared with this sense of continual deterioration, the idea that there is any progress at all is optimistic.

A postmodern perspective helps us appreciate the sense of sitting in physical isolation, tapping into a computer connected to the Internet, and feeling as if we are surrounded by a multitude (Wilbur 1997). It offers a framework for understanding virtual reality, non-physical places and online community.

We return to these issues in following chapters—especially in Chapters 10 and 12. As it is, postmodernism offers one way to look at progress, at technology and at culture as if these concepts were composed of contradictions held in creative tension.

## THE CHALLENGE OF CHANGE

Technology change can often have implications for the past—as well as the present and the future. Our experience of everyday life is so different from what was anticipated a generation ago that some sense has to be made of the shock of the new. One way in which societies make sense of the present is to revisit what was going on in the past and try to rewrite history with the benefit of the new perspectives—with the wisdom of hindsight. We do this because we know that the present has its genesis in the past. If our current life is not what people anticipated 20 years ago, it is because they were concentrating on other issues, or looking for the evolution of different things. When we focus on the preoccupations of those past generations we do so in a 'revolutionary' manner—we are not 'evolving' from where we were; we are changing the perspective, looking for different patterns, and for ingredients other than those which seemed most important at the time.

Thomas Kuhn, Professor Emeritus of Philosophy at the Massachusetts Institute of Technology until his death in 1996, wrote an influential book some 40 years ago [1962] on the 'paradigm shift'—the moment when things are seen differently. It was called *The Structure of Scientific Revolutions* (1996, 3rd edn), but has implications far beyond the realms of science. Different ways of seeing things, resulting from the incorporation of new material into established understandings, are no accidents. We try to make sense of information that challenges our understanding of the status quo (even if only by saying 'It's just another manifestation of postmodernism'). Edison knew enough about electricity to be certain that it had the potential to be a domestic power source, but it wasn't until he had seen the whole picture—and verified the finding of the appropriate filament material—that the paradigm of domestic power provision shifted from gas to electricity. Now it's hard to imagine that a fridge or a washing machine could be gas-powered.

Philosophical cues—ways of looking at the world—engender mental shifts. Once a shift in understanding has been made, it is impossible for us to return to the former state. Although we can appreciate how we once saw something, we also appreciate that an alternative viewpoint is possible. Psychologists have established that, as well as working to achieve a conceptual understanding, we seek to make sense of our environment through our perceptions. The ability to do this is central to human cognition and the examples I am about to offer use perceptual cues to create ambiguity, stimulating a struggle to understand the whole.

Here are a couple of examples of perceptual 'paradigm shifts'. The first (Figure 1.1) is well known. This image can be perceived as the left cheek and jaw line of a young woman with her face turned from the observer, with a narrow throat choker, wearing a feathered hat backed by lacy tulle, and with an oversize furry coat or cape draped off her shoulders. (This is essentially a mid-shot—top of the head to mid-torso.) Alternatively, the image can be constructed as a close-up of a much older woman. The young woman's cheek and jaw become the older woman's nose. The choker becomes a thin-lipped mouth. The young woman's ear becomes some lines under the older woman's left eye, and the young woman's décolletage becomes the older woman's hooked chin. The old woman huddles down in scarf or shawl, which protects her head and the back of her neck from the cold.

The same information is used to construct two very different images. As the reader of this text, instructed to look for competing images, you knew that what you saw at first glance was not the only possible interpretation. Were you aware of a struggle to see an alterna-

Figure 1.1 Wise old woman: 'the crone', and/or young woman with feathered cap and choker

tive picture? Once the change in perception has been achieved, how difficult is it to go back? Is it possible to be a 'naïve' viewer again?

Arguably, change, discomfort and ambiguity are intrinsically related. As information accumulates which indicates that things are not as they once were (for example, marriage is no longer necessarily a commitment for life), so people and society painfully adjust to make sense of the new situation. Vested interests give way to the new circumstances. Old laws are applied to novel situations until the point at which they magnify the problems instead of providing a solution. For example, the 'clean break' philosophy allowed a divorcing couple to end their financial connections, but it left children of the relationship vulnerable to a cycle of poverty. In some societies, a legislative response (such as the Child Support Agency (CSA) in the United Kingdom and Australia) was instigated to deal with the issues arising, 'taxing' the non-residential/ non-custodial parent to ensure they contributed towards the costs of raising their children. (The British CSA website is www.dss.gov.uk/csa/ [June 2001].) The bureaucratic response to changing circumstances often

Figure 1.2 Mystery image (see end of chapter for explanation of this image)
Photographer: R.C. James; from Lindsay and Norman 1977

involves the application of central computer data banks that process information relating to income, employment and taxation. Western society is still coming to terms with what these technologies mean in terms of individual privacy, security and independence from the state. Trying out remedies to address new problems involves exposure to more change and uncertainty. Kuhn describes a cycle of growing discomfort with the changing circumstances, and the trial of new tools to suit the paradigm shift:

> The emergence of new theories is generally preceded by a period of pronounced professional insecurity. As one might expect, that insecurity is generated by the persistent failure of the puzzles [or the problems] to come out as they should. Failure of existing rules is the prelude to a search for new ones . . . As in manufacture so in science—retooling is an extravagance to be reserved for the occasion that demands it. The significance of crises is the indication they provide that an occasion for retooling has arrived (Kuhn 1996, pp. 67–8, 76).

A recent example of a socio-economic paradigm shift occurred in the 1960s–1970s, with the second wave of feminism. Once the contribution of women to society was perceived as being circumscribed by rules about what counts as work, or by what counts as important, it was clear that women's historical contribution was invisible to the people who had seen themselves as recording history—mainly men. A growing academic concern with uncovering women's contribution to history prompted a whole new way of looking at the past, as well as the present and the future. Historical documents, which had previously been seen only in terms of economics, or politics, or religion, were found to also contain valuable information about the women of those times. Sometimes the fact that women weren't mentioned was as informative as if they had been! A generation of scholars has now created a space for women in history to speak to people in the present and in the future.

An equivalent investigation of technoculture is likely to establish that the A, B and C power elites have acquired and exercised the naming rights of what counts as technology, privileging the mythological high-tech boundary-pushing artefacts and ignoring the baby bottle and human language. Back when Thomas Kuhn's arguments about the paradigm shift were gaining ground, cultural theorist Marshall McLuhan (1964) was arguing that 'the phonetic alphabet alone is the technology that has been the means of creating "civilized man"—the separate individuals equal before a written code of law' (1964, p. 84). An inclusive definition of technology, like McLuhan's, makes more of us technologically able, and empowers us to voice our opinions regarding technology policy and debates.

Returning to the original question of the chapter—'What fuels technology change?'—the answer lies in other changes; changes in policy, culture and society among them. According to Wajcman (1994), Marx credited capitalism with fuelling technical change. Effective innovation generates more capital, which funds greater innovation. At the same time, innovation does not prosper in a vacuum—it only generates capital if it produces goods that people want to buy, and can afford to purchase.

Capitalism is an essentially modernist way of looking at history—it is an example of an over-arching coherent narrative that denies the experience of coincidence, piecemeal advance and the interplay of contradictory forces, containing them instead in the myths of technological change. Markets, and the structure of the marketing and diffusion of technology, fit well into a modernist perspective. This is the substance of Chapter 2.

## CONCLUSION

In this chapter we have identified that cultural myths surrounding technology place value upon change and advancement, and celebrate the lives and the achievements of famous innovators. Technological determinists might argue that it is 'scientific progress' that fuels technological change. Social determinists would counter that it is powerful social elites such as the armed forces, bureaucracy and corporate power that play the role of change agents. Postmodernists might suggest that the notion of 'change' is a paradox, since change is a constant and to live is to change.

The notion of the passage of time and technological advance as progress, rather than disintegration and decay, is a secular phenomenon and differs from the medieval conception of a perfect creation that has been constantly breaking down following humanity's fall from grace. A Third World perspective calls the notion of technological progress into doubt, while the concepts of First/Third World and progress/decay are themselves oppositional dualities characteristic of modern (rather than postmodern) thinking.

Using a variety of case studies, this chapter has demonstrated that 'technology' is not neutral. Neither is culture—later in the book we will be addressing the different constructions of culture: high culture, low culture, popular culture, folk culture, etc. Since neither technology nor culture is neutral, it is unsurprising that technocultural tools—writing, the phone, the computer—express the priorities of the elites that champion them.

We have also examined the notion of the paradigm shift, which explains how one world-view is ousted by a new way of looking at the same information, resulting in very different perceptions and ideas. This book celebrates technology and culture as being shifting, and capable of analysis from multiple perspectives.

## NOTE

Figure 1.2 is an over-exposed photograph of a Dalmatian dog, in speckled shade, sniffing at the ground.

# 2

## TECHNOLOGY ADOPTION
## AND DIFFUSION

### PIECING TOGETHER AN UNDERSTANDING OF TECHNOCULTURE

What is technoculture and how can it be explored? We have already seen that technology is a value-laden and multi-faceted concept; so too is culture. Both ideas demand explanation and investigation. The topic is too big to be grappled with globally. Instead, we will address it on a case-by-case basis, looking at specific instances of communication, technology and society often involving consideration of policy.

Case study narratives offer a flexible, shifting and intuitive way to discover more about the relationships between culture, society and technology by answering questions such as: 'What stories do we tell ourselves about . . .?' and 'How would this be different if it had been invented by . . .?'. Sometimes a story will spoof, in a very serious way, the operation of a technology by reversing the cultural roles in the pattern of technology testing and adoption. Such a device serves to illuminate aspects of culture we might otherwise take for granted. That is the technique adopted here by Judy Wajcman:

> The newest development in male contraception was unveiled recently at the American Women's Surgical Symposium held at Ann Arbor Medical Centre. Dr Sophie Merkin, of the Merkin Clinic, announced the preliminary findings of a study conducted on 763 unsuspecting male students at a large midwest university. In her report, Dr Merkin reported that the new contraceptive— the IPD—was a breakthrough in male contraception. It will be marketed under the trade-name Umbrelly (Wajcman 1994, p. 10).

The IPD (or intrapenile device) resembles a tiny folded umbrella which is inserted through the head of the penis and pushed into the scrotum with a plunger type instrument. Occasionally there is perforation of the scrotum but this is disregarded since it is now known that the male has few nerve endings in this area of his body. The underside of the umbrella contains a spermicidal jelly, hence the name Umbrelly.

Dr Merkin declared the Umbrelly to be statistically safe for the human male. She reported that of the 763 students tested with the device, only two died of scrotal infection, only twenty experienced swelling of the tissues. Three developed cancer of the testicles, and thirteen were too depressed to have an erection. She stated that common complaints ranged from cramping and bleeding to acute abdominal pain. She emphasised that these symptoms were merely indications that the man's body had not yet adjusted to the device. Hopefully the symptoms would disappear within a year. Dr Merkin and other distinguished members of the Women's College of Surgeons agreed that the benefits far outweighed the risk to any individual man.

Wajcman comments: 'This report is a parody of medical research into the testing of a new contraceptive. What is striking—some may even find it funny—is that here men are the guinea pigs. In real life, contraceptive technologies have been developed by men for use by women' (1994, p. 10).

This technique makes the normal seem strange by looking at the familiar in a radically different context. These kinds of case studies beg the question of how a situation could be different, or would be different, if other perspectives and social priorities were at centre stage. Sometimes examples exist of such different perspectives in action in another culture. One such case is the Old Order Amish use of the telephone.

## THE SOCIAL CONTROL OF THE TELEPHONE

Diane Umble's study of the role of the telephone in Amish society in Pennsylvania, USA, is one example of the 'resistance and reconstruction' of a technology (1992, pp. 183–94). The Amish are a religiously based community whose lifestyle, technologies and settlements resonate with the rhythms of earlier centuries. The Amish do not use electricity, they speak in a German dialect related to that of Jacob Ammann (who founded the order in 1693), their lives do not include radio or television and they drive horses and carts rather than cars. In 1909, the telephone was banned from Amish homes. The ban was resisted by about 20 per cent of the Old Order Amish community who subsequently broke away/were excluded, and formed the 'Beachy Amish'.

The banning of the telephone from the Amish home was an example of the restitution of the 'old order' over the new, but it involved some difficult compromises. For some twenty years, Amish families travelled to use a public telephone, or borrowed the phone of a non-Amish neighbour. According to Umble: 'In the mid-1930s, several Amish families made an appeal to church leaders for a shared telephone. They argued that access to a telephone was important in times of emergency—calling a doctor or the fire company' (Umble 1992, p. 190). A compromise was reached. Housed in 'little buildings that look much like outdoor lavatories . . . [community telephones] have unlisted numbers, are used primarily for outgoing calls, and are shared by six or seven Amish families . . . Loud call bells to announce incoming calls are discouraged or prohibited' (Umble 1992, p. 184).

The result of the compromise was to allow semi-convenient access to the telephone without allowing it to intrude upon the traditional rhythms of Amish life. The Amish choose to avoid worldly matters, preferring instead to concentrate upon their faith, expressed through the concept of *Gelassenheit*, which 'demands obedience, humility, submission, thrift and simplicity'. In Old Order Amish terms, the home is central to their social and religious experience. There are no churches—when a congregation outgrows the number that can be accommodated in an Amish home, it divides. 'Eating, leisure and work all revolve around the home. It is the centre of faith and life, the scene of face-to-face, often non-verbal, highly contextualized communication. The home is a refuge from the complexities and temptations of the outside world' (Umble 1992, p. 186). The home, in short, is no place for the telephone, which would allow externals to intrude upon this self-contained world.

Umble's argument is that the Amish offer an example of where a technology (the telephone) has been socially resisted and reconstructed to the point where it could be accepted on the terms of Amish society. Amish technoculture, as concerns the telephone, is consequently very different from telephone technocultures in most western societies. Since most societies are less sure about their priorities than the 80 per cent of obedient

Old Order Amish were in 1909, the Amish offer a comparatively rare example of technological resistance through choice. However, even where there is a general social consensus on priorities, it is only rarely possible to control totally the diffusion and use of a new technology.

Where there is no consensus on priorities, technology use cannot be controlled. Julianne Schultz gives several examples of the failure of repressive regimes to control media and communication technologies in their countries. She comments upon the importance of the underground media in 'Iron Curtain' states under communism, and the media's contribution to the fall of the Berlin Wall and of the Soviet socialist system in 1989. The ability of western-based broadcasters to evade the media blocking of eastern European countries also contributed to this outcome (Schultz 1990). All state regulation implies a struggle between competing interests. This is as true in democracies as in totalitarian systems, and these dynamics will be considered further in Chapter 8.

## DISCOURSE ANALYSIS AND THE SOCIAL BIOGRAPHY OF THINGS

Stories which involve the use of the phone in an Amish community are likely to differ from stories which involve the use of the phone in your home, or in mine. Such differences in the ways that different people use a technology, and talk about it, are instructive. Igor Kopytoff (1986), an American academic with extensive experience of African anthropological research, has explored the idea that 'things' have a social biography. In the mid-1980s, Kopytoff was at the forefront of a new interest in consumption studies, an understanding of who consumes (or uses) what, in which circumstances. This perspective offers important benefits in a consideration of how technocultures work.

Discourse analysis is a deconstructive tool, by which I mean it is a way of looking beyond the surface of the meanings that have been constructed, to examine the underlying assumptions and values. For example, the absence (until recently) of historical accounts of women's lives, and the lives of the poor and disempowered, demonstrates that history used to be constructed as a discourse about the doings of rich and powerful men. Discourse analysis is a postmodern (pomo) tool because it allows the existence of multiple realities, and of multiple perspectives, and denies the existence of certainty. Thus the Amish view of the telephone is no more or less valid or true than mine (although an Amish person would find my construction of a telephone highly intrusive, while I would find their construction of a telephone somewhat isolating). Discourse analysis allows us to construct and compare the different cultural frameworks in which the Amish and I use the telephone. What appears to be 'the whole picture' is a subjective and personal construction from the fragments of information that we've gleaned.

The consumption of a technological object is framed in large part by the discourse within which it is constructed—that is, the stories we tell about the object through which its meanings are suggested and communicated. The term 'construction' acknowledges that one effect of a discourse is to frame/showcase meanings created collaboratively through social processes. As a migrant, with my family of origin overseas, I might construct the telephone as a social lifeline, as a way of keeping in touch with my original community. For the Amish, however, the telephone may be constructed as meaning 'an interruption to communication with family', 'potential threat to the community and to traditional values' and 'beyond community boundaries'.

Kopytoff made it clear that discourse regarding cars in the western world differs greatly from that which operates in Africa. For example, a British, Canadian or Australian car might be conceptualised in terms of fuel economy, top speed, safety or price. These functional and economic discourses are familiar from advertising strategies, and tend to influence the way in which people in the West perceive domestic vehicles, and the reasons they give for buying one make of car rather than another. Consider instead Kopytoff's alternative 'biography' of a car:

> The biography of a car in Africa would reveal a wealth of cultural data: the way it was acquired, how and from whom the money was assembled to pay for it, the relationship of the seller to the buyer, the uses to which the car is regularly put, the identity of its most frequent passengers and of those who borrow it, the frequency of borrowing, the garages to which it is taken and the owner's relation to the mechanics, the movement of the car from hand to hand over the years, and in the end, when the car collapses, the final disposition of its remains. All of these details would reveal an entirely different biography from that of a middle-class American, or Navajo, or French peasant car (Kopytoff 1986, p. 67).

This way of looking at a technology places it within the social context of those who use it, and those who are related to its use. It looks at a technology holistically rather than purely in marketing or production terms. In this respect, the social biography approach can address a technology as a cultural artefact, and as interwoven throughout (and offering connections between) human lives.

Since technocultures exist where technologies are used by people to construct culture in a collaborative exchange, technoculture is always interwoven between and within people's lives.

## THE EXPECTATION AND EXPERIENCE OF TECHNOLOGY USE

A similar 'biographical' approach to Kopytoff's can be taken to consider why a computer is bought, for whom, with what ends in mind. This trajectory of intended use may well be at odds with the pattern of use which develops, or which fails to develop (Haddon 1992). For example, in the early years of domestic computers, there were reports of computers languishing in boxes, under the stairs or on top of the wardrobe, as it became clear just how complex they were to operate, and how many skills were required to use them. Murdock et al. cite the experience of one woman, 'who had seen her husband and son lose interest . . . [she says] "they were going to do great things with it [the computer], and make programmes and use it in all sorts of ways. But then they realised what a long time it was going to be to learn to do this, and a long time putting the programme in. They haven't had the time"' (1992, p. 149).

The consumption of a new technology, over and above its purchase, creates pressures upon time and skills. Sometimes these pressures become too great to be overcome by the original 'consumption motivation'. These socio-cultural dynamics tend to be ignored by conventional marketing theory (although they help create 'post-purchase dissonance', where the experience of purchase is at odds with the expectation), but they are central to a cultural studies approach to consumption.

In this section of the chapter, I have constructed technology as being much more than a 'neutral' assembly of functionalities and uses, which together make up an object's technological specifications. Technological artefacts, and possessions generally, represent hopes and fears—projections from the past and present into the future, in terms of desired skills and preferred pastimes. Technological resources and choices inform work, leisure, and social and cultural opportunities. Whether a person is an African car owner, an Amish telephone user or a 10-year-old American Playstation enthusiast, a sense of that individual helps explain the spread of different technologies, and their powerful hold on the imagination.

## THE THEORIES OF ADOPTION AND DIFFUSION

In consumer societies, most technologies come to the market to make profits for developers, manufacturers and retailers. This is not why they are bought, however. They are purchased because the planned (and real) uses of the technology are seen by consumers as life enhancing in some way. The key name associated with marketing theories about the adoption and diffusion of innovation is that of Everett Rogers (1995). In the early 1980s, Rogers and Larsen (1984) began studying the spread of home computers in Silicon Valley in the United States, so the principles of the theory have been applied to practical examples of 'high' technology diffusion.

Both diffusion and adoption are of considerable interest to marketing and consumer behaviour professionals, since they describe (in large part) the take-up of a product and determine its profitability. The prediction of which new products will succeed—and which will fail—is an inexact science, however, and according to Schiffman et al. fewer 'than one in ten new consumer products succeeds, making it vital for the marketer to understand the processes involved' (1997, p. 498).

Hawkins et al. (1994) suggest that the views of others in a social group can be an important spur to experimenting with new, or innovative, products. 'Innovation' can include innovative ways to buy, as well as different things to buy. One example of the use of 'the group' to promote linked selling is www.amazon.com. Although it had years of trading at a deficit, Amazon started the new century as a millennial marketing phenomenon. Its attraction lay in the fact that it did not only offer books, but information about books (and about other people who read the books you're interested in—for example, other books bought by people who buy the book you've heard about). Amazon also offered a chance to invest in a high-profile, new technology company selling established products to a rapidly increasing list of customers. For some time Amazon was the epitome of the new economy, of innovation and of e-commerce success.

As a stock prospect, Amazon had an impressive and growing database of consumers and one of the most widely recognised brand names in the dot.com business. Nonetheless, argues financial journalist Brian Hale, the 'global Internet share bubble' was punctured in 2000, with only a 'rump of Internet companies still standing after share price falls topping 90% for many of them' (2000, p. 58). Hale quotes Lehman bond analyst Ravi Suria as saying 'we believe that the combination of negative cash flow, poor working capital management and high debt load in a hyper competitive environment will put the company under extremely high risk' (2000, p. 58).

Although the dot.coms are looking shakier than they were at the end of the 1990s, according to Morgan Stanley Technology Research (Arens 1999, p. 513, see Figure 2.1) the Internet is the fastest growing communications medium in history. Figures are extremely rubbery, but some data indicate that US Internet use expanded twenty-fold between 1994–99, to over 50 million users (Arens 1999). Figure 2.1 compares the take-up of radio, television, cable and the Internet for the US market.

Figure 2.1 Relative take-up rates of different communications media in the United States

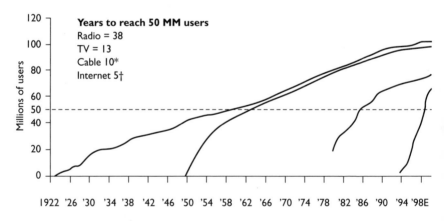

Source: Morgan Stanley Technology Research and Arens (1999, p. 513)

The different stages in which new products and innovations spread through consumer populations together make up the *diffusion process*, while the reasons and decision-steps that underpin a consumer's decision to take up a new product are called the *adoption process*.

## HIGH AND LOW INVOLVEMENT IN TECHNOLOGY ADOPTION

There is a 'classic curve'—or bell curve—which indicates the rate of diffusion over time. It shows an initial period of relatively slow growth, followed by a stage of rapid growth, followed by a final phase of slower growth to reach a point of market saturation (see Figure 2.3 on page 33). This 'typical diffusion' pattern is varied in the case of fast diffusion and slow diffusion, as Figure 2.2 illustrates. Expensive high technology decisions—such as those implicit in hi-tech technoculture—are 'high-involvement' decisions. People are very concerned about the outcome of their investment of time and money. There is more at stake for the consumer than simply the technology; also at issue is the management of public perception about technological competence and the acquisition and display of relevant skills. Often a number of competing products promise a range of benefits which have to be evaluated against each other (is X computer really much easier to use; does that ease of use outweigh the fact that Y computer has much more software available?) Further, high-involvement decisions often involve other people—a computer purchase might involve forgoing a family holiday that year, a child might want a particular model of computer so that they can trade games with friends, or so that the computer can play DVDs. The more people involved in the decision, the greater the 'involvement' in the decision-making, and the more emotional investment in the outcome.

Figure 2.2 Diffusion rate of innovation over time

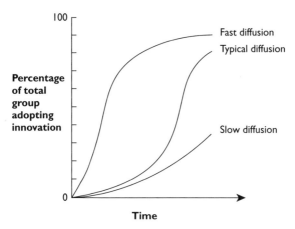

*Source*: Hawkins et al. 1994, p. 414

Rogers' (1995) theory of the adoption process suggests that an individual consumer passes through a variety of stages in arriving at a decision to try (or continue) using a new product. Firstly, a consumer has *awareness* (this is a neutral stage, consumers are aware before they are interested). Secondly, the consumer's *interest* is aroused—they search for information regarding possible benefits of adopting the new technology. Thirdly, a consumer *evaluates* the information they have discovered, to draw conclusions as to the benefits offered by the innovation in relation to its cost. Fourthly, the consumer attempts to negotiate a *trial*: to use the product on a limited basis, with limited risk. Finally, in the *adoption* phase, a consumer either fully accepts, or fully rejects, the product.

This model has been criticised (e.g. by Schiffman et al. 1997, p. 515) in that most consumers recognise that they have a 'problem' to which the innovation offers a potential 'solution' and it is this 'problem-recognition phase' that triggers interest. Similarly, many products (especially services) have to be purchased before they can be trialled. Thus the order of some of the stages might need to be changed. Both evaluation and the opportunity to reject the product are constants in the decision-making process; they don't occur only at the evaluation and adoption stages. Evaluation of the product following purchase is also important, but not included in Rogers' (1995) scheme. This stage raises the potential of 'post-purchase dissonance', where the experience of using a product is at odds with the hopes for that product. Where experience of the product is disappointing, this can be an important factor in halting the diffusion of the product through a population (especially in the early stages) since the product may suffer from poor 'word of mouth' publicity.

Schiffman et al. (1997, p. 515) have suggested a revised 'decision-making model' to overcome these limitations. It also has five stages:

1. knowledge (when a consumer develops some understanding of the innovation);
2. persuasion (when attitudes are formed about the product and its usefulness);
3. decision (this includes activities which lead to a trial of the product);
4. implementation (the consumer uses the product and evaluates it); and
5. confirmation (having reached a decision, the consumer seeks reinforcement for the adoption decision made).

The final stage partly explains why marketers of many high-involvement products see existing customers as an important target for product advertising. It is critical to reassure consumers that a particular high-involvement purchase decision was a good one. Such reassurance increases the likelihood that a satisfied purchaser will recommend the product to friends and colleagues. Many innovators and early adopters are opinion leaders (a concept considered below). These individuals are critical to the process of product diffusion.

Since technoculture implicates the use of technology, and since participation in a specific technoculture (such as online chat) is related to technology access, factors affecting technology diffusion also affect the growth of a technoculture. Table 5.1, 'Worldwide online users by geographical area', indicates the take up of online technoculture in the nineteen months between February 1999 and September 2000. At this point, online communications were no longer new (in the sense of 'just invented/developed') but they were an innovation for the many millions of users worldwide who adopted the online technologies and began participating in online technoculture for the first time.

## ADOPTER CHARACTERISTICS

The early, hesitant period of diffusion marks adoption by 'innovators' (classically the first 2.5 per cent) and by 'early adopters' (the next 13.5 per cent). Schiffman et al. (1997) characterise innovators as being risk-takers (they are less likely to perceive risk, and are more able to cope with loss) and opinion leaders, younger, educated, with a higher disposable income, socially mobile ('upscale') and socially involved (in formal and informal groups). They are active information seekers in their area of interest and likely to be less dogmatic than non-innovators, and to be more open-minded and 'inner-directed' (follow their own judgement). They may seek variety and stimulation. They may need to feel (or self-identify as) 'unique'. Innovation may be a stage they're going through. Some theorists suggest that individuals may move through three stages as they age: embracing innovation; innovation satiation; innovator no more (innovator burnout).

Early adopters share many of the same features as innovators, but they are more likely to perceive the riskiness inherent in technology adoption. They are concerned with the possibility of failure. Innovators and early adopters are likely to have many different channels of communication, including those with people who foster change (e.g., salespeople). They are voracious collectors of information, scouring magazines, newspapers and other mass media for articles and opinions that relate to their enthusiasms. Partly as a result of both their interest and their information search, they have greater knowledge of innovations, and are more likely to be perceived as opinion leaders by others.

Consumer societies foster change by encouraging positive images of 'progress', by valuing advanced technology and training opportunities that support the development of a skilled labour force, and by encouraging a respect for education and science. The desire for 'proof' of benefits and the underpinning of claims by verifiable experience are both important factors for the 'early majority adopters' (the next 34 per cent). These people are more likely to rely on interpersonal communication than upon reports in the mass media. They tend to be socially active, but may be older than innovators and early adopters, less well educated and less socially mobile. The 'rate of adoption' refers to the time it takes for a new product to be accepted by those who will ultimately adopt it. It seems that, in many consumer societies, the rate of adoption for communication technologies gets faster as these societies become more information-driven.

The 'late majority adopters' constitute the next 34 per cent of the potential consumer cohort. They tend to be more sceptical than the earlier adopters, and more reactive to social pressures. These consumers have fewer alternatives. They are often older, with less status and social mobility. They are more inhibited by the risks of adoption. Risks seem greater when consumers cannot foresee the full results of the decision to purchase. Risk may be functional (the product won't perform as expected), physical (it may be unsafe), financial (not good value), social (an embarrassing mistake), psychological (worry-inducing) and time-related (is it a waste of time, will it cost or save me time?). These risks are progressively greater to the laggards (say the next 13.5 per cent), who adopt with reluctance. Such consumers tend to be oriented to the past and have limited (or local) social interactions. The remainder of the market are often 'non-adopters' (the last 2.5 per cent). They are typically older, poorer and resistant to change. The rate of diffusion of a communication technology through society is equivalent to the rate of diffusion of the resulting technoculture.

The term 'laggards' suggests/conveys a judgement by marketers about comparatively late adopters. It implies a social norm of consumption (almost a responsibility to consume!). We will shortly be comparing these value-laden adoption category terms with those developed for 'Values and lifestyles segmentation' (VALS2), a proprietary tool for considering different psychographic characteristics of market segments. Firstly, however, Figure 2.3 illustrates the different categories of adopter—from innovators to non-adopters.

Figure 2.3 Adoption categories for the diffusion of an innovation over time

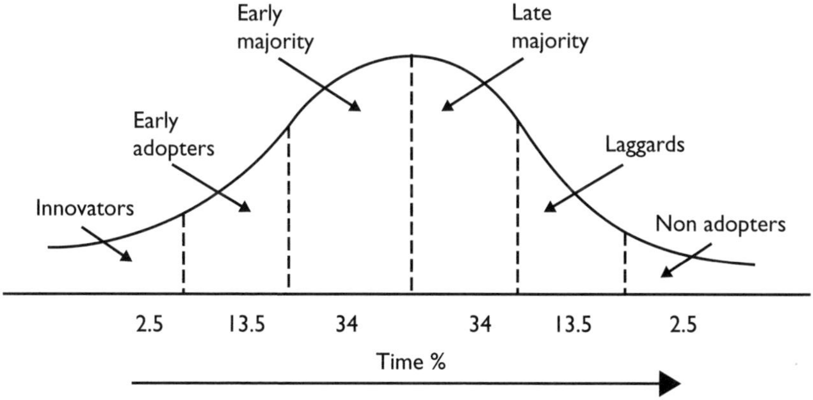

Source: Hawkins et al. (1994, p. 417)

## FACTORS WHICH AFFECT PRODUCT DIFFUSION

Not all products that are new have equal potential for consumer adoption. According to Hawkins et al. (1994), there are ten factors which affect product diffusion (see Table 2.1). Some of these (the first five) are perceived as product characteristics; others relate to consumer characteristics:

### Table 2.1 Factors affecting product diffusion

**Product characteristics**

1. *Relative advantage*
   An innovation should have either a price advantage or a performance advantage. The combination of price/performance *vis à vis* the status quo is called 'the relative advantage'. This is essentially a matter of consumer perception of product superiority.

2. *Compatibility*
   The more consistent the innovation is with consumers' perceived values, beliefs, existing products/technology and skill set, the faster the spread of the product.

3. *Complexity*
   The more difficult an innovation is to use and understand, the slower the diffusion. Complexity is seen as indicating difficulty of use. Nonetheless, if an innovation is perceived to offer significant benefits, then this can alter the consumer's perception of the complexity/difficulty trade-off. This is to say that a highly complex innovation may bring with it benefits that are so great that difficulties in using it, or in learning to use it, are accepted as part of the price to be paid. High-tech products are approached with four particular fears: fear of technical complexity; fear of rapid obsolescence; fear of social rejection; fear of physical harm. Technological complexity may be the most widespread concern among consumer innovators.

4. *Trialability*
   Low-cost and low-risk trials aid diffusion.

5. *Observability (or communicability)*
   The visibility of benefits speeds product diffusion, as does the ease with which a product's benefits can be imagined or described to potential consumers.

**Consumer characteristics**

6. *Type of group*
   The younger, more affluent and more educated the relevant adult population, the greater the willingness to embrace change and innovation.

7. *Type of decision*
   How many people are involved in the decision? The fewer people involved in the decision-making process, the quicker the product spreads.

8. *Marketing effort*
   Extensive advertising and sales promotion help spread innovation.

9. *Fulfilment of a felt need*
The more obvious the need, the faster the innovation spreads.

10. *Perceived risk*
The riskier the product is perceived to be, the slower the rate of diffusion. Risks include: the probability that the innovation will not perform as expected; the consequences of it not performing as expected; and the ability (and the cost) of reversing any negative consequences. Perceived risk can be financial, physical or social.

*Source*: Based on information from Hawkins et al. (1994, p. 417)

In adopting a 'marketing perspective' to interrogate technoculture, we are moving away from the social, cultural, policy and technology viewpoints evident elsewhere in the book. Nonetheless, in consumer societies—especially those built upon an information economy—marketing is a major discourse. In understanding the tools by which marketers explore markets, and create profits from them, we also understand something of why consumers are willing to be part of the markets—and, potentially, pay for membership. The dynamic of the market is also a reason for the dynamism of technoculture, and the accelerating rates of change in communications technology and in the cultures within which such technologies are adopted.

## INTERPERSONAL INFLUENCE

One of the very early theories of modern mass communication, developed by Katz and Lazarsfeld (1955), suggested that a critical role is played by 'personal influence'. This theory argued that some individuals ('opinion leaders') keenly seek out information from the mass media. For most people, it is interpersonal factors rather than the mass media that influence opinion formation. Knowledgeable and well informed, the expertise of media-consuming opinion leaders is recognised by others (the 'opinion followers'). The two-step flow of communication, as the theory became known, attempted to account for the fact that only about one in six people were actively interested in media coverage of the political campaign upon which Katz and Lazarsfeld focused. Those one in six people used personal influence to help the other five people form their opinions. Since those early days, the two-step flow of communication model has been expanded to a 'multi-step' flow model, which takes into account the fact that opinion leaders also seek feedback from opinion followers.

Many Internet users act as opinion leaders to others, introducing them to email, to Internet Relay Chat (IRC) and to online information and entertainment sources. Some opinion leaders will be in Rogers' (1995) innovator and early adopter categories; they will be the first people they know to buy the newest peripherals, or try the coolest Websites. An understanding of patterns of communication and information flow helps explain ways in which these new skills and competencies become more widespread, and the reasons behind the proliferation of Internet technocultures.

The model of personal influence was originally a response to a perception that the mass media were immensely powerful, 'injecting' information and values into passive audiences. The 'hypodermic model' of mass communication (as the injection thesis is now called) developed from attempts to explain the apparent effectiveness of propaganda on different populations in the lead up to World War I, and between the two world wars. This frightening image of power-without-responsibility is often a feature of the 'panic' which accompanies the introduction of a communication technology. The moral panics which accompany the spread of a new technology—such as the fear of children's access to pornography on the Net—are a sociocultural response to the adoption process. They will be discussed later in the book, in Chapter 8.

## Opinion leaders

The role of the opinion leader has attracted considerable marketing and public relations attention. In theory, if professional communicators can win over the opinion leaders, they have gone a long way towards winning public opinion as a whole. What soon became clear, as opinion leaders were investigated more closely, was that an opinion leader in one context (such as which Internet Service Provider (ISP) to use) was often an opinion *seeker* in an alternative context (which physiotherapist to use). The opinion leader and opinion seeker roles vary with the topic of conversation/inquiry.

The hallmark of an effective opinion leader, however, is credibility. People in this role are perceived as objective in the advice they offer (this often rules out salespeople) and they offer both positive and negative information relating to the subject of discussion. Further, they are prepared to offer advice as well as information. Unambiguous advice from an 'informed and trusted person' reduces anxiety and the perception of risk in the opinion seeker. If an opinion follower adopts the recommendation given, they have a clear 'authority' to cite in support of their decision. According to Schiffman et al., 'opinion leaders tend to be consumer innovators' and to speak from experience. They have 'first-hand knowledge' and are likely to try new products in their category of interest as soon as they are released. Their personal characteristics may include a willingness to innovate, self-confidence, gregariousness and a predisposition to stand apart from the crowd ('public individuation'). Social status is likely to be constant between those who give and receive opinions (although this may be a cultural variable) (Schiffman et al. 1997, pp. 480–2, paraphrased).

As to the motivation of opinion leaders, this may lie partly in a personal desire to reduce the post-purchase dissonance resulting from their own consumption choices, to gain attention, to achieve status, to assert superiority, to demonstrate awareness and expertise, and to experience interpersonal power and build personal relationships. In addition to opinions, opinion receivers gain information, reassurance, reduced search-time (in identifying and researching a desired product or service) and the approval of the opinion leader (if the advice is followed). Sometimes 'purchase pals' are taken on the shopping expedition, so that their opinion leadership role is in play at the point of purchase.

Two aspects of research into the role of opinion leaders indicate that there is more at stake than 'information' *per se*. Those who receive advice from others are more likely to offer it to others than those who do not receive advice, and opinion leaders are more likely than non-leaders to receive and seek advice from others. Using a four-way matrix (see Figure 2.4), it becomes clear that some people score high on both opinion leading and opinion seeking, while others score low on both these indicators.

In Internet technoculture terms, a person who is highly involved with life online, and willing to ask advice and support from others, may in turn provide information and support to 'newbies' online. Such an individual is likely to be more gregarious and socially integrated than someone who does neither.

Figure 2.4 Social dynamics of opinion leadership and opinion seeking

| | Opinion seeking | |
|---|---|---|
| Opinion leading | **High** | **Low** |
| **High** | Socially integrated | Socially independent |
| **Low** | Socially dependent | Socially isolated |

Source: Schiffman et al. (1997, p. 485)

An individual is much less likely to seek advice, or to rely upon advice from others, if they themselves have an expert involvement with 'the product'—perhaps through work, or through friendship networks. Perceived 'product knowledge'—such as great competence on the Net—thus reduces the probability of an individual seeking the advice of an opinion leader. These aspects go hand in hand with the fact that the higher an individual's involvement in a decision, the more likely they are to seek advice from a trusted source. The likelihood of someone being motivated to seek the advice of an opinion leader is related to a seeker's (emotional/financial) involvement with the product, their confidence in their personal knowledge of the product, their direct experience of using it, and their involvement in the decision. This relationship can be summed up as shown in Figure 2.5.

Figure 2.5 Involvement and product knowledge related to the seeking of advice from an opinion leader

| | Involvement in product | |
|---|---|---|
| Product knowledge | **High** | **Low** |
| **High** | Moderate likelihood | Low likelihood |
| **Low** | High likelihood | Moderate likelihood |

## VALS (VALUES AND LIFESTYLES SEGMENTATION)

Many markets are segmented on the basis of 'raw demographic variables': age, gender, educational achievement, income. Using these variables, a target market can be identified—for example, families (adults 35–50), with children, and an income of $50 000. Demographic variables are not the only bases on which to segment a market, however. Recently, as an acknowledgement that 'age and stage' may be becoming less and less a predictor of behaviour and interests, market researchers have become increasingly likely to adopt 'psychographic variables' to define their target market. Psychographics attempt to differentiate market segments on the basis of psychological and behavioural variables—values and lifestyles. The complexity implicit in these different ways of segmenting a market is an indication of the art and science of understanding the market. It's not a simple matter of getting a grasp of one jigsaw puzzle; it's almost as though there is an infinity of possible jigsaw puzzles to solve!

Traditional strategies for segmenting markets are very 'concrete': everyone is identifiable according to demographic criteria such as age, gender, income, education, occupation, family life-cycle (to some extent) and geography. Psychographic criteria, based on attitudes, interests and opinions, on the other hand, are not directly accessible in a yes/no mode. Similarly, sociocultural segmentation on the grounds of culture, subculture, class and life-cycle may partly be determined by an individual's identification with that class and culture, and may consequently be more subjective than objective.

One of the most successful (branded) market segmentation strategies of recent years is the Stamford Research Institute International's (SRI) Values and Lifestyles Classification System (VALS). VALS2 is a 1989 refinement of the original model and attempts to predict purchase behaviour on the basis of a division of the (American) population into one of eight categories related to resources available (with Strugglers having the fewest, and Actualisers having the greatest, resources). There are three strands of individual orientation based upon styles of decision-making: principle-oriented, status-oriented and action-oriented. Diamonds intersect to demonstrate market segments that can be considered together (for example, on the basis of resources available, or on orientation).

Resources in VALS2 include psychological, physical and material resources. So the rich, young, fit and mentally inquisitive individual with a voracious appetite for life and the resilience to survive change and reversal has a head start in reaching the 'Actualiser' pinnacle. 'Strugglers', on the other hand, are at the other end of the scale. The presence or absence of resources means that these two groups are beyond the normal categorisation of orientation. Actualisers don't choose between being principle-oriented, status-oriented and/or action-oriented: they are all of these. Similarly, Strugglers don't have a choice—their resources are too limited to aspire to any of these orientations—it is enough of a struggle to get by. The model is shown in Figure 2.6.

Figure 2.6 The VALS2 classification system

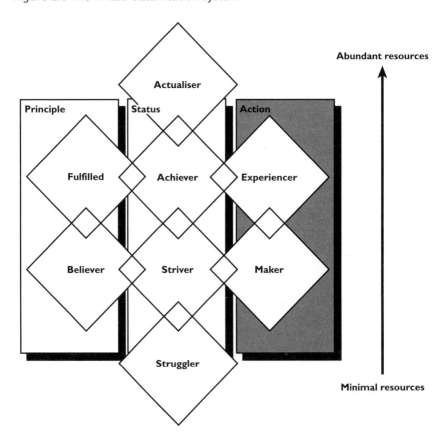

*Source*: Stanford Research Institute International and Hawkins et al. (1994, p. 350)

Horizontal segmentation applies to an individual consumer's basis for decision-making. Some consumers are principle-oriented—they might always choose their actions on the basis of environmental impact, for example, or to benefit their families, or with an eye to other moral/value dimensions. Status-oriented people don't want to miss out on the benefits of a consumer society. They tend to be goal-oriented or they want to be recognised by others as having achieved the good things in life. They work hard and play hard. Experiencers and makers are action-oriented. They like to do/feel/see things. They prefer adventure holidays to a week in a resort; they prefer to make things happen rather than watch other people doing so. They are the ones who commit first and ask questions afterwards. They tend to be optimists, but restless. The interweaving of the diamonds acknowledges that these are not stand-alone categories, but are points in a matrix of resource availability and values, attitudes and lifestyles.

One major difference between the classification of a market in VALS2 terms—compared, say, with Rogers' (1995) terms of innovation and adoption—is that the 'laggards' and 'non-adopters' of the diffusion sequence may well be 'Believers or Fulfilleds' in the VALS2 system. Some potential consumers do not value Internet technology, for example, or the opportunity to participate in online technoculture. They lag behind the market because the market holds no perceived relevance or interest for them. VALS2 suggests that these may be fulfilled consumers, rather than inadequate ones.

The issue of the need to target a market segment is related to the resource-intensive nature of marketing communications. The challenge facing the marketer is to determine which strategies will yield the best value for the market communication dollar: a concentrated approach to target one segment, or a differentiated approach where two (or more) segments are targeted differentially? Very specific segments might constitute a niche market, or a micro market. The process through which segmentation is applied is one of identifying the desirable segment; ensuring that it is sufficiently sizeable and either growing or stable at that size; and (finally) making sure that it is accessible to market communications.

## CONCLUSION

This chapter considered cultural studies approaches to technology and culture. We identified that the actual biography of a technological artefact is likely to differ from the biography anticipated at the time of purchase, and that a comparison of expectation and experience indicates something of the hopes and fears which are part of an individual's use of a new communication technology, and of the resulting technoculture. The dominant discourse in consumer societies, however (and we also looked at what a discourse is, and why it may be relevant), is the economic/marketing approach which informs such academic disciplines as consumer behaviour. This set of theories argues that expensive new technology purchases are high-involvement decisions because the consumer can see the adoption process to be one of social and financial risk. In concluding this chapter, we considered a recent market segmentation strategy and looked at psychographic variables of values, attitudes and lifestyles. Different ways of constructing people's involvement with technology offer different ways of viewing the technocultures created by interacting with communication technologies.

# 3

# DOMESTICATION OF TECHNOLOGIES

## WHAT IS A 'DOMESTICATED TECHNOLOGY'?

Once an individual, a family or a household has adopted a technology, they start to domesticate it. The term 'domestication' echoes the early years of settled human community and the process by which wild herds of animals were tamed to a point where they would reliably produce food, milk and offspring to support civilised society. The domestication of technology includes something of these elements. It implies that the technology has been harnessed to the needs of the people or household groups who sustain it—who keep it out of the rain, keep it fuelled, serviced and mended. There are overtones of predictable, reliable service. The domestication of online computer communication, for example, implies that a specific place has been found for the Internet in the rhythm of family life, and that the technology has successfully been positioned to realise some of its benefits, and to minimise its disadvantages, insofar as that family is concerned.

Most of the scholarly work in this field has concentrated upon the domestication of television, but the domestication of information and communication technologies (ICTs) in general is a common feature of contemporary households. The dynamic of domestication is associated with the private use of technoculture—with uses of the Internet in a domestic setting rather than a place of employment. Domestication carries an implication of individual and household choice. I have used the Silverstone, Hirsch and Morley schema of 'appropriation', 'objectification', 'incorporation' and 'conversion' (1992, pp. 20–6) to address the multi-stage process by which ICTs are integrated within the household. It should be noted, however, that at the same time as a technology is domesticated within the household, so the household is correspondingly technologised: this is a two-way street. The incorporation of an individual or household into a technocultural dynamic occurs in parallel with the adoption and domestication of the technology.

## INTEGRATING TECHNOLOGY INTO THE HOUSEHOLD

The term 'household' is also taken from Silverstone et al.: 'the moral economy of the household is therefore grounded in the creation of the *home*, which may or may not be a family home but which will certainly be gendered' (1992, p. 19, original italics). The implication here is that the 'home' is a construction and understanding shared by members of the 'household', and that the household is consequently the pre-existing entity, and a collection of one or more individual people. As Moores discusses it, however: 'I have tended to use the word "home" as an equivalent to terms like household or private sphere . . . a place which has powerful emotional resonances—usually a strong sense of belonging or attachment . . . beyond something which is merely a physical space occupied by household members' (1996, p. 19). In my usage, the household can represent itself to the world beyond the home. The household has a presence in the public sphere, in a way that the 'home' does not.

Silverstone et al.'s *appropriation* phase includes the household's decision to take—or not to take—a technology into the home. It involves an imaginative projection of the household by its members. Is this a household which 'can afford' and 'will use' the technology? Who makes the decision? Who is seen as using—consuming—the new resource, and in what circumstances? It includes the decision to buy—the adoption phase—and marks the movement of the object from outside the home to within the domestic sphere.

*Conversion* dynamics represent the opposite of appropriation. Both permeate the border between the household and the world beyond (the public sphere, see Chapter 7). Conversion takes the by-products of consuming ICTs and uses them as currency to build social standing, social perceptions and networks of interactions for the household with the outside world. So a computer with a desktop publishing package can be converted into enhanced social status when the computer is used to create a school newsletter, or run a community campaign. In Silverstone's terms, conversion 'defines the relationship between the household and the outside world—the boundary across which artefacts and meanings, texts and technologies pass as the household defines and claims for itself and its members a status in neighbourhood, work and peer groups in the "wider society" ' (1994, p. 130).

*Objectification* relates to the placing of the technology, creating it as an object within the home, and providing/clearing a space for it. The accommodation of a new technology often involves changes to the domestic environment: a desk for a computer; rearranging other items to free up electric sockets. These objectification rituals also herald new dynamics for social space within the household. An Internet-connected computer in a younger teenager's bedroom, for example, identifies the technology as 'theirs', but it also makes it harder for parents to 'know where their child is' while s/he is surfing. The same computer in a communal space within the home is positioned as a 'resource'—suitable for games, perhaps (depending upon the family's rules), but more regulated than in the teenager's private space, and identified as provided for family-sanctioned pursuits such as homework. A kitchen or family room-based computer is consequently less likely to be used to access pornographic or violent images while other family members are present.

*Incorporation* discusses ways in which technologies are integrated within the rhythm of life of a household (and of household members). It is also describes the process through which the household opts to incorporate itself as part of a wider audience, or community of consumption, in terms of relationships and choices made within the domestic context. By watching a television programme such as a soap opera, or the news, the family incorporates itself within a wider community that is also watching that program, and responding to the same information.

Emerging technocultural patterns relating to the adoption/incorporation of a new communication technology are anchored in the choices of individual households. Technocultures emerge as these household patterns are repeated or varied across one or more social systems, creating new cultural configurations as the technology is integrated within individual lives. Technoculture is evident in lives which are changed to accommodate interactions and communication with the new technology. For example, the Internet 'technologises' households by setting the necessary contexts and conditions through which online communications can be accessed. It has the effect of unifying elements of domestic life across different cultures and communities, regardless of location, as a result of the domestification of the technology. Cross-culturally, Internet access requires knowledge and skill, reliable power and phone connections, a dry grit-free environment and some disposable income for both capital and connection costs.

## IMAGINING COMMUNITY

The concept of a household becoming incorporated within a shared audience/user dynamic ties in somewhat with Benedict Anderson's (1991, p. 6) notion of the imagined community: 'It is imagined because the members of even the smallest nation [or audience] will never know most of their fellow members, meet them, or even hear of them, yet in the minds of each lives the image of their communion . . . all communities larger than primordial villages of face-to-face contact (and perhaps even these) are imagined'. Anderson reflected in his work upon 'the origin and spread of nationalism', but a similar process is likely to be at work when a household sees its media consumption habits as a link with a wider technoculture, and with other households who consume media in equivalent or similar ways.

Anderson's framework of an imagined community requires individual people to feel closely allied to other members of the community, who are constructed as 'known' rather than 'imagined'. While the household/community is that gathering of people with whom the individual can discuss shared experience, an imagined community becomes the colourful backdrop which contextualises the household's actions and priorities. This backdrop 'imagining' is built up using hints and raw materials from the media and elsewhere, and the dynamic is further strengthened, argues Anderson, by a person (or household) sharing in a common action of the imagined community. Anderson's example is in singing/ritual, but the example could equally well be in watching a television program, or accessing the Internet in synchronous chat:

> There is a special kind of contemporaneous community . . . At precisely the same moments, people wholly unknown to each other utter the same verses to the same melody . . . the echoed physical realisation of the imagined community . . . How selfless this unisonance feels! If we are aware that others are singing these songs precisely when and as we are, we have no idea who they may be, or even where, out of earshot, they are singing. Nothing connects us all but imagined sound (Anderson 1991, p. 145).

As well as uniting community, communication is critically relevant to the project of community differentiation. Further, this differentiation is both in relation to other communities, and in relation to global culture. As Morley and Robins comment: 'A critical regional or local culture must necessarily be in dialogue with global culture' (1995, p. 41). It is in comparing and contrasting the local with other locales, and with the global, that identity is recognised and celebrated. Castoriadis (1990, p. 29) describes 'the apparent incapacity to constitute oneself as oneself without excluding the other—*and* the apparent inability to exclude the other without devaluing and, ultimately, hating him' (cited in Morley & Robins 1995, p. 22). Castoriadis needs to add the concept of fear to that of exclusion to explain a progression to hatred, and he also needs to allow for less extreme exclusions. Nonetheless, it is theoretically the case that to know oneself one also has to know the differences between oneself and others. This is one of the uses to which the Internet is put in the project of community-building—technoculture can be used to differentiate communities at the same time as uniting them.

Given access to technology, and with the necessary skills in place, Internet communication can be converted into public property and harnessed to the process of community-building in both real life (RL) and virtual life (VL). In this dynamic, the individual uses the information and communication technology (ICT) resource to communicate something about themselves, and their understanding of the community in which they live. The value of this Internet-delivered information for community-building, however, is proportional to how interesting or relevant other people find it. It distinguishes the interested from the uninvolved.

Public communication about a household's relation to the Internet also gives an impression regarding what is 'normal' or socially acceptable. For example, a person who projects themselves as anti-pornography might do so against a background understanding (an imaginary community) that 'most people' would agree with them (notwithstanding the huge popularity of pornography Websites). This person might ostentatiously use filter software to 'censor' access to undesirable (for them) material.

Online communication may be interpreted well, or poorly, by others; however, the introduction of Internet materials means new resources with which to define, refine and communicate individual senses of 'self'. The construction of wider cultural projects is implicated within the expression of technoculture. In an exchange which converts discussion of the Internet into a communication to further the project of developing and defining the self, as presented to the public, the individual communicates something of their own self-image. Further, the public self is expanded when statements are made about what is avoided on the Internet—pornography or hate sites, for example—or when household rules relating to children's access to the Internet are explained.

The household, family, home, is the unit constructed by broadcasters as their conception of 'the audience' when material is produced or consumed, or advertising bought. Morley and Robins (1995, p. 66) credit Cardiff and Scannell with noting that ' "the audience" has always been seen as composed of family units—as "a vast cluster of families, rather than in terms of social classes or different taste publics" ' (1987, p. 161). Advertisers also view consumption as occurring at the level of the 'household' rather than in solitary person-units, or in imagined communities. For technoculture, however, participation and cultural construction occur both at the level of the individual, and the household.

## BOUNDARY MARKERS

Households regulate their members' media and communications access for a number of reasons, and in doing so household members communicate to each other what is and is not important, as well as who does and does not have relative power. Within many households, for example, gender is an organising principle of technological use and appropriation (see also Chapter 10). Domesticated technologies are utilised within the context of a conversation between the genders, and between the generations which constitute the family unit. As Livingstone argues:

> The accounting practices through which people understand and explain the role of domestic technologies in their lives reflect their gender relations and family dynamics. Talk about television or the telephone, for example, is imbued with notions of who lets who use what, of moral judgements of the other's activities, of the expression of needs and desires, of justifications and conflict, of separateness and mutuality (Livingstone 1992, p. 113).

Individual households incorporate the technological material of everyday life into a continuing conversation about power, responsibility, interconnectedness and separateness. Technoculture thus reflects and refracts existing power relations, while introducing new elements which can help change the status quo. The concept of boundary marking is particularly significant to this endeavour:

> For individual household members and for the domestic group as a whole, acts of boundary marking are of crucial importance for the ongoing creation and experience of home. These boundaries may be external 'frontiers' with the public world outside or internal divisions within the private sphere. They can be spatial or temporal, material or symbolic—but each of them is caught up with particular constructions of identity and difference—and they may be tied to dynamics of authority and resistance, or to certain feelings of 'security' and 'anxiety' (Moores 1996, p. 48).

Such communication of boundaries is multi-dimensional, including choices made between ICT products and the balance of media consumption in relation to other activities. Situational factors are also important—many families restrict ICTs in the months leading up to final school exams that regulate entry to university, and to further education and training. Interaction with a given technoculture is thus indicative of other dynamics. As one final-year schoolgirl told me:

> I've got restrictions on it [television] this year because of my TEE [Tertiary Entrance Exams].
> <WHO PUTS THE RESTRICTIONS ON?>
> Mum.
> <DO YOU NEED THAT EXTRA PRESSURE TO GET YOU WORKING?>
> Yes. Yes (Green 1998, p. 156).

A key dimension of the perceived need for adults to control children's access to media and communications is that such consumption is so pleasurable that the child or younger adult might be reluctant to exercise self-control. The pleasure of media engagement combines with elements of anticipation, consummation and fulfilment/release (although the afterglow often includes an element of anticipation for the next episode, access, communication, etc.). The desire for consumption is heightened in circumstances where the individual sees themselves as part of an imagined community, engaged in cultural construction and exchange, and anticipates that the pleasure can be relived through conversation with others who have also shared the experience. It is this inherent pleasure in consuming ICTs—the experience of connectedness and the desire for access—that strengthens the potential role of media and communications channels as a punishment or reward within many households. At the same time, rules about media consumption can be an early site of resistance for young adults keen to take more power for themselves in their own lives. (The balance of power between same-generation adults also becomes visible, but is less axiomatic.)

## TECHNOLOGY AS A BOUNDARY-BREAKER

Media theorist David Marshall has investigated the panic that surrounds many parents' responses to their children's interactions with computing technology. He locates the Internet moral panic, for example, as part of a ritual cycle of panics surrounding new technologies, and his investigation focuses primarily on 'boundaries'. (Chapter 8 investigates moral panics further.) Marshall's emphasis is on the adolescent, 'less innocent and controllable [than the child]', at the boundary of childhood and adult life. The computer is a site of contest between the adult (whose resources often fund the purchase, for educational reasons) and the child/adolescent, who sees it as a games machine: 'The arcade game dimension of the computer shifts its value from information source to entertainment site with a particular [working] class dimension' (1997, p. 71).

Marshall also identifies computer games—'Nintendo (no-friend-o)'—as taking the child out of the family room and placing them (though Marshall identifies this as a predominantly masculine culture) in isolation in the bedroom in the context of a multi-TV set household: at home, but not at home. 'Children's bedrooms [present] a whole new set of anxieties that again operate in the particular middle-class fraction of culture. The bedroom is a complex enclave of security, pleasure, vulnerability and privacy' (1997, p. 74). At the same time, video games echo earlier moral panics about TV violence, with public concern about their violent content leading eventually to a content classification system, akin to films. Nonetheless, films, television and video games increasingly share the same characters and narrative story lines, as related technocultures and popular culture continue to develop in tandem.

Parents commonly worry about their children's future, and about the opportunities available to the next generation. Such concerns combine with a parental fear of exclusion from the spaces, and the culture, of their children. Marshall (1997) argues that a fear of waste surrounds the social construction of new technologies. One aspect of this is fear of a 'waste of time/waste of money' (which can be constructed as a result of game playing, instead of using computers for educational ends). A wider concern is that, unless a young adult understands computers, they can 'waste' their conventional educational skills and strengths. The fear here is that technical computing skills have become an essential starting point for success. According to Marshall, parents believe that 'computer literacy is the passage to a comfortable future' (1997, p. 71). The computer thus becomes a symbol of the 'damned if you do/damned if you don't' battle that parents wage with the future on behalf of their children, and becomes a source of anxiety and panic.

Computer competence is associated with a variety of boundary fears—spatial, usage and also legitimate/criminal: 'The bedroom became the site *par excellence* of computer hacker culture . . . What the hacker represents is out-of-control knowledge, where the general pro-social objectives of education and computer literacy are superseded . . . Cyber has become a prefix that embodies simultaneously the fear and pleasure of the future' (1997, pp. 74–5). Marshall's conclusion is that: 'Youth's public occupation of arcades, or pool halls and pinball arcades articulates a particular menacing presence in the streets [and] . . . these formations of pleasure have been domesticated or *reclass*ified as they have moved into the home and bedrooms' (1997, pp. 72, 77).

It is interesting that so much of Marshall's analysis concerns the threat to boundaries. The classic anthropological study of this fear of boundaries is Mary Douglas' *Purity and Danger* (1978). Douglas demonstrates that a number of cultures share taboos connected with the body, and with matter entering or leaving the body. Hence food taboos exist in many societies ('don't eat in the street'), along with—for example—a prohibition upon having sex, or defecating, in public. Even the public breastfeeding of a baby can cause discomfort to some onlookers. Using boundary taboos to explain social norms about tears, semen, saliva, blood (pre-HIV), menstruation, breastfeeding, farts, etc., Douglas shows that inappropriate public exposure at moments when the boundary of the body is breached often result in an existential panic in the viewer and the viewed. Boundary fears relating to self/other are implicit in individual existence, since existence depends upon preserving 'the self' as differentiated from 'the other'. A boundary has to be maintained to prevent the outside from swamping the self, and to keep the self from dissolving into its surroundings.

Mirroring concerns that Douglas identified relating to taboos and the physical boundaries of the person, Marshall demonstrates that parents have similar existential fears about social and cultural boundaries, and about the ambiguities inherent in these. These fears involve parental attempts to maintain the boundaries of 'home' and 'work/education' and 'legitimate computer use', and can be constructed as fears for the safe passage of (their construction of) their children through (their construction of) their children's future. Such fears can also indicate that parents are hesitant to allow older children the autonomy to choose their own leisure and resource-use priorities.

## POWER AND CONSUMPTION

Parental control over ICT access is often used as a currency to reward or punish behaviour totally unrelated to ICT activity—such as failing to tidy a room, or coming home later than agreed. In this sense, ICT activity serves as a currency, a form of material exchange for 'labour'. The labour to be rewarded is pro-social behaviour required in the context of the household, or industrialised consumer society, or its training ground—school. This dynamic was explained to me by the mother of a primary school child in terms of her son's access to television:

> I went down and saw him [the teacher]—and he said 'Look, it's not that he can't, it's that he won't. It's nothing to do with the fact that he can't.' So I said 'Well, what can we do about it?' And he said 'Well, you know, we've tried incentives, we've tried lollies, we've tried punishment, and it doesn't work with him.' And I said 'Well, the only thing I can come up with is he loves his TV, how about we say—well, you come home with a star each night and get to watch telly? If you don't come home with that star, you don't get to watch telly.' And it worked (Green 1998, p. 157).

Thus one major theme evident when we investigate technology use within households is the imbalance of power between children and their parents. It is much more difficult to restrict access to the Internet, however, on the grounds of the cost of the ISP where an adolescent has an income stream that supports telecommunication and access charges.

Thus, as children become older, the balance of power in some households begins to swing away from their parents and towards them. Further, older children have choices about where they live and rigid rules might precipitate a child's move away from home, against their parents' wishes and better judgement. Participation in technoculture, and according to whose terms, is a reflection of power and autonomy, and changes over time.

One manifestation of the importance of ICT consumption practices within the household is their capacity to demonstrate rhythms of power. Although it would be wrong to imply that relationships between household members are infinitely flexible and renegotiable, it is likely that there is a continuous renegotiation of bonds and of boundaries. Movements in the power balance are not only possible but inevitable, since every household has a dynamic identity, and this impacts upon its own ICT consumption life-cycle. Within this context, information and communication products are used both as a means of integrating different household (and/or family) members, and as a means of differentiation between household members.

Children, for example, may use the Internet to play games, or to research projects while parents might use it for work, or to maintain email contact with others. The differences can also translate as similarities:

> The lack of boundaries both in hunting and gathering and in electronic societies leads to many striking parallels. Of all known societal types before our own, hunting and gathering societies have tended to be the most egalitarian in terms of the roles of males and females, children and adults, and leaders and followers . . . play and work often take place in the same sphere and involve similar activities . . . work and play have begun to merge in our electronic age. Both children and adults now spend many hours a week staring at video monitors [computer screens] (Meyrowitz 1985, pp. 315–16).

At the same time as bonds between household members are negotiated and renegotiated, so the household dynamics affect the bonds which are built with individuals from the wider community. For instance, an adolescent who is prevented from chatting with friends online because of ISP costs would be prevented from participating on equal terms with other members of their friendship circle who are chatters. They would be barred from engagement in IRC technoculture. The loss is more than that of the pleasure of chatting; it is the loss of a potential membership of the chatter community. Further, the reason offered to a friendship circle as to why that adolescent is unable to participate—economic, cultural, etc.—becomes a new element in the public construction of that adolescent's household, and the relationships of that household's members to each other and to people in the community. Such reasons may also impact upon the private sphere, as the 'denied' individual internalises the reactions of others in their friendship circle, and that internalised reaction (and possible resentment) feeds into dynamics within the home.

Technoculture participation consequently becomes a medium through which the priorities and structures of the household are communicated to the wider sphere. It also provides a way in which—particularly vividly—the public sphere is introduced to the household. This dynamic is the paradoxical two-way exchange of the screen, discussed in Chapter 11. The introduction of a new ICT, or of new services and activities involving ICTs, becomes especially relevant, because change illuminates both the rhythm of the present and visions for the future. In talking about newly introduced services, novel insights are forged, even for those who have been used to ICTs. The household is the primary site for the construction of these technological insights. Thus 'the household' talks not only of itself to itself; it contextualises and informs discussions of gender, technology, social conversion, culture and society.

## MASLOW'S HIERARCHY OF NEEDS

Is it important that we feel a sense of connection with others? Maslow's hierarchy of needs is one way of looking at the importance placed upon a sense of social connectedness, and upon interactions with technocultural technologies—telephone, television, Internet and email—that help us feel connected.

Abraham Maslow worked as a psychologist during World War II. The story goes that Maslow noticed that, as food became scarcer, people talked about it more. As food increased in supply and quality, people began again to discuss interpersonal relationships. It was as if hunger meant that the object of desire was the roast beef dinner rather than the latest recording sensation or film star. Once hunger had receded, the pin-up of the roast beef dinner in the serviceman's locker was replaced (again) by the pin-up of the Forces' favourites (Betty Grable, say, or Vera Lynn). This observation about human attention focusing on differing objects depending upon how much food was available led Maslow (1948) to develop his theory of the hierarchy of needs.

Maslow's theory of needs suggests that our basic needs are physiological: air, water, food, shelter. Once these needs are satisfied, attention can be turned to safety needs. Social needs come next in importance after safety, and the basic necessities of life. (Commentators disagree about whether sex counts as a physiological need or a social need.) Social needs help set the scene for ego-driven needs, where a desire to develop a strong and integrated ego is secondary in importance to developing a social circle. The pinnacle of Maslow's hierarchy is reserved for 'self-actualisation' needs. Are you the best you can be? Are you working on improving yourself as your life's project? If so, the chances are that you consume some of the copious self-development popular culture literature—and your basic physiological, safety, social and ego needs are broadly met.

Figure 3.1 Maslow's hierarchy of needs

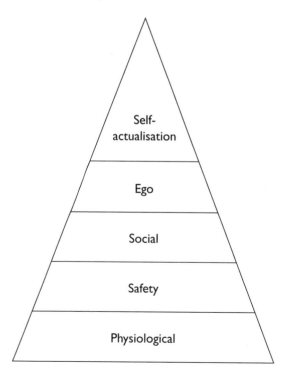

Maslow identifies various triggers as stimulating the arousal of moti-vated behaviour. These include physiological, emotional, cognitive and environmental factors—which are not necessarily mutually exclusive. Maslow suggests a 'hierarchical' approach to needs, where one need is broadly satisfied before the next becomes a focus. The theory of a hier-archy of needs can be criticised, however, on the grounds that we can be working on self-actualisation (for example) partly as compensation for our unmet social needs. Further, ambiguously, we could be enrolled in tertiary study to meet social, ego and self-actualisation needs, but also because we fear our work is changing and that we will face redundancy and food and shelter (physiological) issues unless we change too.

## APPLYING MASLOW'S THEORY TO ONLINE BEHAVIOUR

Although it makes intuitive sense, one problem in relating the theory of a hierarchy of needs to technoculture lies in addressing the difference between needs and goals, and in distinguishing differences between needs, wants and desires. Some people assert that needs and goals are always changing, but that the motivation to fulfil those needs and goals is an enduring constant. Maslow would probably have argued that, where needs and goals are changing, this indicates that the most basic levels of his hierarchy—physiological and safety needs—have already been met. In less specific terms, needs can be divided into physiological needs (generally seen as more basic) and psychological needs. This latter category can be further divided into rational and emotional needs.

Maslow's hierarchy of needs is not the only model with currency. Other theorists have posited the particular importance of a trio of needs for power, achievement and affiliation. All of these can be seen as being met in some ways through participation in technoculture. In particular, technoculture offers both intellectual stimulation and emotional engage-ment—the latter, for instance, is particularly evident in online communities and through email.

Motives that underlie individual needs, however, and the motives for choosing one way to fulfil a need over alternative approaches, are very hard to pin down. Motivational research has depended upon three main methodologies: observation and inference; subjective report; and projec-tive techniques. Even so, some motives (according to psychoanalytical theory, amongst others) are hidden in the 'subconscious' and may not be readily identifiable. Current research into online culture, for example, may observe where Net users go, but it has to deduce their motivations. Interaction with online communities can be seen as socially motivated, and as behaviour which addresses Maslow's hierarchical categories of social, ego and self-actualisation needs.

Although an individual's aspirations may rise as their goals are achieved, Net users may also experience frustration when goals elude them. This frustration can be expressed in a variety of ways, including aggression, withdrawal, projection, escapism and repression. It is possible to argue (and many people do) that engaging technoculturally in online communities may be an indication of frustration with RL. In this scenario, VL is an indication of withdrawal and escapism, and may indicate response to a 'safety' need, in the form of retreat from a hostile world. Those who participate in an online community tend to respond that negative value judgements about online communities are an indication that the person making the assertion is inexperienced in true online engagement, and that VL offers social and personal challenge and support equivalent to that presented in RL. These are some of the issues to be explored further in later chapters.

## HOUSEHOLD VALIDATION AND THE EXPLORATION OF EXPERIENCE

Broadcasting research (especially audience studies) examines ways in which households and individuals struggle to see themselves reflected in media products. One of a range of citizenship information 'rights' discussed in Chapter 7 is the right for media consumers 'to recognize themselves and their aspirations in the range of representations offered' (Murdock & Golding 1989, p. 184). This search for a reflection in the media of the individual, and their household, serves as a public validation of private experience and permits a sense of social 'recognition'. It is this dynamic of recognition which lies behind the desires of ethnic minorities to see themselves represented in mainstream television, and behind women's desires to see themselves valued in the media for attributes other than youth or beauty.

In addition to searching media products for personal recognition and validation, the household harnesses the media as an accessory in the socialisation of younger family members. ICTs allow access to material that can provide a 'common ground' for cross-generational household discussions. Such materials serve an agenda-setting role within which the past and present (and possible futures) can be explored. If a character in a soap opera develops a cyber-addiction, it can prompt a family discussion as to 'What do you think will happen now?', 'What would you do if I . . .?' Families and households use the broadcast programmes to explore their own past and possible future experiences.

The Internet is used by some households, some of the time, to explore their experience of household life and to provide reassurance that, no matter how chaotic family life might appear within the context of lived reality, things could be much worse. Narratives of chaos and catastrophe introduced to the household through the Net, and through broadcast programmes, serve a primary role of reassurance. According to Morley and Robins, it is partly through such consumption and discussion of ICTs that households develop a 'collective identity' (1995, p. 72). To count as an 'identity', the sense of a group to which an individual sees themself as belonging 'must be sustained *through time*, through a collective memory, through lived and shared traditions, through a sense of a common past and heritage. It must also be maintained *across space*, through a complex mapping of territories and frontiers, principles of inclusion and exclusion that define "us" against "them" ' (original italics).

It is within such an ICT-facilitated context that adults (of both genders) use television programming to help indicate to children appropriate social and emotional codes and behaviours. Interaction with ICTs is unlikely to be the main vehicle for this enterprise: parental feedback upon a child's actions and reactions is much more important. Nonetheless, it is clear from individuals' discussions of specific situations that television and Internet information has an important role in providing a socio-emotional context for the household within which this learning takes place. Technoculture is consequently a critical tool for socialisation. While providing common material or information around which household members interact, ICTs also construct a framework on/with which to differentiate one member from another, to differentiate between generations, and to differentiate ways in which power and control can be asserted.

The Internet can be used in a 'game' of giving and withholding attention, and Meyrowitz' (1985) apparently shared family space—with parents and children taking turns to access the technology—can be illusory. People use different ICT access dynamics to tune out others, to funnel attention and to create an individual space in a shared domain. In these circumstances, ICTs can create a psychological haven for the individual at a time when the household may fail to provide a refuge.

Internet access and television programming can serve a similar function to that snippet of an interview famously described by Bausinger: 'Early in the evening we watch very little TV. Only when my husband is in a real rage. He comes home, hardly says anything and switches on the TV' (1984, p. 344, quoted in Ang 1991a, p. 161). According to Bausinger, 'pushing the button doesn't signify, "I would like to watch this", but rather, "I would like to see and hear nothing"'.

## RESEARCHING THE DREAM

As well as offering an apparently safe haven, the Internet can provide images that flesh out nebulous hope for the future. Thus a school student might choose a possible university from an Internet Website, or a family might plan an annual holiday using online images of faraway places. This interactive access to information, and images of 'possibilities', becomes a component of that individual/household's public role. Potentially, household members become identified as people who optimistically focus on goals, and who work to achieve them. Such an identification can influence the way in which household members relate to others in their community, and can mean that a secondary role as 'community resource' or 'information researcher' is opened up for the individual or household in relation to their wider social circle.

The converse is also true. A non-Internet-user can 'convert' a lack of Internet access into a communication—a continuous restatement—about separation from those who use and discuss the technology. Where shared social experience becomes a way of stating identity, opting out establishes a different identity. In our society an individual necessarily communicates something about themself through their reaction to a technoculture such as the Internet. Although there is evidence of people mourning the passing of the pre-Internet age, those who do so are communicating that they have a 'social persona' which desires and values high levels of face-to-face social contact. Thus discussion of the negative impacts of the Internet is used to form links with others, but also to differentiate the self from those others who consume ICTs.

Access to ICTs is one way in which a community can convert media images and information into educational resources to teach community members about life elsewhere. This inside/outside community dynamic, like other border concerns, carries the fear of engulfment. Underpinning these fears of life in communities beyond the boundary is a belief that life in one's own community is substantially different from life elsewhere. A major part of the project of community-building is to use material about life 'outside' to persuade oneself that the home community is the best place to be. In this respect, the Internet—as with broadcasting—offers much RL community-affirming material.

## CONCLUSION

Technology serves as a boundary marker both between and within households, and can be used to express difference along axes of gender, generation and age. Further, it illuminates power relations within the household in terms of who lets whom use what and when. This power is often used as a currency for rewarding good behaviour and punishing poor behaviour. One reason for the power of technology's use as a reward is that it has relevance to so many needs and wants in an information society. Maslow's hierarchy of needs is one way to explain how technology use relates to social, ego and self-actualisation needs.

Households use their media, information and communication resources to understand their own rules and mores, and to explore their experience of 'household' in relation to images of other households offered through ICT channels. Media images can also be used to locate and structure individual and household goals for the future, and as material to persuade household members that their home and their community are good places to be.

# 4

# FRAGMENTING MASS MEDIA IN THE POSTMODERN INFORMATION SOCIETY

## THE MASSIFICATION OF MEDIA AND INFORMATION

Mass audiences, made up of many households, were constructed through the introduction and circulation of mass media—radio, television, newspapers, magazines, films and books—as part of the dynamic creation of mass markets for mass-produced goods. The nature of the mass media, and the homogenisation of individuals into masses, has been seen as compromising the public sphere and laying the foundations of a search for community, identified as an increasingly important preoccupation of the twenty-first century. (These issues will be covered in greater depth in Chapters 7 and 9.) Since the mass media are technologically mediated communication channels—via high technology (Internet), new technology (radio and television) and older technology (press and magazines)—the mass media are technocultural. These technocultures allow ideas, words, sounds and images to be communicated across space to audiences and consumers. The communication can also be stored over time for later access, and creates an historical database. The mass media are both technocultural themselves, and a source of information about the growth, prevalence and importance of other technocultures.

Mass media configure audiences into communities of consumption, which are keenly researched according to a number of agendas. Advertisers like to know what they are getting for their money and, in the famous aphorism, 'the role of the commercial media is to deliver audiences to advertisers'. Thus audience research and statistics are particularly important for the commercialisation of any medium. A social agenda drives research into issues like the effects of consuming media, or of consuming 'too much' media, discussed below. Ang (1991a) describes herself and others as 'desperate' to analyse, understand and describe audiences, but it has only been in the past quarter of a century that the audience has been researched on (essentially) its own terms—in the branch of media and culture studies inquiry called, conveniently, 'audience studies'.

Audience studies methodologies assume that audience participants are sufficiently insightful and sufficiently cognisant of their various pleasures, desires and frustrations to be able to discuss their media consumption patterns with interested researchers. The paradigm takes as read that people have reasons for their behaviours, and sets out to uncover what these are through (often) a variety of interview and observation techniques. This research perspective accords audience membership an importance in people's lives and, in effect, audience studies investigate media technocultures. The nature of the 'mass' audience is illuminated by specific comments and examples offered during the research process by individual audience members—analysed and interpreted by the research team.

When television audiences were first investigated, it was reasonably possible to identify television content as being genred: to distinguish between soap opera, sports, news and current affairs, light entertainment and documentary. With the exception of face-to-face communication, the Internet promises equivalents to all mediated communication available through other channels. It will eventually deliver everything audio-visual from two-way telecommunications through to radio and television broadcasting, coupled with the gamut of text-graphic print products including the letter, the newsletter/circular and the full mass-media printed magazine or newspaper. Internet technoculture promises to reproduce elements of all other media/communication technocultures which have preceded it.

Detailed audience studies, using semi-ethnographic techniques made famous by British consumption studies researcher David Morley (1980, 1986), have yet to be carried out on Internet users. The Internet is paradoxical: one medium serving all the functions of the 'old' mass media, but with the added extra of interactivity. As the Internet becomes all-encompassing, however (in a dynamic familiar to discourses of postmodernism and globalisation, discussed below), so the mass audience fragments. Individual users on the Internet are able to choose between a wide variety of simultaneous offerings and channels, and tend to express difference and individuality. There is no 'normal' way (as yet) to use the Internet, and the construction of user/audience research perspectives will prove a significant challenge.

## TIME, SPACE AND COMMUNICATION

Communication patterns and audience memberships affect the ways we understand our lives, and the ways we experience time and space. Sless' view (1995, p. 4) is that 'each of us, as individuals or as members of communities, inhabits particular communications ecologies'. Arguably, each of us inhabits a variety of such ecologies simultaneously or in succession (depending upon the technology, the community and the communication). Communication ecologies express our technocultural repertoire, our access to ICT technologies and the ease with which we use these.

As a migrant, leaving my birth country at the age of 30 years, one communication ecology supports continuing connection with my family of origin, and mainly depends upon IDD (International Direct Dialling) and associated telecommunications technologies, such as satellites. This is a very different ecology from that which unites me as a parent with other parents in the communities centred upon my children's schools. These different ecologies have implications for the kinds of communication available: face-to-face (unmediated), old-technology mediated (phone, mail) and/or new-technology mediated (cybercommunication).

Innis and McLuhan both argue that the technology used for communication impacts upon the perception and importance of space and time: some technologies are predisposed to communicating across space (e.g., paper), while others persist through time (e.g., stone). Examples Innis (1991 [1951]) gave for the use of these technologies were the stability of the 3000-year-long Pharaonic Dynasties in Egypt, where stone persisted through the ages; and the mobility and spatial extent of the ancient Roman Empire, where orders and instructions could be swiftly despatched on light-to-carry clay tablets, or by an early form of paper. Technoculture can similarly persist in temporal terms, or extend in spatial ones.

As we have seen, McLuhan uses the term 'technology' in a very broad manner to include an argument that written language is technological. Such an argument implies that even face-to-face, unmediated communication may be technological and technocultural, and contemporary communities and convergent technologies further blur old distinctions by using, for example, space-bound (broadcasting) and time-bound (video recordings) communication simultaneously, or in different circumstances. Effectively, the information and communication technologies available to contemporary society ensure that modern communications can extend across space *and* time. 'Communication technology' is no longer specific, but generic, with many different means of achieving communication ends.

The time/space issue became more significant, historically, once technology permitted the separation of the communication from the physical presence of the communicator. Arguably, this was the point at which technoculture became differentiable from the purely sociological. In oral culture, both the communication and the communicator are present or represented (as in the re-telling of a story). Simple messages could be conveyed through sensory channels at a distance—smoke signals, for example, or drum beats—but these were inadequate for complex communications. Further, they were difficult or impossible to record and store.

In written cultures, the thought may be separated from the thinker, but for many generations the written word could only be conveyed as fast as the fastest mode of (human) transport. James Carey (1989) discusses at some length the importance of the introduction of the telegraph in terms of removing the message from the restrictions of human travel. The telegraph also 'allowed communication to control physical processes actively. The early use of the telegraph in railroad signalling is an example: telegraph messages could control the physical switching of rolling stock, thereby multiplying the purposes and effectiveness of communication' (Carey 1989, p. 203). Used for regulating instructions for equipment, the telegraph would be technological, but not necessarily technocultural, since it was not being utilised directly for human communication and the creation of cultural material. In other circumstances, however, the telegraph played a highly technocultural role. Carey notes:

> the telegraph altered literary style. In a well-known story, 'cablese' influenced Hemingway's style, helping him to pare his prose to the bone, dispossessed of every adornment. Most correspondents chafed under its restrictiveness, but not Hemingway. 'I had to quit being a correspondent,' he told Lincoln Steffens later. 'I was getting too fascinated by the lingo of the cable.' (Carey 1989, p. 211)

Carey's comments about 'communication as control' build upon James Beniger's (1986) ideas, discussed in Chapter 5. Beniger examines the implications of the telegraph and other communications technologies in achieving new levels of control of industrial processes, including advertising, production and distribution:

> Control of production was achieved by the continuing organization and preprocessing of industrial operations. The resulting flood of mass produced goods demanded comparable innovation in control of distribution. Growing infrastructures of transportation, including rail networks and steamship lines, depended for control on a corresponding infrastructure of information processing and telecommunications . . . Mass production and distribution could not be completely controlled, however, without control of demand and consumption. Such a control required a means to communicate information about goods and services to national audiences [i.e., mass media] in order to stimulate or reinforce demand for these products, as well as a means to gather information on the preferences and behaviour of this audience . . . The postal system also served as a new medium of mass communication through bulk mailings of mass produced publications (Beniger 1986, p. 285).

Industrial and post-industrial societies are necessarily technocultural.

## MEDIA EFFECTS?

The mass media play a crucial role in information societies the world over. It's hard to imagine how a society could be an 'information society' without a vibrant mass media, and without information packaged as a commodity for sale at a profit. The mass media are just one example of the commodification of ICT technoculture, however. Although the mass media are businesses, and typically account for about 10 per cent of the capitalisation of a western country's stock exchange, they are not 'just another business' (Schultz 1994, 1998).

The mass media (in addition to more individual and personal information sources, like the telephone and letters), set the agenda for our shared discussions as friends, families, neighbours, workers and societies. They provide much of the raw material through which we develop our understandings of ourselves, our place in the world and what it is to be part of an 'American', 'Australian', 'New Zealand' or 'British' nation. The importance of the media in information societies, argue Cunningham and Turner (1993, p. 6), lies in the fact that the media are 'consciousness industries'. We do not passively consume the media; we actively confirm or adjust our mindsets in response to what we see, hear and talk about. The media influence our consciousness.

Between the world wars, the media were seen as extraordinarily powerful and much effort was spent on researching the effectiveness of propaganda and media persuasion (Lasswell et al. 1969 [1935]). This was partly because governments wanted to harness this power, and partly because they wanted to protect their citizens from those who used the media unscrupulously. The belief that mass media have effects remains strong today. It is implicit in every piece of paid advertising, and in film/video/TV and games ratings systems which judge some media products suitable for children while other products can only be seen by adults in regulated circumstances. Media effects theory underpins rules relating to the foreign ownership of media interests, and to the minimum acceptable amounts of programming generated in a country or a region. (These are sometimes called 'local content' regulations.)

Research into media effects over the past 80 years or so has led to the development of complex and subtle models of communication. In the early days, the model used was effectively that of a hypodermic needle, injecting a media-borne point of view into society. This perspective implied that the contents of the media were accepted wholesale by recipients, with very little in the way of critical thought or judgement on the part of an (essentially passive) audience. As research developed, and models such as Katz and Lazersfeld's (1955) two-step flow of communication were put forward, it became clear that there is no simple correlation between media consumption and resulting human behaviour.

Thousands of studies, for example, have failed to find clear, consistent evidence of cause and effect between violence on the screen and violence in society, but considerable debate remains. At the same time, even commentators who believe in the 'active' (powerful, questioning) audience concede that the media operate in a significant agenda-setting role: they circulate topics and provide information about issues that are then debated in the public domain. If we agree that the media form a consciousness industry (even where hedged with qualifiers—'if . . .', 'but . . .'), then it is also important to examine what the media say, and how and why they say it, as they set the agenda. How much might our perceptions be conditioned by our media technocultures, and by the unacknowledged biases of media workers and owners?

## THE OBJECTIVITY OF THE MEDIA

Given that the mass media play a critical role in informing us about ourselves and our nation, we like to believe that media workers are ethical and objective, providing us with enough information to see the complexity of a situation and make up our own minds. In this scenario, it is important that journalists aim for objectivity, do not write nice things just because they have been paid by vested interests, or because they own shares, or because they benefited from a Business Class package to a resort-based briefing. In an ideal world, journalists would investigate their stories fully and report the wider picture.

There are examples where this standard of professionalism has clearly not been reached. In 1999, an Australian talk show host, John Laws, was accused of attacking the banking sector during his programmes on Sydney radio station 2UE while (at the same time) negotiating a public relations deal with the Banking Association. Once the deal was agreed and delivered, the radio show attacks stopped, and Laws started presenting the banks' side of the story. When challenged about this practice, Laws claimed that he was an entertainer, not a journalist, and thus not bound by any codes of conduct prohibiting the sale of editorial opinion. He also argued that audiences know that commercial radio operates on this sort of sponsorship. Both these arguments were thoroughly discredited in the inquiries and hearings set up to investigate this misuse of the mass media for individual and commercial gain (www.aba.gov.au [June 2001]).

Michael Galvin's case study of media coverage of the 1991 Gulf War offers a more global example of bias. Since the Gulf War involved a number of western powers, the national interest (rather than personal gain) was the likely journalistic excuse for the subjectivity of reporting. Even given the national interest, however, western journalists' coverage of Iraqi soldiers during the fighting was not at all balanced or objective:

> Despite the high-tech features of the war, much of its coverage in the media was as distorted and propagandist as any previous conflict. For example, it has been shown that, in one single week during the conflict, the British press used the following terms to describe Allied troops and Iraqi troops:
> '*Allied troops*: boys, lads, professionals, lion-hearts, cautious, confident, heroes, dare-devils, young knights of the skies, loyal, desert rats, resolute, brave.'

'*Iraqi troops*: troops, hordes, brain-washed, paper tigers, cowardly, desperate, cornered, cannon fodder, bastards of Baghdad, blindly obedient, mad dogs, ruthless, fanatical' (*Sunday Age*, 10 February 1991, p. 8).

However, such blatant propaganda and disregard for the full facts has probably been true of many wars and most participants for as long as the power of the media to influence events has been recognised (Galvin 1994, p. 185).

Wars themselves are expressions of communication, technology and society, just as the media reports which discuss them are an expression of technoculture).

## THE MEDIA AND GLOBALISATION

CNN, an American media organisation with global reach, was about the only media agency able to get independent images (i.e., not filmed from the Allies' attack vehicles or equipment) out of Iraq during the Gulf War. With CNN and 'smart bomb' cover, the war became a global media event—as have most recent wars that involve soldiers from the western world. The dynamic of the global coverage of the war was to 'localise' in some ways the issues involved (although it was the Iraqis who did the dying):

Did the Gulf War take place in Kuwait, Baghdad or Washington? Was the site the Middle East or the whole globe? This is a particularly vexing point. If Iraqi commanders order a SCUD missile launch via radio-telephone from Baghdad, the signal may be detected by orbiting US satellites. Another satellite detects the launch using infra-red sensors. Information from both will be down-linked at Nurrungar in South Australia. From there it will be relayed to the Pentagon, then again to US command HQ in Saudi Arabia and to Patriot missile bases in Saudi Arabia and Israel (Wark 1991, pp. 6–7).

As early as 1968, Marshall McLuhan and Quentin Fiore commented: 'Today, electronics and automation make mandatory that everybody adjust to the vast global environment as if it were his little home town' (1968, p. 11). Communications media return to us images of village-like encounters, but on a global scale, with American teen sensation Britney

Spears and Prince William Windsor more easily recognisable than neighbourhood young adults. British sociologist Anthony Giddens describes globalisation as 'the intensification of world-wide social relations which link distant localities in such a way that local happenings are shaped by events occurring many miles away and vice versa' (1991, p. 64). Globalisation is quintessentially technocultural.

In these terms, the global media are particularly American and/or British, and many commentators are concerned about this concentrated association of global media with the interests of these powerful western nations. American critical scholar Herb Schiller (1991), in particular, argues that the western mass media act a little like an invading imperial force, subjugating and crushing all cultures that stand against them. The McDonaldisation of the world (Ritzer 1996), and the power of English as a spoken language, are two trends he uses to support his thesis. The thesis that Schiller propounds is called 'cultural imperialism' (addressed in Chapter 9).

## THE LOCAL IN THE GLOBAL

Even though Schiller has a point, the situation is less uni-dimensional than his analysis implies. As well as being technocultural, globalisation is 'meta-narrative', or a modernist over-arching story. Like capitalism, or communism, globalisation is an essentially modern way of referring to a phenomenon that is more complex than the theory initially acknowledges. Audience studies of the reception of global products indicate that a more fragmented, less predictable process is also in operation. Addressing the meanings that recipients make from global media—without denying the power disparity between producers and receivers of mass media messages—researchers identify a radical disengagement at the local level from what might be termed the 'global message' (see *The Young and the Restless* case study in Chapter 9). Worldwide audiences are not mindlessly receptive of American culture. The experience of peripheral countries is that cultures do survive—sometimes through resentment—the disproportionate influence of the media from other nations, British or American. We may watch *Ally McBeal*, we do not live it.

In his research into the attitudes of Hong Kong viewers to foreign television programming, Paul Lee's findings are that: 'most Hong Kong people consider that foreign television has a good impact on Hong Kong culture and individuals' knowledge. Seven in ten (72%, N = 189) thought that foreign programmes could enrich local culture, and eight in ten (82%, N = 196) considered that foreign programmes could increase their knowledge' (1995, pp. 72–3). Arguably, the introduction of mass media popular culture is one way of finding out more about both the 'self' and the 'other'. Lee suggests that the result of his survey 'contradicts the thesis of communication imperialism, [but] it may be a unique case. Nevertheless, if the theory of communication imperialism is to become a general, rather than a local, theory, it needs to incorporate the varied experiences of receiving foreign cultures in different cultural settings at different stages' (Lee 1995, p. 80). In other words, Lee asserts that the cultural imperialists may themselves be culturally imperious by not paying adequate attention to the experiences and opinions of those outside the critical scholarship discourse of their core cultural area.

The image of a hypodermic injection of media messages into the psyche of passive consumers has repeatedly been discredited. The postmodern interpretation of media effects involves a call to ethnography—the study of 'the irreducible dynamic complexity of cultural practices and experiences' (Ang 1991a, p. 161). Ang asserts that the globalisation of culture:

> should not be conceived as a process of straightforward homogenisation, but rather as a checkered process of systematic integration in which local cultures lose their autonomous sovereignty and become thoroughly interdependent, relying for their active continuation precisely on the appropriation of global flows of mass-mediated forms and technologies (Ang 1991b, p. 5).

Ang suggests, for example, that the 'curry eastern' is an appropriation by Indian cinema of the conventions of the American spaghetti western, while the burgeoning popularity of martial arts movies for Cantonese audiences incorporates and transforms 'James Bond style film narratives by using fists and martial arts as weapons, as well as drawing on traditional Cantonese values' (Ang 1991b, p. 6).

It may be that the more globalised the communication, the more local is the interpretation of the message. Perhaps the more homogenous the product, the more fragmented are the meanings taken from it. The dominant reading (the intended or obvious interpretation of the media text from the point of view of the producers) is frequently resisted or subverted. Media products become the site of a struggle between homogenising forces and those that fragment wholes which have become too unwieldy. Postmodernism invokes its own oppositions to discuss these issues, addressing both globalisation/localisation and homogenisation/fragmentation. A postmodern perspective is available through the rich, deep consideration of homogeneity and fragmentation—the tension of the global in the local and the local in the global.

## POSTMODERNISM AND THE INFORMATION SOCIETY

While postmodernism resists the overarching as an explanation for anything (including the differences between the modern and the postmodern), it is worth indicating some differences in a comparative table (see Table 4.1). Both the modern and the postmodern are technocultural, but the technologies involved may differ.

**Table 4.1 A comparison of modern and postmodern characteristics**

| Modern | Postmodern |
| --- | --- |
| Industrial society | Information society |
| Production | Consumption |
| An overarching meta-narrative: communism, capitalism, etc. | No integrating story explains the postmodern experience |
| Unambiguous | Ambiguous |
| Cause and effect | Chaos, random |
| Certain | No certainty |
| Depth | Surface |
| Exchange | Commodification |
| Borders and boundaries | Overlapping layers, shifting meanings |
| Mass media | Niche media |
| Alienation | Fragmentation |

Ann Game, in her book *Undoing the Social: Towards a Deconstructive Sociology*, starts with 'the basic semiotic assumption that culture or the social is written, that there is no extra-discursive real outside cultural systems' (Game 1991, p. 4). In other words, the way people construct the issues that concern them creates a 'text' that is analysed. Game is arguing, in essence, that there is no 'certainty' or 'reality', apart from what we choose to see that way. Deconstructive philosophy and discourse analysis—postmodern tools—address the construction of these social texts. Such tools can be applied to the analysis of the modern, as well as the postmodern, and to analyses of technoculture.

Identifying Edvard Munch's image *The Scream* as quintessentially modernist, Frederic Jameson (1984), one of the first English-language postmodern theorists, comments that the modern involves the 'alienation of the subject' (1984, p. 63). Modernist texts include the early industrial city, mass production, mass broadcast communications, the assembly line and the theories of Marx and Freud: individual *angst*. Modernism offered some (alienating) boundaries between home and work, labour and capital, workers and bosses. Postmodernism, on the other hand, displaces the alienation of the subject 'by the fragmentation of the subject' (Jameson 1984, p. 63).

A filmic illustration of the difference between the perspectives might be a comparison of the 'modern' *1984* with the 'postmodern' *Brazil*. *1984* is the story of Winston Smith, who futilely opposes both 'the system' and its figurehead—Big Brother. In sombre and depressed/depressing tones, *1984* offers a tale of heroism defeated, and the eventual subjugation of the human will. *Brazil*, in contrast, features an inept bureaucracy that is deadly for all that it is incompetent. While Winston Smith takes the system on in *1984*, in *Brazil* the battle of the individual against the system is the result of random outworkings of a clerical error. There are issues of right and wrong, but the drama is not played out in the context of right versus wrong, but in the context of it all being a 'terrible mistake'. The greyness of *1984* becomes a positively flamboyant use of colour in *Brazil*, and drama, pastiche and theatre are most likely to break out in the more tragic moments of the tale. A first viewing of *Brazil* is likely to evoke the question 'What was that about?', whereas there is no doubt about the intent of *1984*. Both films have the power to unsettle, however.

Postmodernism fragments both 'the subject' and 'the self' and has been dubbed 'the philosophy of inverted commas' (Scruton 1994, p. 504). According to Jameson, this means:

> the end for example of style, in the sense of the unique and the personal, the end of the distinctive individual brushstroke (as symbolised by the emergent primacy of mechanical reproduction). As for expression and feelings or emotions, the liberation, in contemporary society, from the older *anomie* of the centred

subject may also mean, not merely a liberation from anxiety, but a liberation from every other kind of feeling as well, since there is no longer a self present to do the feeling (Jameson 1984, p. 64).

## POSTMODERNISM, PEASANTS AND THE PROLETARIAT

Although we talk about the information revolution, the information economy and the information society, it can be hard to remember just how different our contemporary methods of technocultural and social organisation are from those that precede them. Whether or not we accept that the postmodern exists, if we accept Game's perspective then both the modern and the premodern eras are texts that we have constructed. The premodern epoch tends to be seen in rosy terms as harmonious, communal and natural, grounded in agriculture and the church. The plague, the Inquisition, fire, famine and the lack of human and civil rights are generally ignored in this romantic reinterpretation. In comparison with this positive view of the premodern, modernist perspectives—as we have seen—communicate negativity and loss.

Using work by Japanese theorist Yoneji Masuda (1972), futurist Barry Jones has made a useful contribution in comparing and contrasting the means of production, social structure and values of the agricultural, industrial and information eras. Jones is a former Australian Minister for Science and first wrote his treatise on 'technology and the future of work' in 1982. It remains a best seller, and is regularly updated. Table 4.2 is included in the revised edition of his classic text, *Sleepers, Wake!*

Naturally, there is no suggestion that each layer of social organisation should be seen as entirely obliterating the former one. New systems of production co-exist with the remnants of former system(s). Similarly, the theatre continues to exist following the introduction of the cinema, and the cinema retains a role even after the widespread use of television. The Internet has yet to make all other ICTs redundant.

Throughout human history, most agricultural societies were characterised by face-to-face communication patterns, where information travelled at the same speed as the human who carried it. In such communities, important communications took place between an individual and their immediate social network; there was little need to send messages outside the town or village. Only a small proportion of people were geographically mobile, and travel for any distance involved danger

**Table 4.2 A comparison of information society with agricultural and industrial society**

| | Agricultural society | Industrial society | Information society |
|---|---|---|---|
| *Production power structure* | | | |
| Production power form | Land production power (farmland) | Production power of motive power (steam engine) | Information production power (computer) |
| Character of production power | Material productivity | Material productivity | Knowledge productivity |
| | Effective reproduction of natural phenomenon | Effective change of natural phenomenon and amplification | Systemisation of various natural and social functions |
| | Increase of plant reproduction | Substitution and amplification for physical labour | Substitution of brain labour |
| Product form | Increase of agricultural product and handiwork | Industrial goods, transportation and energy | Information, function and system |
| | Agriculture and handicraft | Manufacturing and service industry | Information industry, knowledge industry and systems industry |
| *Social structure* | | | |
| Production and human relations | Tying humans to land | Restricting man to production place | Restricting man to social system |
| Special character of social form | Compulsory labour | Hired labour | Contract labour |
| | Closed village society | Concentrated urbanised society | Dispersed network society |
| | Permanent and traditional society | Dynamic and free competitive society | Creative and optimum society |
| | Paternalistic status society | Social welfare type controlled society | Social development type multifunctional society |
| *Value outlook* | | | |
| Value standard | Natural law | Materialistic satisfaction | Knowledge creation |
| | Maintenance of life | Satisfaction of sensual and emotional desires | Pursuit of multiple social desires |
| Thought standard | God-centred thought (religion) | Human-centred thought (natural science) | Mankind-centred thought (extreme science) |
| Ethical standard | Ecclesiastical principle | Free democracy | Functional democracy |
| | Law of God | Basic human rights; ownership rights | Sense of mission and self-control |

*Source:* Jones (1995, p. 33), after Masuda (1972)

and difficulty. Literacy levels were often low, and the social system was comparatively inflexible.

Industrial cities brought a completely new challenge in terms of organisation and communication. Subsistence-farming communities, whose notional surplus had been used for the enrichment of the church or the aristocracy, were caught up in changes associated with the creation of a new urban market. The accompanying agricultural revolution allowed the hundreds of thousands in the cities to be fed by a much-reduced population working the land. The flow of primary products from the rural periphery to the industrial core, and of manufactured goods from the core to the periphery, characterises industrial societies. (Core/periphery theory is addressed in Chapter 6.)

## THE INFORMATION ECONOMY

Information societies are post-industrial societies: their wealth relies not on industrial labour but in the processing, packaging and use of data and information. Information markets and management dominate post-industrial economies, and their technologies demonstrate the importance of communications. In a society where information is the major key to wealth (and where information workers include managers, lawyers and teachers as well as stockbrokers and IT consultants), information has never been more plentiful or more accessible. The paradox is that generally available information is not necessarily (or even usually) the information that is required. Moreover, much information cannot be trusted and the effects of a glut of information—information overload—are becoming increasingly serious.

Although our economy is an information economy, and information continues to proliferate and accumulate, it is often the withholding of information that has the capacity to generate the greatest value. As with stockmarket 'insider trading', those who have accurate information possess an advantage over those who do not. Progress (social, political, economic) in an information society depends upon education and access to information. Frequently, these parameters include consideration of the range of available communications networks, and technological access and competence—all of which tend to be related to economic wealth. In these circumstances, the information rich can get speedy access to high-quality information, while the information poor often don't know where to start looking.

The ready availability of information has the capacity to impact socially and psychologically upon the wider society. People are no longer restricted to social networks dictated by proximity—to some extent, the 'tyranny of distance' has been overcome. Instead, neighbourhoods of affect and interest—'psychological neighbourhoods'—are engendered by technologies such as the telephone, email and Internet chat. The electronic environment is enhanced by digitisation (which allows information to be standardised for multiple applications and transmissions) and by miniaturisation (which allows the incorporation of electronic components into more and more areas of life). One reason for the power of the information society is that information provides such a versatile basis for levering economic prosperity within the capitalist system.

## COMMODIFICATION IN THE POSTMODERN

Neighbourless electronic neighbourhoods, the trading of vital information for capital gain, the packaging and sale of images (of famine, disaster and catastrophe, for example)—all these are aspects of the commodification of individual lives. They are also examples of the conjunction of technology and culture. Newsworthy or potentially profitable events and information are extracted from their context, then refined and packaged for sale. The disembodiment of the communication from the communicant, of information from the informant, is sometimes seen as a prime constituent of the postmodern, and of post-industrial society. The postmodern promotes surface impact rather than contextual depth, commodification rather than exchange, and consumption rather than production. Put crudely, it reduces human society to its icons and to its material possessions. According to Frederic Jameson (1984), postmodern communities no longer need members, they need consumers.

In describing postmodernism, Jameson does not celebrate it. Instead he perceives the dissociation of form from content as a political development. Comparing Munch's *The Scream* with Andy Warhol's (postmodern) images, Jameson comments that Warhol's work 'turns centrally around commodification, and the great billboard images of the Coca-Cola bottle or the Campbell's Soup Can, which explicitly foreground the commodity fetishism of a transition to late capital, *ought* to be powerful and critical political statements' (Jameson 1984, p. 60, original emphasis). The politics behind postmodern theories are essentially oppositional to the interests of elites that benefit financially from the promotion of consumption. In deconstructing the postmodern moment, commentators such as Jameson (who was writing in the *New Left Review*) hope to offer strategies and perspectives which will empower resistance.

Fragmentation and commodification are appropriate conceptual frameworks for examining the technological realities of Internet access, mobile phones, global networks, transnational capitalism and international markets, among other indicators of technoculture and the information society. Fragments and surfaces in many respects characterise the technologies, and the lives, of people today. Our postmodern society is in contrast to the modern (industrial) and premodern (agricultural) societies which, in the West, can be constructed as preceding the information society.

Our concern with the information society continues into the next chapter where the 'information' in the information society is problematised and interrogated, and where we consider the role and nature of information policy, education, privacy and intellectual property.

## CONCLUSION

This chapter has investigated the technocultural role of the mass media in information societies, and the objectivity of media workers. We rely on the media as agenda-setters and to provide information which we use to construct our sense of an imaginary community, against which backdrop we position our own lives. The media are implicated in the project of globalisation, both because they globalise local information and because they deliver global information within a local context.

Information societies have been identified as postmodern, as the industrial society has been dubbed modern and the agrarian society premodern. We have compared and contrasted some elements of these different social systems and identified some characteristics of information societies that are especially postmodern. Both modern and postmodern societies are technocultural, however. Where information becomes the raw material for economic prosperity and advancement, so the commodification of non-material goods assumes greater importance.

# 5

# INFORMATION POLICY IN THE INFORMATION SOCIETY

## THE NATURE OF INFORMATION

The control of information is an index of power in contemporary societies since information allows policy-makers and bureaucrats to regulate markets, institutions and individual behaviour. It is the power implicit in the collection and processing of information about individuals, for example, which makes Tax File Numbers and Social Security data such important privacy issues, and which has seen the enactment of Freedom of Information legislation in many western countries. According to Beniger (1986) it was the need to control information relating to mass production, distribution and markets that set up the dynamic for the control revolution, which eventually resulted in the development of information technology, and the establishment of an information society. Thus information can be seen as essentially related to power and control, as well as being the quintessential material of high-tech technoculture.

The concept of information implies a capacity to inform: once a piece of information has been communicated and is internalised as knowledge, it has fulfilled its informative potential. Consequently, what is information for one person may be existing knowledge to another, and even redundant. Similarly, what may be relevant information in one context may be an irritation or pollution in another. For a communication to be information, the recipient must be able to make sense of it, use it, and develop ideas, understanding and/or knowledge through it. Given that all communication involves patterns of perception and attention, it follows that an individual actively participates in the acquisition and incorporation of information as knowledge. By extrapolation, knowledge is an artefact, constructed by the individual as part of their paying attention to data, cues and stimuli in their environment, and using the raw material gathered via their senses in knowledge-construction.

All information critical to an information society reflects the society that produces it. Like technology (see Chapter 1), information expresses the nature of the elites who create it, and who control it. An English encyclopaedia of the Victorian era, for example, says more about that social system than it does about Indigenous Australians when it comments (in the two sentences referring to Aboriginal people, in the entry on Australia): 'The aborigines [sic] of A. belong to the Papuan, Austral-negro, or Melanesian race. They rank very low in the scale of humanity, and fast disappear when brought into contact with civilisation' (Eastwick 1895, p. 233). Changes in social attitudes, and in what counts as information, have made it uncomfortable to read such sentences and impossible to write them. Yet these sentences communicate volumes about the nature of imperialism and its foundation upon racism. Their informative role has shifted over the decades.

Kuhn's notion of the paradigm shift is one way of explaining the mechanism by which an informational sea-change occurs. Before the paradigm shift happens, there is a jockeying for ascendancy of ideas, theories, ways of seeing. The shift to a new paradigm demonstrates change in the dominant power. The fact that the paradigm has shifted does not make the new information less of an artefact: it indicates that the artefact is created by a different group of people, or by the same group of people in different circumstances. This is the kind of shift which has occurred in terms of the Victorian view of a 'scale of humanity', and our view of human rights.

The information society is predicated upon information as a commodity, and upon the lion's share of paid employment involving information collection, dissemination and manipulation. It also marks the ascendancy of those individuals and elites who control information. The passing of the industrial society (with its economic foundation in the production of material goods) and the coming of the post-industrial society (with its informational foundation) coincide with electronic methods of information storage, retrieval, production and communication. As information becomes the pre-eminent commodity, so it becomes central to a plethora of control technologies designed to restrict access to it, to enhance its value, and to exercise power through it (Beniger 1986; Roszak 1994).

Relationships between individual citizens and their information are complex and reflexive. While the individual has some control over the information they provide, the information provided can then be used by bureaucracy and power elites in an attempt to control the behaviour of that individual. The choice—whether or not to communicate information—has implications for the future, according to potential uses for the information. Whereas the individual can resist or object to the collection of information at the personal level (on a form, by interview, in having to show an identity card), the national and international data flows are not controllable by individuals. Once it has been shared, it is almost impossible to control, follow or retrieve information. One of the most difficult facts to be faced in privacy issues, for example, is that information divulged for one purpose to one agency is then used in quite a different context by another agency, often without any record of its transfer.

As Japanese futurist Yoneji Masuda (1978), credited with being 'an architect of the information society', points out (in Jones 1995, pp. 186–7), the growth in the quantity of information rests upon four properties not found in industrial goods. Information is:

1. *inconsumable*—information is not consumed through use—it remains available to be used again, however much it has been used;
2. *untransferable*—information is not transferred. Once information has been received, and internalised, it can be passed on without being lost to the original recipient;
3. *indivisible*—information may be partially transferred, but for something to make sense as information it has to be transferred as an entity—transferring every fourth data element does not transfer one quarter of the whole;
4. *accumulative*—the addition of new information means more than simply the sum of the parts and can create new knowledge, as well as greater amounts of information. Further, because information is inconsumable and untransferable, it accumulates even while being used. (This is the opposite of material goods, where consumption equates with destruction.)

Once these four properties of information are combined with the properties of information technology, the result is an exponential multiplication of information. Masuda comments that, while 'information has always had the property of self-multiplication, computer-communication technology has rapidly increased the speed and quality of self-multiplication because the technology itself has added four more properties to information: (1) concentration, (2) dispersion, (3) circulation and (4) feedback' (Masuda 1978, cited in Jones 1995, p. 186). This means that:

1. information can be concentrated—it may be handled more efficiently with technology than without;
2. information can be dispersed—it need not remain at the site of collection, or be used only for the purpose for which it was acquired;
3. the circulation of information means that more people can work with information simultaneously, exponentially increasing the speed of processing and use; and
4. the feedback properties of technology allow information to be cross-referenced and internally manipulated to create new levels of value-adding using huge databases not accessible to non-technological analysis.

So far, we have addressed the 'semantic' definition of information—concepts of information that concern meaning. This way of looking at information allows us to judge its quality, usefulness and significance. The semantic definition is contrasted with that definition relating to 'classic information theory'. Here the issue is not the quality of information, but its quantity. Further, that quantity can be judged exactly because the 'meaning' of information is irrelevant to classic information theory. Instead, information is a flow of 'bytes' and the volume of information exchanged can be measured as a transfer of bytes (see Figure 5.1). Eight bits equals one byte. Eight bits are necessary to convey an alpha numeric character.

Figure 5.1 Screen grab from an online session

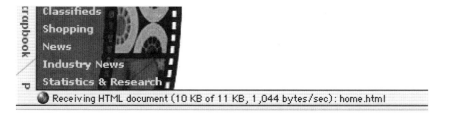

## FROM CHAOS TO WISDOM

The classic information theory definition is the one used by Stonier (1990, p. 21), who claims: 'Information exists. It does not need to be perceived to exist. It requires no intelligence to interpret it. It does not have to have meaning to exist. It exists.' For those who prefer a semantic approach, the classical definition describes 'data' rather than information. Both perspectives can be represented on a chaos–wisdom continuum (Figure 5.2).

Figure 5.2 Chaos–wisdom continuum

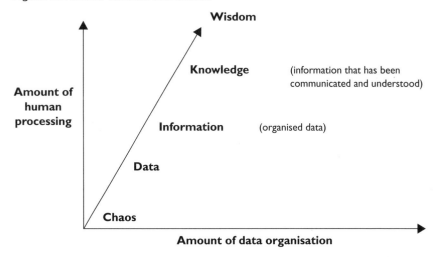

This progression starts in *chaos* where there is no discernable pattern or organisation, and where bytes of information are fragmented, and unable to be processed readily by human or machine. *Data* occurs where the symbols have been processed in such a way that they conform to the requirements of a transmission channel, such as a modem. Data is a quantity, rather than a quality. *Information*, on the other hand, refers to data organised into meaningful chunks—specifically, chunks that have meaning to humans rather than machine applications. Information becomes *knowledge* when it has been successfully communicated to, and understood by, the by now more knowledgeable recipient. Knowledge is the product of information plus thought and ideas, used to inform communication and action. It implies a value judgement because knowledge marks the processing by a human of 'useful and relevant' information. *Wisdom* is the final stage on the continuum. Here there are two sets of value judgements: the first in terms of the transition from information to knowledge; the second in terms of knowledge being used in the making of sound judgements. The 'information revolution' can be seen as an explosion of information at the lower levels of the chaos–wisdom progression. The kind of information involved in the technocultural realm depends upon sense-making and meaning, and relates to upper levels of the continuum.

## THE TECHNOLOGICALLY CONVERGENT SOCIETY

The growth in the amount of information available, and the use of machines to foster the development of knowledge and the getting of wisdom, all contribute to the accelerating pace of social and technological change. As accessing information becomes more important, so the standardisation of information becomes more relevant. Information is created or stored in digital forms to enable processing in many ways by a wide variety of ICTs. With the standardisation of processing procedures, a greater array of technologies can be used to record, process, store and communicate information and the information revolution speeds up.

The unparalleled dynamism of technological change in the fields of media, computing and telecommunications, and a continuing acceleration in this change, have been dubbed 'convergence'. Increasingly, ICTs are developed in such a way as to synergistically lever their power, and add value to existing processes. A beneficial cycle has been created whereby improved telecommunications leads to better computing power and access, while more efficient computing spurs the development of improved media and telecommunications while the media publicise both telecom and IT advances, attracting investment and stimulating innovation. With intelligent systems, differentiating between telecommunications, IT/computing and the interactive media and information held in (and accessed through) ICT networks becomes more and more difficult (Barr 2000, pp. 22–31).

The 'digital imperative' that pervades contemporary technoculture dictates that everything from phones to televisions be reconceptualised as 'digital'. Digital technology permits audio, video, data, graphic, multimedia and other information to be manipulated and communicated via computer-controlled equipment and telecommunications. The common use of digital information across applications means that all communication and storage uses involving these disparate media are based on essentially the same principles. Further, digital information can be delivered through a variety of channels including cable, satellite, microwave and other telecommunications systems, with the platform of delivery being less relevant than the bandwidth capacity of the delivery channel.

The technical dynamism inherent in convergence (which characterised the last decades of the twentieth century, and which continues apace) has its roots, according to American professor James Beniger (1986), in the early nineteenth century and in the development of the telegraph. For the past two hundred years, argues Beniger, the development of one aspect or another of ICTs has precipitated 'a crisis of control'. Beniger identifies the early crises as relating to the 'massification' of the market, and a desire to control the processes of marketing, production, distribution and packaging where these processes are orchestrated by information about demand, relating demand to the other elements.

As (for example) mechanised production outstripped the ability of the marketing machine to find customers, so mass media were used to create mass markets so that consumers could be informed about the availability of mass-produced goods. As demand was stimulated, so distribution channels had to be developed and controlled so that retailers had confidence in supplies, and manufacturers knew how much product to ship, and when. Once the market operated at the level of the 'mass', rather than the 'individual', then it needed increasing levels of integration—including information and communication integration—to deliver maximum efficiencies of scale. The 'control imperative' driving the information society is the reduction or removal of blockages to the collection, communication and application of information and knowledge in order to provide a 'leading edge' of information management that confers an advantage. Beniger argues that:

> inseparable from control [of the mass production and mass marketing processes] are the twin activities of information processing and reciprocal communication . . . Because technological innovation is increasingly a collective, cumulative effort whose results must be taught and diffused, it also generates an increased need for technologies of information storage and retrieval (Beniger 1986, p. 434).

This demand for information storage and retrieval of larger and larger amounts of information fuels huge increases in the storage capacity of computers and drives both the miniaturisation of size, and the magnification of power, of computer processing units. More and more powerful processing and communication software packages are required to handle the volume of information and a growing range of applications (for example, connections with the Internet). In turn, these stimulate demand for further increases in power. Computer-based technocultures thrive and proliferate as the technology increases in power and in pervasiveness.

## FILLING THE BLANK AREA IN MEDIATED COMMUNICATIONS

Some years ago, Peter Morris (1996) argued that online communications were a threat to the long-term continuation of printed newspapers. This was not because newspapers would fall out of favour with readers, but because they would fall out of favour with advertisers, who would prefer to advertise on the Web. Since up to 70 per cent of the cost of a newspaper is covered by advertising (although this proportion varies between 50 and 70 per cent around the western world), a dramatic decrease in the volume of advertising involves a dramatic increase in the cover price. If the price of a newspaper began to reach that of a magazine, circulation figures would plummet, further affecting advertising revenues. Effectively, newspapers would cease to be a mass medium, and would be repositioned as a niche medium for consumers prepared to pay for a daily magazine.

Instead, the Internet, radio and television would absorb the role of providing the daily services (information, entertainment) currently associated with newspapers. In support of his argument, Morris reproduced a diagram to show the communication niche which the Internet is supremely placed to fill (see Figure 5.3).

The 'blank area' is a niche suited to a medium serving from 10–10 000 people with information from minutes to one week old. Much of the information from other media and communication modes (outside the blank area) can also realistically be transferred electronically. Such a model has implications for the future of the press, and for a shake-up of other traditional media. It explains why so many media (content) companies are forming alliances with telecommunications (channel) and IT (process) companies. They are trying to second-guess the future, and become future-proof (Barr 2000, pp. 24–5).

## THE INFORMATION WORKFORCE

In an information age, where an increasing proportion of the workforce is paid to process, use, add-value and apply information products (Porat 1977), it is not surprising that national governments perceive that future prosperity rests, in part, upon an effective information infrastructure and a technologically literate workforce. The change in composition of the workforce in Australia is shown in Figure 5.4.

Figure 5.3 New electronic media 'blank area'

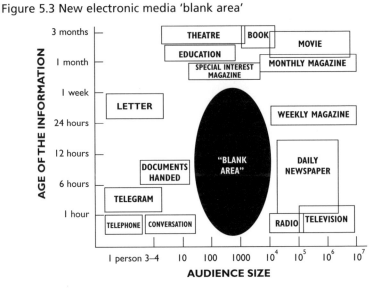

Source: Tomita, Tetsuro, *The New Electronic Media and their Place in the Information Market of the Future,* from Morris (1996, p. 11)

Figure 5.4 Australian labour force in paid employment, four-sector analysis, 1891–2000

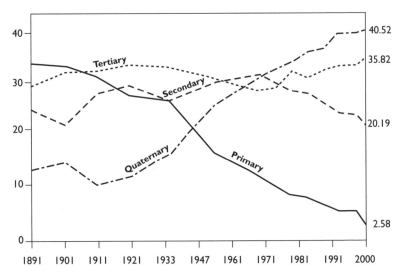

Source: Adapted from Jones (1995, p. 58) and data from the Australian Bureau of Statistics (2000)

Jones' definitions of the different sectors indicated are (1995, pp. 56–66):

- *primary*: includes the cultivation and harvesting of raw materials; farming, mining, etc.;
- *secondary*: involves mainly manufacturing and construction;
- *tertiary*: 'tangible services'—maintenance, transport, storage, retailing, utilities, security;
- *quaternary*: information processing, including politicians, public servants, teachers and media workers.

Jones goes on to comment: 'In the global economy the United States is still Head Office. When the United States carries out basic research and development in vast industries such as aerospace, telecommunications, computers or defence hardware, it does so for the entire world' (Jones 1995, p. 65). The status of the United States as the pre-eminent information society is clear from Makridakis' diagram of the percentage of the workforce engaged in different industry sectors (Figure 5.5). The service section here includes the information economy, and the growth of that sector is earlier, and more pronounced, than was the case in the United Kingdom (Figure 5.6), with the US workforce accelerating the flight from agriculture at the turn of the 1900s.

Figure 5.5 Percentage of the workforce engaged in different industry sectors: United States (1820–1995)

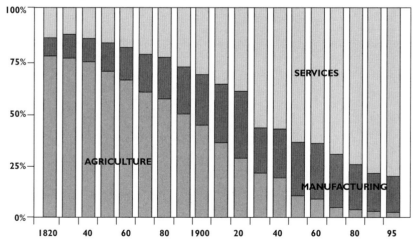

*Source*: Makridakis, personal communication, based on Makridakis (1995)

Figure 5.6 Percentage of the workforce engaged in different industry sectors: United Kingdom (1801–1995)

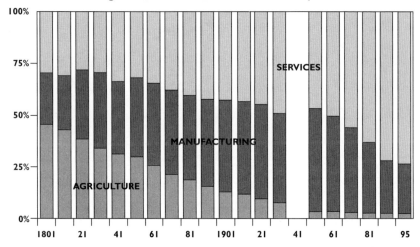

*Source*: Makridakis, personal communication, based on Makridakis (1995)

The strength of the United States and Canada as players in the quaternary sector can also be gauged by the relative numbers of online users in different geographical regions. Even so, the rate of Internet take-up elsewhere in the world is accelerating, as the comparative figures (in Table 5.1) demonstrate, and it is no longer the case that there are more online users in Canada and the USA than in the rest of the world combined.

**Table 5.1 Worldwide online users by geographical area**

| Worldwide online users (in millions) | Feb 1999 | Sept 2000 |
|---|---|---|
| Africa | 1.14 | 3.11 |
| Asia/Pacific | 26.55 | 89.68 |
| Europe | 33.71 | 105.89 |
| Middle East | 0.78 | 2.40 |
| Canada and United States | 87.00 | 161.31 |
| South America | 4.50 | 15.26 |
| **Total** | **153.68** | **377.65** |

*Source*: Adapted from NUA Internet Surveys at www.nua.net/surveys/how_many_online/index.html and Barr (2000, p. 122) (who also used NUA Internet Surveys)

## INFORMATION AND EDUCATION

Along with the growth of the Internet, and as part of a different vision for the future, the 1990s witnessed the burgeoning of new ways of looking at education. 'Just in time training' and the 'flexible delivery' of 'open learning systems' are all shorthand for saying that educational institutions face radical change. The old ways of doing things are becoming extinct. It is no longer appropriate to identify three years of degree study as preparing someone for 35–55 years of work. (I use the 55 year upper limit time frame because we have yet to learn the effect of baby boomer retirees, and voluntary retirement policies.) 'Open' learning suggests universal access without unnecessary prerequisites, with people able to achieve recognition for working at their own level. Flexible delivery systems use relevant technologies to provide access to information and education at the point where it is needed. They effectively reposition the education system as a high-tech technoculture. One futuristic vision of this principle in operation is included in *The Matrix*, where the knowledge Trinity needs to fly a helicopter is delivered intracranially, via an uploaded computer file, a split second before the skills are required.

While education systems move towards being just in time, they also need to embrace the idea of flexibility. Here the issue is accepting individuals as already having diverse skills and expertise, auditing those skills, identifying gaps and providing education and training to plug those gaps. In principle, policies which recognise prior learning free people from having to relearn skills which have already been mastered, and speed up the educational process. They also mean that educational products need to be tailored more specifically to the needs of the individual student. Higher education is likely to be provided in the future by education brokers. According to information scientist Julie Johnson:

> The education broker brings together course offerings from a range of providers, negotiates accreditation of the selected materials with an educational institution or professional association and handles the copyright, licensing, authentication, security and electronic payment processes. Students build their course of study from a repository of course materials drawn from a variety of countries and institutions. They collaborate electronically with teachers and other students who may or may not be completing the same course of study and who could be physically located anywhere (1998, p. 70).

These concerns are all 'information age' technoculture issues about the need for lifelong learning and the flexible delivery of education and training. They also address citizens' abilities to contribute to the development, extension and diffusion of high-tech technoculture. In an era when workers are likely to occupy at least three to five different jobs during their working lives, lifelong learning becomes an absolute imperative. Jones cites a European Parliament report arguing that only 30 per cent of knowledge and skills in the workforce remain relevant over a seven-year period (Jones 1995, p. 151). An uneducated workforce is an obsolete workforce. Governments, teachers and students grapple with the twin pressures of the necessity of continuing education, and its accelerating redundancy.

Education is not a stand-alone industry, but is central to the operations of culture and society, as well as being a major conduit for the dissemination of technological skills and competencies. Digital culture is integral to the future development of the education sector in information societies. Not only is education one of the largest sectors of the information economy, it operates as the powerhouse for driving the skills and training through which the rest of the information infrastructure develops.

## BUREAUCRACY AND INFORMATION

The bureaucracy is arguably the workforce category most closely associated with the collection and processing of information (with marketing departments coming a close second). Information societies consider an efficient bureaucracy central to issues of effective governance—taxation, welfare benefits and car licensing, for example. The bureaucracy has been identified (see Chapter 1) as one of the A, B and C of social power elites. Its importance has grown in proportion to the growth in importance of information, and its power lies in information collection and processing and the following through of policy decisions. The power of the bureaucracy to accumulate information about individuals should be differentiated, however, from its power to collect *quality* information.

Information tends to be less informative in proportion to the requirement for it to conform to a standard information collection procedure—such as a form or survey. Indeed, where any information is standardised, it tends to conform to the lowest common denominator.

Everybody in the country might, at a given moment of time, be categorisable as either single or married. (Legally it is impossible to be both, or to be neither.) Yet this level of 'information' is barely satisfactory, either for the bureaucracy or for social uses. Where the range of options is expanded to single/married/widowed/divorced/de facto, it appears to offer more sensitive discrimination of individual circumstances. Indeed, in social usage, these categories are refined further to indicate the status of developing or waning relationships, or experiences of loss or transition. In reducing the complexity of individual lives and choices to binary opposites on a form, however, much complex information is lost, while other information—the information brought into existence by the options available on the form—is created. Forms create misinformation as well as information. As David Sless comments:

> Forms are used directly by government to control the behaviour of citizens. Tax and social security forms are not just a nuisance, they are the direct instruments by which the state apparatus controls individual behaviour . . . One of the simplest kinds of resistance manifests itself in error rates. It is not generally realised that error rates on forms are extremely high . . . [sometimes] every single copy of the form processed by the bureaucracy has at least one significant error per form filler (1988, pp. 66–7).

The information extracted from individuals—and it is often like having teeth pulled—frequently involves a degree of resistance. The local control of information by people completing forms and surveys may be under-researched, but Sless's comment on error rates indicates that the purposes and/or meanings of the forms are both actively constructed and actively resisted by the users. People control information provided by themselves, about themselves, by making errors on data collection forms. This power may appear minimal compared with that of the database compilers, but people use it, regardless.

## THE CENTRAL DATA BANK

Changes in the collection and accumulation of information have accelerated in the post World War II era, as the emergent information society has become more prevalent. Clarke suggests that: 'For twenty years [from the late 1950s] computers were mainly used to address needs within individual organisations. Gradually . . . it was feasible to share data between systems in different organisations, and even to conceive systems which crossed organisational boundaries' (1994a, p. 117). Initially, individuals were protected because each organisational system identified individuals—customers, clients, patients, citizens—with different codes. Clarke (1994a, p. 118) continues:

> As Representative Frank Horton commented, in a submission to the 1966–7 hearings on a proposed national data center in the U.S.: 'One of the most practical of our present safeguards of privacy is the fragmented nature of present information. It is scattered in little bits and pieces across the geography and years of our life. Retrieval is impractical and often impossible. A central data bank removes completely this safeguard' (Frank Horton, cited in Rule et al. 1980, p. 56).

The willingness of individuals to provide quality information for 'central data banks' should not be assumed. Neither should the good faith of the data collectors. The voracious appetite bureaucracies have for collecting and cross-referencing information indicates that they construct the form filler as unreliable, and see one of their key roles as catching the form filler out in an inconsistent response. Trust is based upon information, and the information most likely to build trust—either of the form fillers or the bureaucracy—is not the information produced by the systems which characterise bureaucracies in information societies. Further, much processed information is not accessible to those who most need reassurance: the poor, the less educated and socio-cultural minorities. While all citizens require information, the information poor tend to have fewer alternatives if the bureaucracy does not meet their needs.

Increasingly, individuals are accessing information from systems—such as computer networks and data banks—which demand a level of technological competence over and above pressing a button and making sense of the content. Here basic access to (leaving aside control of) information is related to education, to gender and to class, with young, highly educated, white, middle-class males (still) having the greatest advantage. These people are often characterised as the information rich, with older women of a working-class background, low levels of education and/or English as a second language at the other end of the continuum. The growing divide between the information rich and the information poor is one of the greatest challenges confronting the information society (see Chapter 6). There is increasing concern that people who most need relevant information have the fewest skills to access it, and the least training in interpreting it. Melody suggests that 'ignorance based on misinformation will be the pollution of the information age. Overcoming it will be a formidable challenge' (1990, p. 18).

A 'technological determinist' mindset helps to make social choices regarding the control of information invisible, thereby effectively removing them. Combined with the economic and administrative efficiency imperatives, it is as if the potential of bureaucratic technology to control individuals through their information—through 'dataveillance' (Clarke 1991)—is necessarily realised. The use of a range of technological apparatus may obscure the human will implicit in the process, but technocultures which create, manipulate and communicate information about individuals both embody and express the priorities of the elite who employ the bureaucracies of clerks and keyboard operators.

## PRIVACY, INFORMATION SECURITY AND FREEDOM OF INFORMATION

Arguably (and depressingly), privacy is a modern right sacrificed as part of the price of participation in postmodern information societies. Dataveillance, defined by privacy advocate Roger Clarke as 'the systematic use of personal data systems in the investigation or monitoring of the actions or communications of one or more persons', is now endemic (1994b, p. 83). Although many societies have privacy laws in place, these provide little protection to individuals who are as concerned about the legislated and legitimate bureaucratic uses of their private information as they are about possible breaches of the law.

Some people are excluded by their circumstances from certain privacies that others take for granted. For example, in Australia, a person on a sole parent's pension can legitimately be watched to determine whether or not they are 'cohabiting'. The presumption is that someone in a cohabiting relationship is part of a shared household, supported by their partner, and thus not entitled to support from the state in the form of sole parent's benefits. The bureaucratic definition of cohabiting, however, may differ substantially from that of the individuals concerned, and a relationship that involves financial reciprocity is likely to take considerable time to establish. Thus an individual might legitimately not be in the kind of cohabiting relationship which makes the sole parent's pension unnecessary (and which makes claiming the pension a matter of fraud), but may nevertheless be identified as a 'social security cheat' because of a pattern of cohabitation, or even because of a short-term sexual relationship. Inquiries into highly personal matters are an integral part of many government welfare provisions for sole-parent families.

In 1999, the American Civil Liberties Union (ACLU) campaigned with other groups and individuals to persuade the US Congress to reject a plan 'to federalize driver's licences and turn them into the precursors of a national I.D. card'. Nonetheless, six states require social security numbers on the driver's licences they issue, effectively allowing cross referencing of data. According to the ACLU website (www.aclu.org [June 2001]), 'most of the large states have moved away from such a requirement in order to protect their drivers' privacy, reduce fraud, and inhibit I.D. theft'.

Computer matching allows governments to check the records of two or more agencies. If a person on unemployment benefits is also paying significant taxes in a paid job, then that person would show up both in tax records and in welfare payments. It is likely that the individual would eventually be investigated further. Profiling is defined by Clarke as occurring when 'a set of characteristics of a particular class of person is inferred from past experience, and data holdings are then searched for digital personae with a close fit to that set of characteristics' (1994b, p. 86). The steps involved in profiling can be identified as:

- describe the class of person sought;
- use existing experience to define a profile for that class of person;
- express the profile formally;
- acquire data concerning a relevant population;
- search the data for a digital personae whose characteristics comply with the profile; and
- take action in relation to those individuals (Clarke 1994b, p. 86).

The FBI creates profiles for terrorists and serial killers as part of its law enforcement activities; marketing departments create profiles to decide whom to target with their direct mail postings. Both activities can raise legitimate privacy concerns, although the possible benefits in the former case may well outweigh the social costs.

Most western countries have some privacy legislation in place to reassure the public that the administration's ability to use a range of means to identify and prevent crime (especially fraud) is balanced by a commitment to protect the private information of law-abiding individuals. Depending upon the country concerned, these privacy laws may concern:

- government use of data;
- storage of data;
- record-keeping and the individual's right to access their own data;
- freedom of information requirements;
- the activities of credit reporting agencies and credit providers; and
- commercial and business uses of information about private individuals.

Many organisations require information workers not to disclose personal information about individual customers—for example, library borrowing records or video hiring patterns. In business and private situations, it is not legitimate to use information given for one reason for another purpose. Thus joining a club should not mean that an individual's details are onsold, without their consent, to a mailing list broker. Privacy considerations would suggest that all intended uses of information should be disclosed at the time information is collected, and that organisations which misuse consumer data may be guilty of misrepresentation, as well as invasion of privacy.

## COPYRIGHT AND INTELLECTUAL PROPERTY RIGHTS

Copyright and 'IP' is a matter of considerable concern to 'content providers'—for example, writers, artists, video producers, Website designers. It has given me some specific worries in the writing of this chapter, since I have been quoting some lecture-based work of a friend and colleague, Julie Johnson. The issue raised is this: where does the use of another person's work become theft? It is a moral issue as well as a legal one. As Julie indicates in her course guide: 'In addition to the obligations placed on you by the *Copyright Act* you are under a moral obligation to acknowledge the contribution which the work of others has made in the preparation of your own work' (Johnson 1998, p. 89).

In a knowledge economy, it may be impossible (still) to copyright ideas and information generally circulating in discussion and debate, but it is possible to protect the intellectual property of individuals. For many workers in the information industry, intellectual property is the only tangible result of their labour. A book or an article, a music disc or a software package might represent a significant portion of a working year, or of a working life. Copyright is the content producer's equivalent to a patent or a trademark, and copyright represents an investment in time and money, as do patents and trademarks.

During 2000, international bands such as *Metallica* (www.metallica. com/[June 2001]) argued that Websites such as Napster (www. napster.com/ [August 2000]) and Gnutella contravened their copyright by providing download software that did not distinguish between copyright-free music and the copyright-protected music that forms the backbone of their income. Napster's response was that its Website builds music industry sales by introducing fans to new artists and new music. Such an argument recognises that copyright laws are concerned to act in support of the public interest to ensure the free flow of information, and this impetus balances the desire of copyright-holders to restrict access only to those who have paid for it. (However, the bands, their recording companies and, ultimately, the court failed to agree with Napster, which has now closed down (Rimares 2001).)

A newspaper comment on this case, headlined 'Napster's mobile music fans show inadequacy of laws' (syndicated, *Los Angeles Times* 2000), raises the possibility that the western world may increasingly become a culture of plagiarism. Such a culture would be characterised by unauthorised (and possibly unacknowledged) copying of other people's work. Audiotaped music and programming from the radio, videotaped movies and TV programmes, photocopying of printed materials other than for personal use, home-copied CDs of games and other software, unfettered transfer of digital music files—all of these may indicate the widespread abuse of other people's intellectual property. The *Los Angeles Times* article quoted music industry lawyer Russell Frackman as saying: 'One of the arguments we made to the court all along is that Napster was training people that piracy is acceptable'. He maintained that, 'if Napster's users simply moved to Gnutella and other services . . . people far smarter than I will have to figure out how copyright law can assert itself'.

The issue of copyright arises when people want the information (article, music) but not necessarily the product (newspaper, CD), and where the two are separable. Debate is stifled if it is no longer possible to circulate photocopies of articles (being a fraction of the whole printed product) without getting permission from the publisher and/or author, or without buying multiple copies of the newspaper, magazine, etc. Further, freelance journalists themselves take issue with newspaper proprietors' use of 'unfair contracts' to acquire syndication and republication rights in freelance material. In March 1999, this was the subject of heated dispute between the National Union of Journalists (NUJ) (www.gn.apc.org/media/nuj.html [June 2001]) and *The Guardian* newspaper in the United Kingdom, with an independent inquiry finding in favour of the journalists (www.gn.apc.org/media/9903GDN.html [June 2001]). In addition, journalists working for wire services Reuters, AAP, UPI, etc., argue that much of their work has an invisible presence in the mainstream press, being picked up and printed without being acknowledged by the paper publishing it (Pusey, 1995). The rights of content providers versus publishers remain a vexed terrain.

Digital technoculture did not invent copyright problems: copyright has been a hot topic ever since intellectual property was identified as such. The first copyright law was passed in England in 1709 (and was probably copied by other countries thereafter!). Even if digital society did not invent copyright problems, however, it has exacerbated them, and is making it even easier—and more tempting—for people to infringe copyright.

## CONCLUSION

This chapter began by looking at the nature of information. The semantic definition of information was contrasted with that of classic information theory, and both were further explored through the use of the chaos–wisdom continuum, through chaos, data, knowledge, information and wisdom. Over the years, as information has become easier to collect and to manipulate, so concerns about privacy and rights over personal information have multiplied. One response to this public concern has been the burgeoning of Freedom of Information legislation from the 1980s onwards. Government approaches to information regulation can often include a legal requirement for individuals to provide personal information, balanced by *Privacy* and *Freedom of Information Acts* so that individuals can (in theory at any rate) monitor what governments do with that information.

Another important way in which national governments get involved with the enacting of information-related legislation is in the fields of copyright and intellectual property. We considered this challenge from the viewpoint of the 'content owner' wanting to protect the fruits of their intellectual and creative labour, and from that of the desirability of freely circulating information within an information society. Copyright legislation tries to balance these imperatives, but faces increasing challenges from information transfer in the digital domain.

## NOTE

I recognise the particular contribution that Julie Johnson's work has made to this chapter.

# 6

# THE PUBLIC INTEREST AND THE INFORMATION DIVIDE

## THE PUBLIC INTEREST

The concept of *the public interest* has an increasingly out-of-date feel to it—an association with nanny statehood, where the state looks after citizens incapable of looking after themselves. It suggests that the role of government might be more than simply balancing the books and determining a taxation structure; that social and community concerns *are* relevant and that the state has a part to play in promoting and nurturing these. The public interest was once perceived as an obligation to consider social costs and benefits wider than company profitability or government efficiency, but times have changed.

The public interest is one justification for policies that promote universal access to information, computers in the classroom and well-stocked public libraries. It is the concept of the public interest that opens high-tech technoculture debates to wide participation. This perspective asserts that the whole of society benefits from addressing inequalities in the distribution of technological and other resources, and from providing a quality education. The public interest includes concepts such as *minimum service provision* (MSP, discussed below) and *community service obligations* (CSO, see Chapter 8), and suggests that these are important elements of the social fabric and should be instituted even where there is no prospect of service delivery at a profit. Public service privileges the needs of 'the public' regardless of their financial status, whereas customer service considers the needs of people rich enough to be customers. The introduction of user-pays changes a public service into customer service.

In the twenty-first century, consumer society policy-makers are increasingly likely to argue that 'small government' is in the public interest, and market forces should regulate access to information and services as much as possible to ensure efficiency and competitiveness. Differences between a social equity model and a market-driven model of public service centre upon a belief as to whether or not the market can provide all that society needs. Market-driven models of the public interest suggest that those who are not motivated (or financially able) to participate in the market may be responsible themselves for their resulting disempowerment and reduced access to resources. This scenario can be played out within nations, and internationally—between nations.

The discussion so far has foregrounded public interest and policy development discussions in the wealthy nations of the First World. The issues of information and communication access are relevant in all societies, but in poorer societies there are pressing health, education and welfare priorities with a more urgent claim upon the national purse. It is conceivable that a 'Maslow's hierarchy' of needs/priorities can be developed which charts a policy progression for Third World nations. This would likely include pure water, food and shelter at the physiological level, and health and security at the level of safety. Education might equate to social needs, while a communications and information infrastructure could be included at that level, or considered as an 'ego' need required for integration and development. The First World/Third World divide will be addressed as the chapter progresses, but debates about CSOs and MSPs tend to be luxuries that only developed nations can afford.

## JUSTIFYING THE PUBLIC INTEREST

Communications researcher William Melody argues that there are two primary elements to debates about the public interest, 'but in most cases [these] are absent':

> One is the perspective of those groups in society that may be significantly affected by the policies adopted, but which do not have a sufficiently organised financial vested interest to mount a representation, e.g. users of the public telephone service, children's interests in television or probable victims of technological change. This perspective is necessary to ensure that in the final balancing of interests underlying most policy decisions, the interests of important public segments are not omitted.

The second perspective is that of society as a whole, focusing directly on the overall structure of benefits, costs and consequences for society. This would include an evaluation of economic externality, public good, social and cultural consequences of policy options (1990, p. 16).

Is there still room for such a vision in western society? What benefits does it confer, at what cost? Free-market democracies are consumer societies, driven by both competition and choice (Barr 1994). These two drivers, however, depend upon maintaining both scarcity and desirability, and good consumers are defined as such by their capacity to pay for what they consume. (Society holds a dim view of those who consume goods without paying for them—by theft, for instance.) Those who promote the free market as being a greater public good than policy intervention argue that the interests of the wider society are protected by an effective business sector which keeps costs low through competition. By providing a choice of products, services and payment options, the free market competes for and services a range of market segments; it also fosters national prosperity by delivering profits and developing potential export markets. Thus the public interest, as Melody defines it, is replaced by the profit motive—public good is only served insofar as a bureaucracy or corporation finds it profitable to do so. In these circumstances, do we have the technocultures we need—or only the technocultures which create profit for those involved in their development?

The impetus of competition could be used to drive socially desirable objectives, customising 'redundant' computers for secondary uses in ways that empower the information poor, for example. Competition can help a society to achieve policy objectives quite apart from financial and economic ones. Deregulated information and communication practices have the potential to include people in wider discussion and decision-making, thus helping to foster community ownership and the public good. A participative democracy demands information, debate and involvement, and even information society bureaucracies should work for the benefit of the people who live in them, rather than the information they use.

## REDEFINING THE PUBLIC INTEREST

Academic and technology commentator Trevor Barr warned in 1994 that a democracy should include 'open debates about the costs and benefits of technological change . . . The slippery redefinition of the public interest which states that what is good for the market is good for us all could prove, in the long run, to mark the end of . . . a democratic information society' (1994, pp. 102–3).

Some six years after first writing these words, in the face of unprecedented deregulation (with much of the decision-making occurring in commercial/government forums that are secret and closed), Barr comments: 'At the beginning of the twentieth century telecommunications was considered too important to be left to the *private* sector, at the end of the century telecommunications has come to be regarded as too important to be left to the *public* sector' (2000, p. 216, italics in original). Barr sees these changes in a national and an international context:

> Governments of nation states are attempting to reposition their economies within the new interdependent global information economy so as to increase their relative share of wealth and power . . . Paradoxically, at a time when virtually every government in developed countries is embarking upon greater privatisation, deregulation and liberalisation of their communications industry, and withdrawal from their traditional roles, most governments have been constructing national communications development strategy plans (2000, p. 169).

The assumption behind this strategic planning, suggests Barr, is that 'no future economy will grow substantially, or attract foreign investment and technology, unless it has a world class communications infrastructure' (2000, p. 169). High-tech technoculture, in short, will become increasingly important. This 'world class communications infrastructure', however, can involve the tradeoff of the social agenda against that of economic development. It prioritises customer service over public service; consumer satisfaction over democratic participation; and shareholders' dividends over the public interest. The price to be paid when handing over a national communications infrastructure to free market forces includes possible misuse of information, invasions of privacy and a growing gap between the information rich and information poor—with a marginalisation of those whose disposable income is too small to make them attractive customers. This scenario is a long way removed from Melody's concept of the public interest, where it is those who lack the wherewithal (economically and socially) to represent themselves who deserve the greatest consideration.

Increasingly, such public service concepts as CSOs or MSPs seem quaint and old-fashioned throwbacks to the days when there was such a thing as 'a national telecommunications carrier'. These days, when service providers are expected to do battle in a free market, and customers are fickle creatures to be wooed and won, 'the public' is less visible and (perhaps) synonymous with such phrases as 'the great unwashed'. Stakeholder is the new catchcry: it is no longer chic to be a public.

## INFORMATION POVERTY

The information poor tend to receive token representation in issues of public interest, but they are unlikely to represent themselves. The concept of information poverty tends to be applied—by those with access to information—to 'others', people other than the information rich. Such commentators erroneously put themselves in the place of people with far fewer information resources, and imaginatively reconstruct how they would feel if they were in such information-reduced circumstances. An approach like this emphasises the circumstances of people with access to fewest information resources—whether or not these information-less individuals are actively demanding more equitable distribution. It builds upon a model of 'laggards', rather than one of 'fulfilleds' (see Chapter 2).

This situation—of feeling for the information poor—has become more extreme as information societies project the current rate of change, and the growth of the rich/poor divide, into the future. In searching for future strategies to address inequality, policy-makers ignore the difference they could make immediately to the lives of those experiencing a reduction in information access. By developing strategies to intervene at the point where existing information and communication resources are lost, policy-makers could quickly lever the benefits of intervention.

For some time there has been an identifiable, existing group of 'losers' (in terms of winners and losers) whose information and communication needs are inadequately addressed under current resource-allocation provisions. These people, with recent experience of information loss, may usefully be referred to as the 'nouveau information poor'. (Their sudden, low-visibility, information poverty is in contrast with the conspicuous consumption characteristic of the 'nouveau information riche'.) Addressing the putative needs of those with the least information access may result in over-servicing people who do not experience themselves as information poor, while at the same time under-providing for others who, as a result of certain identifiable events, may be in great information distress.

People in transition—for example through a reduction in their economic and social circumstances—may be denied effective access to information and communication resources that had hitherto been a part of their everyday lives. (Moreover, such access to information may be a crucial component of any attempt to regain their former socio-economic status.) Whilst not actually on the bottom rung of the information society ladder, the 'nouveau information poor' may have slipped so far, so fast, as to experience information deprivation at an intensity unknown to those who have never had significant information access—and who are untroubled by the absence of such resources. In effect, people who have been participants in digital technoculture can become locked out of it, as a result of a range of life events.

## INFORMATION ACCESS

The public good to be achieved in addressing information deprivation rests in a joining of competence with need. It is sometimes argued, as a matter of fundamental equity, that all people should have trouble-free access to information, because that would promote equality. Access to information is a necessary, but by no means sufficient, condition of equitable participation. To talk simply in terms of equity of access ignores the fact that effective interaction in the information society requires high levels of motivation and sustained effort. Such keenness to interact with the technology of information cannot be assumed. Continuing motivation is perhaps the key determinant of successful participation—more important than access *per se*.

Far from making life easier, a new technology can add frustration, guilt and excuse-making to the daily agenda. Many households who have invested their own time and resources in computers and other ICTs (and whose motivation can consequently be inferred) have had negative experiences with the technology's ease of operation and consequent usefulness. Providing greater access to technology is not, by itself, sufficient to lessen information poverty.

In France, where Minitel was designed with social equity in mind, the idea was to offer the whole nation the benefits of the information society. According to Julianne Schultz, the system:

> is used by millions of French citizens to search a telephone directory, reserve a ticket, teleshop, bank, learn a foreign language, receive news and send mail. Although Minitel is not without its problems—and is used least by the new underclass at whom it was originally targeted—the success of the French system has demonstrated the limitations of a commercially driven approach (1994, p. 109).

From the perspective of the information rich, 'the people who most need this information' are the ones least likely to use it. Access to technology does not necessarily lead to its use, and information does not necessarily fuel self-empowering activity.

This conundrum may reflect—as many commentators have suggested—the distorting dynamic of information-production in the information society. Information is not produced in accordance with need, but to make a profit. The nature of the information produced (e.g., who is dating whom in Hollywood) may also explain why so few of the information poor stridently demand better information access. Nonetheless, the institution of further MSPs with regards to information and communication resources does not of itself alter the dynamics of information production and distribution. It would be prudent to investigate thoroughly the circumstances of 'those who are to benefit' from increased service provision, to ensure that they want the services to be provided, and that they are motivated to learn and use the technology involved.

There are formidable obstacles to providing universal access to a new technoculture. Murdock et al., addressing the theories underlying patterns of technology diffusion of computers, comment: 'The maintenance of particular forms of computer use will depend in large part on access to other users who can offer advice, encouragement and practical support. Conversely, users who are isolated from or marginal to such networks may find it difficult to acquire competencies and sustain interest over time' (1992, p. 150). As demonstrated in Chapter 2, models of technology diffusion and adoption are incremental. Nonetheless, once the diffusion 'bell curve' is breasted, late adopters, laggards and non-adopters find themselves in a society where the benefits of the technology are readily apparent and where there is a comparative wealth of people willing and able to support the process of technology adoption.

In terms of telephones, television and radio services, they were already widely spread before they became established as MSPs. While younger, middle-class, educated consumers in free-market societies are more likely to see the benefits of using the Internet, and have relevant skills and support networks, it is premature to start seeing domestic access to the Internet as a new MSP. Nonetheless, access through libraries, schools, etc., remains an important priority—and in the public interest. In a sense, a technology or service only becomes recognised as having become the minimum level of service when almost everybody already has it.

'Consumers and citizens do not walk around with holes in their lives waiting for broadband services to arrive,' argues David Sless, pointing out: 'Many today work far more hours than their parents did and develop ways of avoiding extra information services, not acquiring new ones' (Sless 1994, p. 6). Yet some citizens do walk around— metaphorically—with exactly these communication holes in their lives. Those are the people who have experienced some measure of infor-mation wealth, and whose transitional circumstances have plunged them into what they experience as extreme information poverty.

## TRANSITION, STRESS AND INFORMATION POVERTY

The western world is revisiting Descartes to update *Cogito ergo sum* for the twenty-first century: 'I'm stressed, therefore I am.' Stress has become the *sine qua non* of the information society, and some reasons for this will be discussed further in Chapter 12, in terms of the clash between modern expectations and postmodern experiences. There are still, however, key transition points which carry within them an evident and added 'extra' burden of stress. This stress is frequently exacerbated by sudden information deprivation at a time when information would help to address the stressful situation—that is to say, in a way most likely to lead to its successful resolution.

Stressful transition points include a dramatic decline in economic position—such as sudden unemployment or redundancy, the onset of chronic (disabling) sickness, marital separation or bereavement; and/or an upheaval in social circumstances—migration, moving from the city to regional (or remote) areas, leaving home, graduating from college or university. A consistent component of these stressful changes is the having and the losing of information and communication opportunities and resources. Further, since information access is an effective way of overcoming or ameliorating economic crisis and bridging physical and social distance, the loss is accompanied by frustration that the communication resources disappear just when they are critically needed. These dynamics can conspire to produce feelings of helplessness, often associated with depression.

If information withdrawal is one characteristic of acute crises resulting from social transition, another is that there are reduced economic incentives for manufacturers and service providers to target these 'nouveau poor' populations. Newlyweds and new home buyers are far more attractive markets for sales and promotional campaigns than the recently separated, or those who are reluctantly moving into state housing. (There is also a stress associated with positive transitions—a new job for example, or marriage, but these often go hand-in-hand with an improved financial position, and greater access to resources, and do not involve loss of access to information.)

There is no research that would allow us to guesstimate the effect of applying some sort of MSP to those who are undergoing traumatic social and economic transition. Nonetheless, it has been established that access to information helps to empower decision-making, and that this fosters a sense of control and competence (without which it is hard to reverse a decline in material and social circumstances). Making information technology accessible to those who want it, and who know how to use it, has the effect of reducing the subjective perception of neediness, helplessness and passivity.

Further, in the context of their straitened economic circumstances, the nouveau information poor can act as innovators within their recently acquired (poorer) social circle, becoming Murdock et al.'s (1992) 'other users who can offer advice, encouragement and practical support [enabling new users] to acquire competencies and sustain interest over time' (1992, p. 150). They can become effective conduits for the dispersal and maintenance of skills in accessing and using information and communication goods and services. Barr links the success of future information and communication services to 'how the organisations that offer those services understand the behavioural practices and needs of consumers and citizens. The real question for our communication future is not what the *technologies* are going to be like, but what *we* are going to be like' (2000, p. 233, italics in original).

## THE INFORMATION DIVIDE

Improved communication options for some go hand in hand with an increase in communication barriers for others since communication brings together some people at the expense of separating those who are not connected. From Roman road-building onwards, a communication channel may link two points, with division as a side effect—clearly demonstrated by the distance between the two sides of a busy six-lane highway. Literacy allowed people to communicate across space and time but created a gulf between those who could read and those who couldn't, while the introduction of a mail service created a professional demand for letter readers and writers. Most recently, the capacity to communicate via email and the Net has become a touchstone for those who are—or are not—part of cutting edge conversations. Techno-cultures exclude people, as well as uniting them.

Poverty, in an information society, is linked to gender, age, social class, cultural grouping, education, disposable income, ethnicity and indigeneity, and geographic location. These are all factors that help determine relative access to ICTs, and to skills and experience in using the information gathered for social, cultural and personal ends. While there is undoubtedly an information divide, there is no certainty that providing access to a 'minimum service' will bridge it, as Minitel demonstrated when it failed to recruit poorer French citizens into the ranks of digital information users.

Interestingly, the information poor who are frustrated with their circumstances are unlikely to participate in discussions about information and communication policy (even where they have that opportunity): they protest instead. It is much easier for the information rich to apply the label of 'information poverty' to those who accept their status, and appear comparatively unfazed by their circumstances. The label is most likely to be worn by those who are indifferent to it.

The people who find information poverty unacceptable, and start making demands to redress the situation, are not categorised as 'information poor', but as 'unreasonable' or 'unrealistic'. An example of this at the international level is the (all too brief) history of the NWICO (New World Information and Communication Order). In the 1970s and 1980s, Third World nations used a UN education and cultural forum, UNESCO, to demand greater global equity in terms of access to, and distribution of, information and communication resources. Their actions resulted in the United States and the United Kingdom deserting

UNESCO, and depriving it of funding on the grounds that it had been 'politicised' (Savage, 1989).

Information poverty, as the NWICO countries argued, is a two-edged sword. Not only is there a lack of access for the poor as consumers of information and communication products, but there is a corresponding lack of access for the poor as producers of such products—and no realistic editorial control over the content produced by information-powerful others. The information rich control the representations of the information poor, and select images congruent with pre-existing perceptions. This leads to a predominance of 'passive', 'helpless', 'needy' images of the developing world, which represents one western conception of the information deprived. (Sinclair et al. (1996) argue that such a perspective may merely represent the myopic viewpoint of the information rich, unable to recognise the peripheral product.)

A similar dynamic can be seen to operate when considering the relatively poor population groups in western societies. They control neither the agenda, nor the content, of public debates. In a sense, their silence is a *prima facie* indicator of how greatly they need the information which they are currently unable to access, and may partly explain why there is not more popular debate on information and communication policy. The suspicion is that the information poor should be demanding greater equity, but are not—possibly because they are not aware that such a debate is available. Alternatively, they may simply feel that communications and IT are not priorities in their lives.

The information rich are those who are wealthy according to indicators of technology access and other measures, so they are more likely to be perceived as 'rich', as well as 'information rich'. It may not predominantly be technology access that makes them rich—instead, their technology access may be only one of a number of traits, happenstance and privilege that reveal wealth, rather than confer it. Most of the information rich in consumer societies are ignorant of the lives and aspirations of people they class as information poor. Apart from the socio-economic data gathered to ensure that relatively disadvantaged individuals are not double-dipping—or defrauding—social welfare programmes, little research is funded into the lives of the information poor, partly because they are not targeted consumers of information, communication and up-market products. People make assumptions, however, and some of these are discussed in terms of their/our constructions of the 'First World' and the 'Third World'.

## THE THOROUGHLY MODERN FIRST, SECOND AND THIRD WORLDS

The phrase 'First World' implies an order, or sequence. It might refer to the temporal domain, but human society is not thought to have started in any First World country—maybe in Africa, or China. So the phrase 'First World' can be deduced as referring to a sense of pre-eminence, or importance. Not surprisingly, it is a term resisted by Third World countries. They also see the label 'developing' as a possible pejorative, and doubt they want to develop like the developed world, in any case.

Developing countries prefer the term South for themselves, and refer to the rich nations of the North. In resisting the terms First/Third and developed/developing as reference points, the South is resisting the core–periphery dynamic implicit in both, and attempting to replace it with a spatial relationship. (While having sympathy with this argument, I tend to use 'western' as a synonym for the developed and First World because the terms have ready meanings for readers in information societies.)

The core–periphery dynamic predates discussions and debates about the First World and the Third World. It has always been possible to construct a history of human society through core–periphery relationships, but that construction became particularly dominant in the modern era, at the time of the Industrial Revolution. At that point, the city was the core, and the country became peripheral to the industrial heartland. The core–periphery duality was then reproduced in colonial practice. The First World/Third World divide largely rewrites the power imbalance first practised in empire. Empires depend upon soldiery, specialised administrators and rigid divisions of labour. By the time imperial theory and practice had become incorporated into the British Empire, it was undoubtedly modernist and indisputably organised according to a core–periphery model.

The phrase 'post-colonial' signals a postmodern perspective where the erstwhile periphery has assumed centre stage. There is also an implication that the post-colonial approach differs significantly from the 'modern' colonial perspective. Although core–periphery theories may be modern, they also tend to be politically radical. They use a political economy theory of power and influence, which is to say that they see power and influence as a kind of currency used by key players and elites to negotiate political advantage. A political economy perspective analyses the political costs/benefits of interactions and exchange, including those that take place in a core–periphery context.

Like many other modern perspectives, core–periphery discourse includes oppositional dualities—along the lines of 'First/Third' and 'developed/developing'. (Table 4.1 in Chapter 4, comparing the modern and the postmodern in terms of dualities, is itself a modern approach to that task.) One aspect of core–periphery theory constructs oppositional relationships between peripheral places or cultures, and that/those at the core. Cores are constructed as benefiting at the expense of their peripheries.

Colin McArthur (1985) discusses the creation of the periphery (Scottish people—*homo celticus*) by the core (English/French society—*homo oeconomicus*) in terms of binary oppositions: 'Oppressed people the world over know this discourse to their bitter cost . . . What is important is that the Celt (or African, or Polynesian, etc.) is allocated his/her place, is constructed, in a discourse enunciated elsewhere' (1985, p. 65). McArthur's oppositions are followed and adapted in Table 6.1 to compare conceptions of *homo informaticus* (First World) and *homo incommunicaticus* (Third World).

**Table 6.1 Discourses relating to the First World/Third World divide**

| Homo informaticus | Homo incommunicaticus |
| --- | --- |
| Urban | Rural |
| Civilised | Wild |
| Developed | Developing |
| Rational | Emotional |
| Christian | Non-believer |
| Astute | Gullible |
| Innovative | Traditional |
| Technological | Untechnological |
| First | Third |
| Rich | Poor |
| Generous | Needy |

This duality is not offered as a 'real' explanation of differences between the First and Third Worlds, but as a demonstration of how a periphery can be/is constructed in opposition to the core. Such a construction demonstrates an ignorance that results (in part) from an economic bias—the Third World receives scant attention from the First except as a potential market or as the recipient of aid. The information poor and the information rich rarely communicate directly, partly because the Third World lacks communication access. People in the Third World have less information, and less access to information technologies, and the technology they can buy (with 'soft' loans and an increasing debt) is western technology, and benefits the key elites that create it. High-tech technoculture is a predominantly First World feature.

According to the core–periphery model, globalisation offers nothing new, just more of the same. Globalisation has been defined by Featherstone as 'the increase in the number of international agencies and institutions, the increasing global forms of communication . . . the development of standard notions of citizenship, rights and conception of humankind' (Featherstone 1990, p. 6). This implies a 'western liberalisation' of the world, but the haves are still exporting poverty to the have nots, at a profit.

Even if the Third World could equalise technological resources and technology use with the first, it would not necessarily wish to do so. Given that the Scots resent being constructed by the English, then *homo incommunicaticus* also resists being modelled by, or in the image of, *homo informaticus*. The either/or duality is a genuinely modern problem— if the information gap continues, the First World is (morally) untenable; if the gap is filled, the Third World is (effectively) engulfed. There is a compartmentalised division between the core and the periphery. The boundaries are hard to blur, except at the price of difference itself.

Further, this core–periphery duality is inadequate for conceptualising power disparities, or interdependencies, in the networked globe. The common experience of individuals living in contemporary nation states is one of dislocation and fragmentation within and between societies. Boundaries are illusory. There are elements of information poverty within all First World countries, and tranches of information wealth within the Third World. There were capitalists in the second (Soviet Bloc) world and revolutionary socialists in the first. A theory appropriate to the analysis of post-industrial life—networked and excluded—would take account of this fragmentation.

Modernist, industrial verities of core–periphery theory—endorsing such geographical certainties as the Iron Curtain and the Free West— have given way to the postmodern condition of indeterminacy and uncertainty. A psychological mesh without a centre encircles a technological network without a core in a globe that has no periphery. The one truth offered globally is that there is no one truth: everything is negotiable and all perspectives are relative to the discourse through which they are constructed. The discourse of high-tech technoculture is one that sees the First World as continuing into the future, and as clearly beneficial for humanity—but the excluded are not part of the picture.

This is not to claim that core–periphery theories are entirely bankrupt: they have their uses. In an analysis constructed upon the dicho- tomy of have/have not—upon comparisons—modernism is an appropriate discourse. Where the nature of the information-driven, post-industrial, late-capitalist society is under discussion, however, postmodern analyses offer fruitful ways forward. (These will be considered further in Chapter 12.)

## BUILDING INFORMATION WEALTH: MALAYSIA

The old divisions of First World/Third World are looking increasingly dated, however. Since 1997, Singapore has been envisioning itself (see Chapter 7) as 'Beyond the Internet'—hard to position in terms of an information divide. Malaysia, too, set itself clear information society targets at the beginning of the 1990s and is progressing towards them. The case study reported here was supported by the Canadian Development Research Centre, and discusses the impact of *Vision 2020* upon information technology and access in the Sarawak region of Malaysia.

Malaysia's *Vision 2020*, announced by Prime Minister Mahathir Mohammad (Mahathir 1991), provides a blueprint for Malaysia to achieve the status of a 'developed and industrialised' country by 2020. This time frame was more realistic than many of the millennial visions, which used the 2000 watershed as an almost-magical benchmark. Although the aim includes that of becoming an industrial nation, Malaysia is using *Vision 2020* to drive technological literacy and build a knowledge-based economy 'equipped to perform in a global environment'. Malaysia has built a Cybercity with fast (road) connections to the capital Kuala Lumpur, and instituted the MSC (Multimedia Super Corridor) in the hope that it will become the 'Silicon Valley of Asia'. In addition to these high-profile initiatives, the Malaysian Education Ministry (Malaysia 1997) has plans to convert all 10 000 primary and secondary schools in Malaysia to Smart Schools by 2010 (Khoo et al. 2000, p. 57).

The Smart Schools project sets out to 'wield technology effectively in transforming and improving teaching practices, school organisations and student performance; accelerate the development of student learning, critical thinking and creativity; and increase IT literacy and penetration' (Khoo et al. 2000, p. 58). The policy faces formidable challenges. As with other nations, commentators have identified a 'digital divide' between the information rich and the information poor within Malaysia itself. This division parallels that of urban/rural, as well as reflecting wealth, education and other factors. Thus Khoo et al. (2000) offer a useful case study of the challenges faced by governments in developing countries who are trying to ensure that their nations can participate in the global information economy, and in the further development of technoculture.

There are a number of isolated regions in the Malaysian state of Sarawak (situated in Borneo). SMK Bario is the only secondary school in the Kelabit Highlands of Sarawak and was established in 1967. It caters mostly for students from Bario's twelve villages and offers lower secondary school education. Since July 1999, the school has provided boarding for its entire 158-student population. It has amenities such as piped water, medical care services and two diesel-operated generators to provide electricity. At the start of 2000, the computing facilities in the school were five 486 PCs, two dot matrix printers and one scanner.

At the turn of the century, the only means of telecommunication available in the school was via Very High Frequency (VHF) radio services. Telecommunications services are consequently a top priority since neither the school nor its pupils can connect with the Internet given the current information resources. *Vision 2020* offers a goal for Malaysia's online future which, given the time frame, may continue to prove inspirational for the achievement of information and computer literacy. It has already yielded significant results, and the teachers in the schools appear enthusiastic about working towards future goals, such as Internet access. Nonetheless, developing nations will continue for some time to question the equity of discussions of information policy, and information priorities, in the west.

## CONCLUSION

This chapter has addressed the issue of the public interest, and its relevance to discussions about ICTs. Although there is a growing tendency for governments to argue that what is good for the market is also in the public interest, this perspective does not address the needs of those who are not customers in the market. The concept of information poverty is a relative term, especially in a country where most people have access to radio, phone and television. Nonetheless, there are clearly people who experience differential levels of access to, say, the digital domain, and high-tech technoculture.

As well as an information divide within First World countries, there is an information divide between countries of the First and the Third Worlds. Brief mention was made of the NWICO movement of the 1970s and 1980s. The chapter ended with a case study of IT access in a secondary school in Sarawak, a regional area of Malaysia. High-tech technoculture is pervasive only in the western world, and in westernised areas of Southern countries. Technoculture divides the globe, as well as uniting elements of it.

# 7

# MASS MEDIA AND THE PUBLIC SPHERE

## THE PUBLIC SPHERE

The public sphere is an issue of relevance to technoculture since technoculture is a major site through which the public sphere operates. The public sphere is the space between 'the private' and 'the state', and is a locale within which the state can be criticised. Formally, the public sphere is a concept put forward by critical German philosopher Jurgen Habermas (tr. 1989), whose views on its origins and nature hark back to an earlier (theoretical?) society when state and business interests were unable to control a public sphere of free-flowing ideas and information. (See below for Habermas' definition.) Loosely speaking, the public sphere concerns that which is not 'private'—the world of communal, economic and political life rather than intimacy and familial relations. A healthy public sphere is both necessary for, and an indication of, the exercise of the rights of free speech and of participatory citizenship. It is also an indication of 'modern' notions being in play, of boundaries and dualistic oppositions between public and private.

In the west, free speech has been identified as an important component of the public sphere, although an absolute right to free speech is generally qualified by 'the national interest' and by issues of social harmony. The mass media are technocultural sites for the creation of the public sphere—providing a framework within which the public issues of the day are discussed. The question Habermas raises, however, is whether the mass media are so dominated by the political system—by the government and the corporate realm—that the public sphere is compromised. Are the mass media sufficiently free of state power, and of corporate influence? Habermas says not.

In his writings, Habermas is highly critical of the mass media. These concerns are echoed by David Holmes' argument (see Chapter 9) that broadcasting 'cellularizes' social interaction into domestic groups—the groups within which broadcasting is consumed. Indeed, Holmes suggests that: 'The greater the dependence of the individual on television, the less dependent s/he becomes on the public sphere which is being displaced in practice; and the more such a public sphere, particularly in its architectural/compositional aspects, withers away' (1997, p. 34). Holmes interprets the growth of the Internet as being evidence of a hunger for community resulting from the breakdown of the public sphere by broadcasting. In effect, Holmes sees the growth of technoculture as resulting from the withering of face-to-face social culture.

## HABERMAS' IDEAL OF A PUBLIC SPHERE

Habermas sets up an ideal vision of the public sphere in order to comment upon the 're-feudalisation' of the public, brought about—he argues—by their enthralled relationship with television. The press, with its roots in the eighteenth-century movement of the Enlightenment (where traditionally accepted ways of doing things were subjected to scrutiny in a new light of inquiry), is considered by Habermas to be far more supportive of a public sphere than television.

The radical genesis of the press is evident in the term 'the fourth estate'. This is a historical reference to the role of the press as independent of government, and to the political importance of the press in being able to call governments to account. The three estates which made up the Estates-General in France at the time of the French Revolution were the nobility (first estate), clergy (second estate) and commoners (third estate). The press claimed authority—as the fourth estate—to be an essential element of the revolutionary political process, monitoring the other estates and acting as the communication channel between parliament and the people. Indeed, in countries where the press is not currently free, journalists still risk their liberty—and sometimes their lives—to live up to the notion of making their governments accountable to the people.

Unlike many commentators, who see the *agora* or public space of the ancient Greek city-state of Athens as the ideal of democratic participation, Habermas situates his 'imperfect' example of the public sphere in the lively political debate which characterised the eighteenth-century London coffeehouse. Literary and political intellectuals gathered in the coffeehouses to read the news-sheets of the day and to debate the important topics. As in the Athenian *agora*, the people engaged in this debate were men, freed from the requirements of earning their daily living. In Athens, this was through the slavery of others and in London through colonial trade in slaves and other 'goods', and in the fruits of the Industrial Revolution. In both examples, participation in democratic debate was secured by virtue of gender, geography and social standing and at the expense of other people's (enforced) labour. Corner's comment is that London coffeehouse society was 'limited to a small elite in a period of extensive public illiteracy well before the enfranchising of the majority of the population' (1995, p. 42).

Habermas judges the political health of a society on the basis of the nature, scope and accessibility of its public sphere—a perspective echoed by British academic Nicholas Garnham. 'We would find it strange now if we made voting rights dependent upon purchasing power or property rights; yet access to mass media, as both channels of information and forums of debate, is largely controlled by just such power and rights' (Garnham 1990, p. 111). In practice, Habermas' concept of the public sphere has often been appropriated by those who wish to celebrate the achievements of the mass media, and who hope for equivalent—or greater—gains in democratic freedoms and expressions from the Internet. This discourse constructs technoculture as a liberating force, promising freedom and political power to the people.

## GOVERNMENT, CITIZENSHIP, INFORMATION AND THE PUBLIC SPHERE

Information, citizenship, government and the public sphere are all inter-connected through technoculture, and through the mass media. Corner summarises Habermas' view of these interconnections and the public sphere as being 'the space within a society, independent both of state power and of private, corporate influence, within which information can freely flow and debate on matters of public, civic concern can openly proceed. The concept is . . . central to Habermas' idea of the rights and duties of citizenship' (1995, p. 42).

According to British mass communication researchers Graham Murdock and Peter Golding, the commercialisation of information and communication services speaks to 'people predominantly through their identity as consumers, both of the communications and infor-mation products they buy and of the products promoted in the expanded advertising system that finances many of the new services. In the process, the system marginalizes or displaces other identities, in particular the identity of the citizen' (1989, p. 180). Citing Marshall (1949), they identify three dimensions to citizenship: civil, political and social. All of these rely, to some extent, upon information, a healthy public sphere and a supportive technocultural environment.

Civil rights concern an individual's freedom of action, freedom of association and movement, freedom to own and dispose of property and freedom of thought and speech. Political rights address an individual's right to engage in political activity and to help form the laws under which they are governed. These rights 'are what separates citizens from subjects. The latter may have the right to protection under the law, but only citizens can take part in determining the nature of the laws by which they will consent to be governed' (Murdock & Golding 1989, p. 182). Marshall's third set of rights, 'social rights', is identified with the twentieth-century development of welfare state style rights in industrialised nations. According to Marshall they cover 'the whole range from a right to a modicum of economic welfare and security to the right to share to the full in the social heritage and to live the life of a civilized being according to the standards prevailing in society' (1949, p. 11). In effect, citizens have rights to participate fully in society and the public sphere at every level of policy and culture. These rights imply the possibility that access to technoculture is a social right in western society, and that the development of cyber-democracy is an important technocultural goal.

Leading on from their discussion, Murdock and Golding identify three kinds of relationship between communications and citizenship, all of which are threatened by the privatisation of communication and information and its repackaging as part of a commodity exchange. The first relationship requires that 'people must have access to the information, advice and analysis that will enable them to know what their rights are in other spheres and allow them to pursue these rights effectively'. The second relationship requires access to 'information, interpretation and debate on areas that involve political choices', and also to channels of communication so that citizens can freely 'register criticism, mobilize opposition, and propose alternative courses of action'. Murdock and Golding's final relationship is one of representation in the media: people 'must be able to recognize themselves and their aspirations in the range of representations offered within the central communications sectors and be able to contribute to developing those representations' (1989, pp. 183–4).

According to this analysis, any information and communication arena which makes a significant contribution to the public sphere needs to be accessible to all citizens. If some people are excluded, then they are being denied their citizenship rights. The emphasis upon privatisation, claim Murdock and Golding, presents 'the freedom to choose among competing products as the central and defining liberty of the modern age'. Potentially, good information policies affecting the development and promotion of future digital technocultures offer a way beyond this, provided relevant information is publicly accessible, without charge, in places such as libraries, schools and government offices. Here, if citizens are to participate, the level of interaction with the public sphere must be two-way—both to retrieve information, and to introduce and circulate it as part of the creation of technoculture.

Many information societies include policies to create such accessible information channels within their plans for national information infrastructures. Although access needs to be combined with technological competence and confidence to be truly emancipating, government online services offer some solutions to citizens' information problems that seemed pressing until comparatively recently (social welfare information, for instance).

## CYBERSPACE AND THE PUBLIC SPHERE

Jan Fernback (1997) justifies her view that 'Cyberspace is essentially a re-conceived public sphere for social, political, economic, and cultural action' by commenting: 'Cyberspace has become a new arena for participation in public life . . . users can act as media audiences . . . yet users are also authors, public rhetoricians, statesmen, pundits' (1997, p. 37). Participation in cyberspace has none of the prerequisites of power and property criticised by Garnham—beyond access to technology, education, electricity and the accoutrements of the First World.

The public life lived in cyberspace is a very particular manifestation of society, fraught by qualifications and contradictions. Nonetheless, it is more difficult for the state to regulate and control the Internet than to regulate the mass media; consequently, it may more closely approximate the 'ideal' of a public sphere. The Internet's effectiveness as a forum for radical debate has been demonstrated, for example, by the successes of the Electronic Frontier Foundation (www.eff.org, see Chapter 8), and by examples of concerted political action, such as the disruption of the World Trade Organisation summit in Seattle in November–December 1999. British journalist and cultural commentator Joan Smith noted the role of the Net in coordinating national and international action:

> 'All the WTO's [World Trade Organisation] money and power and influence wasn't [sic] enough to move all those concerned, committed people out of the way', crowed Sam Corl, designer of the [Ruckus] society's website last week. Other organisations, such as the Seattle-based People for Fair Trade and Network Opposed to WTO, also used the Internet to invite volunteers to converge on the talks. Website graphics included world maps, allowing activists to click on to individual countries and find out where and when smaller N30 events—named for November 30, the first day of the summit—were being organised . . . Perhaps WTO leaders—those of them who know their way around the Internet—had begun by then to absorb the contents of the protest's main website, with its alarming pledge: 'May our resistance be as transnational as capital' . . . If this is anarchy— and groups such as Anarchy Now! were involved in the preparations—it is organised anarchy, turning the information technology which has fostered the growth of globalization into a formidable weapon against capitalism. 'Globalize this!' the demonstrators demanded, deliberately appropriating not just the methods of transnational corporations but their rhetoric (Personal communication, basis for article by Smith & Gumbel 1999, p. 16).

Accepted norms of free speech relating to the expression of radical and dissident ideas often vary over time, even within a given cultural framework. One example of this is the postwar Hollywood blacklists of people who held pro-Communist views during the McCarthy era. A British example includes the differential treatment of Gerry Adams' views and of Sinn Fein (the political wing of the Irish Republican Army), depending upon the socio-political context within which the Northern Ireland/North of Ireland debate was being framed at that time. Where a public sphere is regulated, as with the mass media, it reflects the culturally acceptable—at least as regards political elites.

As well as varying over time within one national context, nation states also have marked differences between their concepts of free speech, and in the relationship of free speech to their public spheres. Singapore, for example, celebrates being an information society, but conceives the public sphere in a way that differs greatly from the West—free speech is less important than community harmony and the avoidance of express dissent. In a sense, the public sphere promoted and embraced by a nation partly creates that nation's 'invisible community' and expresses elements of its national identity.

## THE PUBLIC SPHERE AND NATIONAL IDENTITY

Nations identify themselves and others according to a variety of stereotypical criteria. People in the West tend to identify themselves as liberal, *laissez faire*, free-trade, parliamentary democracies. Other nations, not subscribing to these tenets, are often categorised as communist, Third World or developing countries, or variations on these themes, such as newly industrialised, emerging or post-colonial nations. For some of these developing countries, the recent experience of colonisation—almost always by nations of the North—continues to affect their international relations, just as the experience of being a (past) colonial power continues to confer benefits upon many former colonial economies.

Countries with a recent history of colonisation are often governed by a Westminster-style parliamentary democracy—a legacy of their colonisation—but may combine this with elements of social organis-ation at odds with the western model—for example by outlawing opposition parties. Whereas western-style freedoms are usually based upon a 'for' and 'against' style of parliamentary debate, with visible winners and losers, such a perspective is less acceptable in consensus-style cultures where social cohesion, and traditions of respect and saving face, may be of greater importance. Arguably, the West has a lot to learn from the ways in which such consensus societies resolve crises. It is hard to imagine a western country in which an event equivalent to the Fijian hostage crisis of May–July 2000 would have ended with such little loss of life, even given that civil rights and the processes of democracy in Fiji continue to give cause for international concern.

Singapore media specialists and commentators Ang and Yeo note that, although 'freedom of speech and expression' is granted under the Singa-pore constitution, 'Parliament may pass law restricting freedom of speech and expression for the following reasons: interest of the security of Singapore, friendly relations with other countries, public order, morality, restrictions designed to protect the privileges of parliament or to provide against contempt of court, defamation, [and] incitement to any offence' (Ang & Yeo 1998, p. 18). An acceptance of restrictions on freedom of speech is a key distinction of many consensus-driven, developing societies. This differentiates them from western-style democracies where individual communication and information freedoms, such as freedom of speech, are enshrined in the national constitution (as in the United States, McCarthyism notwithstanding).

In a newly industrialised nation such as Singapore, strongly adversarial speech is experienced as threatening to the social fabric. In countries such as the United Kingdom and the United States, however, the sting of losing a verbal engagement is mitigated by the socially accepted opinion that spirited debate is healthy, and such clichéd comments as 'everyone is entitled to their own point of view', and 'at least it's out in the open'. Even in western culture, however, the adversarial exchange is being softened by a growing acceptance of the value of consensus-building procedures. Signs of this include the increasingly important committee stage of parliamentary process and policy-making in Westminster-style democracies, and experimentation with mediation and conciliation as part of the processes of (for example) the resolution of disputes over children, custody, access and property following marital breakdown. The general spread of no-fault divorce in the West, based on the grounds of irretrievable marital breakdown, signals a move away from an adversarial proving of right and wrong as part of deciding the outcome of marital disputes.

Regulation of the public sphere in developing nations may demonstrate where tensions lie between the press (in their role as a 'fourth estate' watchdog) and the government (who may construct the role of the press as supporting the emergence of a society-wide consensus). Ang and Yeo note one example from Singapore where a 'reporter took the Ministry of Health to task for declaring that the period of uncertainty when AIDS could be detected was about 30 days when in fact it was almost three months. The Minister of Health described the report as "fairly irresponsible" and his Ministry wrote a letter to the newspaper demanding a retraction and apology' (1998, p. 22).

Ang and Yeo do not state whether the retraction and apology were provided, but do comment that the reporter was 'not sanctioned'. The lack of sanction was contrasted with past practice where 'reporters have been denied access to information when the Ministry in question found that they had written reports it considered erroneous' (1998, p. 22). In a sense, both parties (minister and reporter) were able to save face; the minister may have had/got his 'apology', but the reporter was not sanctioned—an implicit recognition that the reporter was accurate in their comments about the AIDS window of uncertainty being 90 days.

In societies such as Singapore, there is often an acknowledged hierarchy of 'heavier versus weaker' regulation in different social spheres. According to Ang and Yeo, these heavier/weaker dyads operate in: home/business, children/adults, public/private. Heavier regulation in the home, rather than business, differs from the expected priority of many western countries. This ordering of heavier/weaker: home/business refers to Singapore's emphasis upon its export economy, and recognises that a competitive business strategy might involve businesses operating under a more lenient regulatory regime (for the export market) than is applied to domestic consumption. 'Information for the home is considered less critical so censorship of such information is deemed to have less deleterious effect' (Ang & Yeo 1998, p. 17).

We can draw the inference from Ang and Yeo's commentary that the putative outcome of Singapore's media regulation is the 'enlightenment' of the audience: 'Events like these [reporting the Singaporean execution of a Filipino domestic help convicted of murder, which caused huge protests in the Philippines] are therefore seen as justifying the need for the controls on the media as the unimpeded flow of ideas can sometimes have negative consequences instead of leading to enlightenment' (1998, p. 16). The assumption that one person, or group of people, can decide upon what material is enlightening, and in which circumstances, runs counter to most western ideas. In liberal democracies, information access is seen as a public good, since citizens (in an ideal world) need unbiased information circulating in the public sphere to make individual decisions regarding important political issues. Different restrictions on the technoculture of Singapore's public sphere, compared with the British/American/Australian technocultural realm, reflect cultural differences as well as differences in social and political priorities.

## TECHNOLOGY IN AN INDIGENOUS PUBLIC SPHERE

Eric Michaels died young, in 1988, at the age of 40. Before he died, however, he spent some six years with the Warlpiri people of Yuendumu in Australia's Northern Territory, investigating how 'television' would have looked if Australian Aboriginal people had invented it, and the contexts within which video was used by the Warlpiri community. His work had far-reaching effects, and remains groundbreaking. Amongst other outcomes, it set the scene for innovative Australian legislation to deal with the issue of broadcasting in Indigenous communities. Michaels' work was used as evidence to support the assertion that Indigenous Australians should have 'local control' of television. In this way, it is a further example (along with Umble's 1992 case study of the Amish, referred to in Chapter 2) of a community assuming social control of a technology developed outside the user-community, and potentially threatening to its values.

Michaels documented the Warlpiri's appropriation of video/television and the way in which the community consumed broadcast products, videotapes, etc., and created cultural documents through their use. His writings include accounts of programme making which indicate significant cultural differences between western modes of production and Warlpiri video-making. One of these is the account of filming the *Coniston Story*, produced and shot by Francis Jupurrurla, and dealing with the events of 1929 when about 100 Aboriginal people were massacred in retaliation for the murder of Frederick Brooks, a 'white trapper and dingo hunter':

At the appointed moment Jupurrurla arrived at my camp with four carloads of people, and together—him, old Japangardi [the narrator], 26 more Warlpiri men, women, and children, and myself—we headed off to Coniston to undertake a major epic production . . . Although very few of these people would be participating directly in the videotaping, either in front of or behind the camera, everyone had to be present to authorize the product . . . Everyone had rights to both the story and the land on which—of which—it speaks. The credibility of the resulting tape for the Warlpiri audience is dependent upon knowing that these people were all participating in the event, even though the taped record provides no direct evidence of their presence . . . Any story comes from a particular place, and travels from there to here, forging links that define the tracks over which both people and ceremonies travel. Jupurrurla models his electronic discourse on exactly such principles of orientation (Michaels 1994, pp. 113–14).

The taping of this story allowed it to circulate in a new way, and in a new medium, within the public sphere.

As well as documenting video production culture, techniques and processes, Michaels analysed the policy implications of video production and consumption and communicated his observations directly to the regulatory and decision-making forums which were, at that point, masterminding the introduction of satellite broadcasting to remote Australia (and to Aboriginal communities). The introduction of broadcast television to Indigenous Australia raised a number of potential problems for the Warlpiri. These included the broadcasting of 'western' content and language, and the depiction in drama, soap opera and documentary of taboo relationships, such as incest. Such concerns might be seen as a fear of 'the corruption of culture' by channelling the 'outside/global' into the local Aboriginal community, and contaminating the Indigenous public sphere.

The fear of the 'outside coming in' was matched by the fear of the 'inside moving out'. The use of Aboriginal culture by non-Indigenous broadcasters and its representation as 'exotic', 'other', 'poor', 'different', and so on was perceived as both demeaning and disempowering by the Warlpiri. Mass media representations of Aboriginal people often include images which break Indigenous cultural taboos relating to information (who is allowed to say what in which circumstances) and 'recording and showing' (for example, of sacred rituals, and of people who have since died). The re-broadcasting of programmes which include Aboriginal people and Aboriginal content—interpreted, edited and packaged by conventional television production techniques—has the potential to cause huge community distress.

In traditional Aboriginal culture, information is not 'transferable' in the way that it is in western society (see Chapter 5). Only certain people hold 'copyright' on particular pieces of information. These individuals may have the authority to communicate that information to specific people in a given time, place and context but that communication does not give information recipients any rights to the re-telling. Aboriginal people who had authority to talk to documentary makers in the time and place where they were filmed were thunderstruck to find the culturally important information they had shared was desecrated by being broadcast in inappropriate times and places to whomsoever might be watching. Michaels argues that such practices constituted a 'culturecidal' threat to traditional Aboriginal culture:

Aborigines who now are regarded by their countrymen as having leaked information into the public network are accused by their fellows as having 'sold their Law'. Fights, social upheaval and elaborate paybacks can follow the desecration of a ceremony or even a design that occurs when it is broadcast. The problem is grave, serious, and 'culturecidal' . . . Traditional people care not a whit what trendy and pro-Aboriginal rhetoric is used to frame these desecrations (1994, p. 33).

Australian debate in the 1970s and 1980s concerning whether or not to introduce a domestic satellite—AUSSAT—concentrated on issues of cost/benefit and 'national pride'. Little policy consideration was initially given to cultural sensitivities. An 'equivalent' nation, Canada, had its own satellite system from the mid-1970s, and the domestic control of satellite broadcasting seemed a fitting advance for Australian broadcasting, rather than continuing to hire Intelsat capacity. In any case, although Intelsat was used to broadcast the public service channel (ABC) to larger remote towns, the government cut-off was a population of 1000, and smaller communities were excluded from federally funded access. Use of Intelsat required the purchase of a very expensive town-based satellite-downlink to capture a signal that was then re-broadcast terrestrially using a community re-transmitter. The Australian domestic satellite, however, could be received by an individual household at a relatively affordable price.

Because of the costs of servicing smaller settlements using Intelsat, most traditional Aboriginal communities had not experienced broadcast television. This was all about to change, however, with the commissioning of the domestic satellite, and the availability of household-priced dishes. As Michaels wrote at the time, 'Aboriginal societies are to be included in the Government's plans to assure every Australian the "right" to watch ABC television. Many people fear that this curious "right" may jeopardise the maintenance of Aboriginal values, language and law in remote communities' (1984, p. 51).

In 1987, these culturecidal concerns resulted in the federally enacted Broadcasting in Remote Aboriginal Communities Scheme (BRACS). This legislation allowed remote Aboriginal communities to vet incoming programmes for offensive content, or for topics and sequences which transgressed traditional cultural practice and law. Programmes judged suitable were then rebroadcast within the community—together with local production, often in an Indigenous language, concerning topics of relevance to Aboriginal people living traditional lifestyles. Such a scheme might offer some reassurance to Habermas' supporters that television and the public sphere are sometimes compatible in socially grounded technocultures.

Aboriginal elders hoped that the BRACS strategies would help turn satellite-delivered broadcast programmes from a threat into a television service more allied with the project of cultural maintenance and development. The legislation also meant that Aboriginal people acquired the right (held by no other Australian community) to record and censor broadcast television as part of a decision-making process as to which programmes were—and were not—suitable for public consumption. According to Indigenous media specialist Helen Molnar: 'BRACS was established in 1987, and the installation of the BRACS units in eighty remote communities was completed in 1992' (1994, p. 11). There have been continuing concerns about under-resourcing and lack of federal commitment to the scheme, but its existence is a testimony to the effectiveness of Michaels' life and work.

Parallels exist between the BRACS debate and issues raised by emerging industrial nations such as Malaysia, and Malaysian television's refusal to accept the BBC dictat that either a BBC news bulletin is broadcast whole, or not at all (see Chapter 8). Western assumptions about information ownership, rights, obligations and free speech are brought into sharp focus by contact with cultural perspectives that construct corresponding rights to retain control of information (even after it has been shared), and rights and obligations to 'turn off' free speech where that speech might cause offence, community discord or undermine culture in other ways. Indigenous Australians' use of broadcasting can make clear the inappropriateness to other cultures of many western attitudes. Technoculture is not ubiquitous; neither is one cultural manifestation of a technoculture universally acceptable.

This section has demonstrated that technoculture has the capacity to reflect significant differences between separate cultural groups in a nation or country. The next segment addresses the role of technoculture in relocating participants within different psychosocial realms. Regardless of physical location, for example, a 'domestic' phone call can relocate the speakers psychologically to the private realm of the household.

## THE SOCIAL SPHERE AND IMAGINED COMMUNITY

Some decades ago, Hannah Arendt commented: 'The distinction between a private and a public sphere of life corresponds to the household and the political realms . . . but the emergence of the social realm, which is neither private nor public, strictly speaking, is a relatively new phenomenon' (1958, p. 28). In recent generations, the telephone has been the technology most associated with the development and maintenance of a social sphere. Gillard et al. argue that for some people the phone is a way of extending 'private boundaries . . . beyond their home to family and friends [who] were welcome to call any time' (1994, pp. 21–2). The impression here is that the phone is used to 'capture' a friend/household member and bring them into an elastic, psychological domain of social space. A 'private' call has the effect of relocating the other psychologically within the socio-domestic sphere; a 'business' call psychologically propels a home-based individual from their domestic context into the public sphere.

In community-building circumstances, the telephone is not being used as a message-communicator, but as a tool for the more fundamental task (according to Maslow's [1948] hierarchy of needs) of relating. In western societies, communities tend not to be based purely (or at all) upon daily face-to-face contact. Geographically dispersed social systems rely upon mediated communications for their existence and their strength, and email also offers an extension of private boundaries in the public realm; a private email can be equivalent to a private phone call in propelling the recipient into a different social space. Digital technoculture can be used to maintain the oldest community links—ties of blood lines and kinship—across geographical space.

Whereas mail can maintain community at a distance—with the inevitable time lapse between exchanges—telephone calls offer simultaneity, but at a price, and with possible complications of time zones over extended distances. Following the introduction of email and the Internet, nonsynchronous psychological communities extend from the remotest corners of the networked globe through the towns, cities and country areas of information societies. Further, once the hardware has been purchased and the ISP contracted, the unit cost of sending and receiving an email is very cheap. Rath (1985, p. 202) argues: 'frontiers of a national, regional or cultural kind no longer count: what counts much more is the boundary of the transmission . . . which increasingly bears little relationship to the geographical territory of any given nation state' (cited in Morley & Robins 1995, p. 61). Indeed, nation-state boundaries are all but irrelevant to the construction of online communities.

Psychological communities link together people who share ties of family, interest and/or affection. Whether they are termed psychological communities, 'virtual' communities, 'horizontal' communities, online communities or electronic communities—and in whichever ways they are mediated—communities of shared interest are of growing importance for social sustenance. The next case study, dealing with the use of particularistic media in diasporic communities, demonstrates how a 'micro-public sphere' is maintained by circulating shared items and cultural fragments as media elements. This technoculture uses a variety of media and artefacts to provide cultural constancy and cohesion.

## PARTICULARISTIC MEDIA AND THE MICRO PUBLIC SPHERE

Dayan's (1998) study of 'Particularistic media and diasporic communications' is one indication of how people (in this case, those involved in a cultural diaspora) work hard to communicate between generations as well as time zones, and without regard to geographical place or local circumstance. By implication, particularistic media are not shared by the 'mass' of people in the geographical country within which they circulate. Among particularistic media identified by Dayan are: audio and video-cassettes, newsletters, holy icons, letters, photographs, telephone calls and exchange of travellers. Particularistic media are especially valuable in maintaining community and connection across space, and are 'particular' to the society concerned. They are discussed by Dayan in terms of a 'micro public sphere' (1998, p. 103).

Dayan describes particularistic media as elements that circulate understandings between people who have already constructed a shared past—media used to keep a group in contact, rather than media used to form a group of like interests. These are 'media whose aim is not to create new identities but to prevent the death of existing ones' (Dayan 1998, p. 110). Email, and correspondence via Websites (for comparatively wealthy diasporic community members), can be added to the elements Dayan identifies as supporting a micro public sphere. Such studies of diasporic communities have relevance to studies of other psychological, dispersed and virtual communities and technocultures.

Almost every cultural group has a diasporic community associated with it, living away from the geographical region identified as the heartland of its cultural tradition. The dispersal may have been a result of political or economic persecution, or voluntary migration, and may have occurred two, twenty or 2000 years previously. A diasporic group (as opposed to assimilated migrants) retains an affinity with its notional homeland, whether or not that homeland continues to exist as a political entity on the world map. Such a group may identify with both the 'host' nation—where it may have lived for many generations—and the diasporic homeland. The Jewish nation constitutes a classic example of diaspora in western history.

Members of a diaspora are often especially visible at times of racial tension in their adopted country. People identifying with the Indian diaspora living in Fiji, for example, have recently been the focus of world concern. For most of the time, however, and in most of the world, diasporic communities are welcomed for the cultural enrichment they offer the host nation. In the absence of persecution, the survival and maintenance of a diasporic culture as 'a diaspora' is a matter of choice on the part of the community members who may identify both as 'Chinese' or 'Jewish' or 'Irish' or 'Indian' and as American, British, Australian or Malaysian. Dayan comments that 'a diaspora is always an intellectual construction tied to a given narrative' (1998, p. 110). In other words, a diaspora is dependent upon an individual's understanding as to who they are, and where they belong, in which circumstances. This personal construction of the self, and of the self's historical narrative, is more important in determining diasporic community membership than any given demographic index (such as geographical location).

Many members of a diaspora have never belonged to a geographical community in which their culture represents the 'dominant' or majority identification; they may always have seen themselves as having been 'dispersed'. The belonging-to is a mythological 'given narrative', a reconstruction of a community 'as it might have been' pieced together from fragments dispersed through time and space. Diaspora functions as a discourse, constructed in similar ways to Benedict Anderson's (1991) imagined community (see Chapter 3).

Dayan perceives the construction of diasporic identity as a process: production, confrontation (between alternative discourses of identity, including those produced in the host culture) and adoption. This process starts with differentiating constructions of identity produced autonomously by the diasporic community from those produced by the (possibly hostile) majority. The second stage is a choice between a range of identities on offer in the public sphere. For an identity to be individually 'owned', however, the individual community member must involve both the private sphere and the public sphere . . . 'where the intimate meets the historical'. This may happen in popular culture narratives, and in individual decisions about name use, language, food and religion. Dayan refers to this process as the rediscovery or reinvention of tradition. Holmes' (1997) reductionist comment that online technocultural interactivity involves isolation at a workstation is an observation that relates purely to the physical plane, ignoring the sense of psychological belonging and connectedness associated with the experience of community-at-a-distance. People who passionately collect and exchange particularistic media (whether or not they have access to the Internet) are unlikely to agree with Holmes that Internet interactivity is 'an extension of the cellularization of social interaction via the workstation as well as household'. Instead of cellularisation, their experience in the exchange of the particular is one of communing, and of community. Holmes' perspective also ignores the fact that many people feel threatened and rejected by those with whom they live in physical proximity. Geographical co-presence is no guarantee of community, or of access to the public sphere.

## CONCLUSION

This chapter examines the notion of the public sphere and its relationship to technoculture. In particular, it investigates Habermas' original ideal, and addresses the possibility that cyberspace—if it were more genuinely accessible—might provide a model of such a sphere, beyond control of the state and of corporate power. Technocultures can be created by a variety of individuals (agents), to express a range of cultural priorities. To operate as an effective public sphere within a national context, however, technocultural forums have to interrelate with political and regulatory systems.

The public sphere is conventionally differentiated from the private sphere—but it can also be differentiated from a social sphere and/or a 'micro public sphere'. In the first case, the social sphere is seen as being bounded by communication and interaction with a social purpose. In the case of the micro public sphere, an example of diasporic community was used to suggest a community-driven context with the rationale of shared culture, but without the benefit of geographical proximity. Such social and diasporic communities illuminate Benedict Anderson's philosophy of 'imagined community', and inform discussion (later in the book) about the validity of 'virtual community' given that there is no physical co-presence.

# 8

## COMMUNICATION POLICY AND REGULATION

### REGULATION AS A CONTEST OF INTERESTS

Technocultures do not proliferate in a haphazard and uncontrolled way. Instead the norms and regulatory priorities of the society that forms them influence the development of technocultures and other socio-cultural institutions. Len Palmer (1994, p. 78) makes the point that 'regulating' is an intensely political act. He argues that the 'process of regulating' is a far more dynamic concept than 'regulation' and includes within it the idea of different groups and interests working in conjunction to achieve (or avoid) a particular result. Regulation only ever occurs where there is a possibility that a trajectory of activity and events will lead to a questionable, undesirable or less than optimum outcome.

Where things will always end in the best possible way to the best possible benefit of all participants there is no need for formal regulation procedures. Nonetheless, the 'best possible way' tends to reflect the value judgements of the power brokers. The value judgements currently in vogue may include market forces, a social contract or being environmentally friendly. Thus regulation is required when:

- there are two or more players who are working to achieve potentially conflicting outcomes;
- a regulatory body or process can possibly influence these outcomes by applying rules and sanctions; and
- regulation fits within an acceptable socio-political framework to achieve outcomes judged appropriate against one or more (value-judgement) parameters.

Regulation may be considered where the interests of an organisation, institution or individual may differ from those of the general society, or the regulators' view of the public interest. In fact, it is in the act and process of regulation that many stakeholders make themselves and their priorities visible. For example, governments are given (or take) the power to regulate communications, information and media 'in the public interest', or 'in the national interest'. An administrator's view of 'the public interest', and the regulators' or industry's or institution's definitions of public interest may differ widely, but the public interest generally remains the rationale behind regulatory activities.

One of the reasons why much regulating involves extensive consultation (apart from the fact that there are so many direct/indirect stakeholders and interested parties) is that many countries recognise that regulation is a form of social gambling—the definition of 'good outcomes' is both highly negotiable and society-dependent. Regulation often involves unintended consequences, and regulators are unable to guarantee or predict outcomes. Palmer (1994) credits Scandinavian scholar Cees Hamelink with recognising that regulatory and policy choices involve 'a decisive element of gambling social resources for social outcomes'. Palmer comments:

> Let us be clear about Hamelink's argument here . . . knowledge and choices are necessarily shaped by the culture, the period in history, and the people who make those choices. Such people, be they men, policy-makers (usually the same) or entrepreneurs, are influenced by their respective positions, interests and cultures, including assumptions about progress, growth, economic rationality, etc. . . . The dominant models for technology policy, based on belief in certain knowledge and certain outcomes, amount to Russian roulette. Because such policy is unacknowledged gambling, it is gambling without considering the costs of wrong choices. The costs of social gambling include wasted government research, subsidies and promotion, and lost profitability, productivity and jobs . . . Hamelink's thesis [1988, pp. 101–3] does not lead to avoiding the gamble, but to building in the possibility of the failed gamble. Flexibility, openness to reversals and modification of policy, and learning from errors are the necessary responses to the gamble (Palmer 1994, p. 79).

Regulation involves research, investigation and policy formation as well as the codification and application of rules arising from these. It concerns business, academia, politicians, and pressure groups as well as 'official' regulatory bodies. Acts, Reports, Codes, Charters and self-regulatory regimes are all implicated, in addition to regulation through parliamentary, religious (e.g., in some theocratic systems) and governmental instruments. Since regulation is so integrated within the contemporary international mediascape, it is likely to present itself in a variety of guises. From the protests of those who say regulation has gone too far to the moral panics surrounding allegations that the authorities have yet to take a problem seriously, the clamour to regulate better, or differently, makes the news. Almost every issue of every newspaper has a regulatory story in it, and regulation affects all aspects of human life and endeavour. High-tech technoculture is no different from other forms of social expression—domain name registration, for example, is part of a regulatory process, even though the Internet is traditionally depicted as 'unregulated'.

**Figure 8.1 The western regulatory cycle**

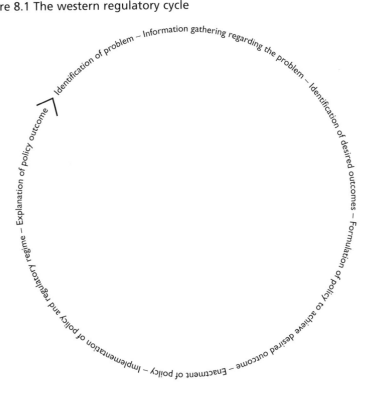

Regulation is dynamic. It is never over, since novel circumstances, new technologies and changing times throw up issues and problems that demand a regulatory response. Accordingly, it is as important to understand the process of regulating, and the reasons behind it, as the regulations themselves. We need the skills to research current regulation, so that changes in the regulatory environment do not catch us unaware.

When the regulatory process is investigated a clear cycle emerges: in western democracies, regulating tends to start with a problem (although other societies might start with the awareness of a potential problem). Problem recognition is followed by the gathering of information to evaluate possible solutions (committees, inquiries, consultation with stakeholders, reports, etc.). Consultation eventually results in the identification of desired outcomes. Governments formulate policy to achieve the outcomes, enact and implement the policy, and evaluate results. Often this cycle then starts again since the results raise a further problem.

Defamation, copyright, official secrecy, sedition and censorship laws all regulate what can be said, written, copied, networked, broadcast and transmitted. Western legislatures argue, for example, that the desire of business and commerce to make a profit by covering attention-grabbing, circulation-boosting, titillating stories needs to be balanced in the public interest by a requirement that published information should be honest, fair and decent. The appeal to the public interest recognises that 'the public' tends to be represented by individuals and by groups who speak on its behalf, including parliamentarians, civil libertarians, pressure groups and special interest organisations. Some elements of the public— young children, for example—do not have a legitimate voice in policy and decision-making themselves so they necessarily need others to be their advocates (see also Chapter 6).

## REGULATING TELECOMMUNICATIONS: THE LANGUAGE OF DEBATE

One area where regulation has been a hotly contested area 'in the public interest' is the field of telecommunications provision. Is the public best served by a large organisation accountable to government, or by more entrepreneurial companies accountable to shareholders? And should 'the public' be seen as the poorest, least privileged citizens, or as those most likely to generate wealth and advantage from a sophisticated, interconnected telecommunications system? Effective information access is closely related to an individual's ability to access telecommunications systems. As economic, technical and educational markets increase their reliance upon technoculture, this puts considerable pressure on the telecommunications infrastructure of a nation. Over the final fifteen years or so of the twentieth century, telecommunications in the western world underwent a radical shake-up with almost all developed countries *deregulating*. A deregulation initiative that gives a market more self-regulation is often termed *liberalisation*. The result of deregulation/liberalisation is that governments and regulatory agencies allow market forces to play a bigger part in service provision, and in determining the cost of services.

As their markets were liberalised, many of the national carriers (e.g., British Telecom (BT), Telecom Australia (Telstra)) had their *monopolies* broken up. They faced competition, and if they had been a monopoly at the time of deregulation, they faced competition for the first time. In the United Kingdom, competition was marked by the entry of Mercury into the telecom market, whereas Optus played the role of second carrier in Australia. With the death of the monopoly, the consumer gained choice. For many carriers, consumer choice meant that if they offered poor customer service then customers would move their business to a competitor. Liberalisation generally raised *customer service standards*—provided the customer was in a profitable market (commercial; towns and cities), and provided carriers were willing to compete for the customer's business.

Often—soon after deregulation, liberalisation and the introduction of competition—the erstwhile national telecom carriers also faced *privatisation*. One rationale behind this was that privatisation allowed the once-national carrier (BT, Telstra) to compete on an equal footing with its private competitor/s for capital funds to fuel investment and expansion. Private individuals were able to buy shares in organisations that had been developed and funded over the years as publicly owned (or nationalised) bodies. The board of a publicly listed company (which is the term for a company that has shareholders, and is quoted on the stockmarket) has the maximisation of the return on shareholders' investments as one of its main objectives. Policy-makers who were pro-telecom privatisation believed those shareholders, and the new board of the once-national telecom company, would drive the privatised telecom carrier into commercial activity and the adoption of a commercial culture. For some commentators, the term 'deregulation' is a misnomer. They prefer to see the process as reregulation—with market forces in the driving seat.

There was some concern, in western democracies, about *community service obligations* (CSOs). These were obligations that monopoly telecommunications carriers had been obliged to fulfil, partly in return for operating in an environment without competition. Once the monopoly disappeared, and shareholders demanded a maximum return on investment, some of the CSOs became hard for the telecom companies to justify on commercial grounds, even where the government attempted to regulate the CSO into the licensing framework. In Australia, for instance, this situation led to widespread complaints from people living in remote and rural areas. They argued that Telstra no longer offered an adequate or reliable service outside the boundaries of the larger towns and cities. In the United Kingdom, there were constant complaints that public phone boxes were not maintained and repaired.

One of the most significant CSOs in many western countries was the commitment to provide *universal service*. This commitment recognised that phones play such an important role in the operation of contemporary society that it is a social obligation to provide the service to anyone who wants it, at an affordable price. Regardless of how inaccessible someone's home might be, or how much the service actually costs to provide, most western countries have a maximum charge for 'putting the phone on'. Participation in telecommunication is an important first step to participation in a range of technocultural activities. A universal service commitment often makes no financial sense for the carrier (otherwise they would be willing to put the phone on under commercial operating procedures) but it makes social and political sense to the government. Thus a commitment to universal service is in the *public interest*.

The discussion here on the deregulation of telecommunication carriers is a model of what happens as information and communication policy, the public interest and maintenance of the public sphere are taken to their logical extent in a regulatory regime which operates within a free-market economy. The postmodern nature of information societies complicates this process (notions of the public interest, and of regulation, are essentially modern), not least as a result of *convergence*, but telecommunications is often heralded as the quintessential deregulation success story. For most people living in western countries, the deregulation of telecommunications has seen a dramatic fall in service cost, an improvement in customer service and the burgeoning growth of digital, virtual and (increasingly) mobile communications. Customers have benefited—but those who could not afford to become customers are even more excluded than they were.

The convergence issue relates to the dissolving of borders between media (content) telecommunications (carriage) and IT/computing (process) (see Chapter 5). In de/regulating telecommunications, governments are also deregulating media and IT applications. This dynamic raises more questions about the relevance and applicability of regulation within a global information environment, and the capacity of governments to regulate any or all of the 'convergent elements' given the transborder nature of contemporary information and communication flows. How far are current technocultures accessible to national regulatory regimes?

## A GLOBAL INFORMATION INFRASTRUCTURE

In 1995, the United States developed a vision for a *Global Information Infrastructure* (GII). Barr comments:

> The plan is based on five principles:
>
> 1. encouragement of private investment,
> 2. promotion of competition,
> 3. creation of a regulatory framework that can keep pace with rapid technological and market changes,
> 4. provision of open competition to the network for all information providers, and
> 5. ensuring the provision of universal service.
>
> These five principles now consistently appear in so many economic development national blueprints that they have virtually become international communications policy benchmarks (Barr 2000, p. 171).

To some extent, this framework spells out an approach that had already been followed in many developed nations during the preceding decade relating to the deregulation of the telecommunications industry. The GII grew out of the NII, or US *National Information Infrastructure*. The national policy was developed in the early 1990s, and its principal features were outlined in the NII Advisory Committee Recommendations, since updated at www.benton.org/Library/KickStart/nation. home.html [June 2001]. The equivalent Canadian blueprint document was called *Building the Information Society: Moving Canada into the 21st Century* (The Canadian site is strategis.ic.gc.ca/SSG/ih01103e.html [June 2001]). Singapore aimed in 1992 to become 'the intelligent island', and followed this up in 1997 with *Singapore One: Beyond the Internet.* The Singapore Ministry of Communications and Information Technology Website is: www.gov.sg/mcit [June 2001]. The Australian National Library Website maintains links to current reports, recommendations and policies at www.nla.gov.au/lis/govnii.html [June 2001]. The number of relevant national Websites continues to grow since many countries have an 'open government' approach to making their information policy available on the Web. In practice, most governments are keen to foster vibrant technocultural growth and ICT regulation aims to promote this, rather than inhibit it.

Regulation is so implicated within the operation of information, communication and media policy that one of the definitions of a 'US media institution'—such as NBC or CNN or Fox—might be 'susceptible to regulation by USA mechanisms'. Consequently, regulatory style is intimately associated with the project of national identity, even though many of the businesses and technocultures regulated are effectively global in scope.

## REGULATION AND NATIONAL IDENTITY

National regulatory regimes themselves make clear the priorities of elites in the society concerned, in much the same way as the promotion or languishing of technology does. Thus the Oscar-winning sci-fi film *The Matrix* (M) is classified as 'advised for audiences of 15 plus' in Australia, but the use of the M rating (rather than MA—mature adult) means that under-15s are allowed entry unaccompanied. Nonetheless, the audience is advised that the film is suited to 15-year-olds and over. In Australia, MA indicates that the viewer must be either 'over 15' or 'in the company of an adult parent or guardian'. In the United States, *The Matrix* received an R rating, where R indicates 'Restricted'. There, people under 17 years who wished to watch *The Matrix* required an accompanying parent or adult guardian.

Australian censors noted 'medium level violence'. The US censors commented upon 'sci-fi violence and brief language' (meaning that there were brief episodes of bad/offensive language). The United Kingdom has a different regulatory regime, without a rating equivalent to Australia's M. In Britain, *The Matrix* was judged 12, indicating that only those over 12 could see it, but they did not need an accompanying adult to do so. In Malaysia, however, the same film (apparently uncut) had a general classification as 'suited to all levels of the population' when it was screened as the in-train movie in January 2000 on a trip between Kuala Lumpur and Singapore. We can speculate that representations of violence (and there are some in *The Matrix*) are of significant concern to the British and American film classification authorities, and note-worthy for the Australian censors, but are less worrying to Malaysian regulators. On the other hand, a film with a M 15+ 'sexual content' tag in the United Kingdom and Australia (the spoof Bond-genre spy movie *Austin Powers: The Spy Who Shagged Me*) is completely banned in Malaysia, indicating anxiety/taboo over visual representations of (and jokes about) sexuality.

Comparative studies of different regulatory regimes operating in different societies offer insights into the fears and concerns of the societies involved. The apparent tolerance of film representations of violence and sexuality in Australia and the United Kingdom contrasts with the philosophy of China Entertainment Television Broadcasts, which prides itself as being 'no sex, no violence, no news', and which is committed to 'government-friendly, family entertainment' (Atkins 1995, p. 59). This approach espouses a very different philosophy of journalism and the media from that of the fourth estate, and fits into a very different vision of national identity.

Will Atkins, who has worked both as a well-respected journalist and an academic, has made a study of Rupert Murdoch's Asian activities as owner of the Star TV satellite service. In 1993, News Corporation's purchase of Star TV, operating out of Hong Kong, brought Murdoch into close contact with many Asian governments and regimes. Star TV had a satellite broadcasting footprint covering 2.5 billion people, most of whom were forbidden to use satellite dishes. Murdoch tried to reassure local regulators that he was sensitive to their cultural values, hoping to receive official sanction for his television services. He claimed that 'Star TV would not become a vehicle for outside interference in Asian affairs' (Atkins 1995, p. 58), and that his television channels would be a 'service which governments in the region would find both friendly and useful' (Atkins 1995, p. 56).

At almost exactly the same time, however, Murdoch was also telling the British political and media establishment that: 'Advances in the technology of telecommunications have proved an unambiguous threat to totalitarian regimes everywhere . . . The Bosnian Serbs can't hide their atrocities from the BBC, CNN and Sky News cameras . . . the extraordinary living standards produced by free-enterprise capitalism cannot be kept a secret' (Atkins 1995, p. 58). While each of these pronouncements might be appropriate to a reading of the national identity of the countries/governments to which they were directed, the fact that each audience is aware of the statements to others has continued to cause Murdoch some embarrassment. It is one thing to be aware of differences in national identity, and of the impact that this has upon regulatory issues; it is another to be seen as trustworthy across a variety of regulatory contexts. Different technocultures, and individual responses to these, can swiftly illuminate principles and values.

## REGULATING FREEDOMS OF SPEECH AND COMMUNICATION

As we have seen in Chapter 7, with the case study of Singapore, the sensitive juncture between free speech, maintaining good international relations and the reporting of objective news is contested territory in terms of postcolonial theory and perspectives. These issues have many ethical ramifications. For example, should an international news organisation (by definition grounded in western culture) allow news products to be censored and cut by the society which rebroadcasts them, to fit more closely with that society's cultural priorities? These issues were brought to the fore in the mid-1990s by conflict between some international news organisations (i.e. transnational corporations) and various nation states in the Southeast Asian region.

In one case, a near-diplomatic row resulted from the relationship between the BBC and RTM, Malaysia's national broadcaster. The BBC had entered into an arrangement in Malaysia under which RTM rebroadcast the BBC's world news bulletin. The row concerned the editing out (without BBC consent) of the lead item of a daily BBC report, 'featuring labour protests on the Indonesian island of Sumatra, involving tens of thousands of workers. The segment showed the lynching of an ethnic Chinese businessman and the vandalism of Chinese-owned shops by factory workers demanding money.' The

BBC's argument was 'that the news must be run in its entirety or not at all . . . censorship by governments undermines the credibility of its brand name' (Atkins 1995, pp. 61–2). This perspective illustrates a significant difference in journalistic culture between the BBC and RTM, arising from different conceptions of the national interest and of corporate identity.

The Malaysian government spokesman justified the cuts to the BBC bulletin by saying that the material 'was damaging to Malaysia's good relations with Indonesia, but also harmful to the racial harmony of Malaysia'. Further, he claimed, there was no problem losing access to BBC material since it could be replaced by rival news programmes. Ted Turner (then chairman of Turner Broadcasting, CNN's parent company) made his viewpoint on such issues clear in 1994: 'I personally don't believe that any country is in a position to tell any other country what to do. I'm a great believer in live and let live' (Atkins 1995, p. 60).

Questions remain about whether these western news values are a bastion of democracy (as the BBC argues, for example) or an example of cultural imperialism—where one cultural model is imposed upon another as part of a dynamic of relative politico-economic power/ weakness. Is cultural imperialism, in any case, better or worse than a 'live and let live' media institution proving itself to be 'friendly and useful' to a government regardless of its record on social justice and human rights?

## UNDERMINING GOVERNMENT: MEDIA AND COMMUNICATIONS UNDERGROUND

Although many countries restrict the carriage of print and tape media across national borders, electronic communications historically have evaded these controls. Thus the revolutionary importance of the under-ground printing press became less critical once fax machines could be combined with photocopiers, as Litchenberg demonstrates with respect to resistance to President Noriega's regime in Panama, following the close-down of the country's independent media: 'A Panamanian exile managed to produce an alternative newsletter and sent it to facsimile receivers in banks, law offices and travel agencies throughout the country. Within hours up to 30,000 photocopies of the paper were on Panama's streets' (Litchenberg 1991, p. 372, cited in Schultz 1994, p. 111).

The fall of the Berlin Wall has been attributed in part to the inability of the Soviet authorities fully to block western broadcasts (Schultz 1990). Examining the fall of the Wall, McKenzie Wark contrasts the ('equally real') territory, or physical spaces of Berlin, and the inhabitants' psychological map. According to Wark, people use both physical and mental schema to locate themselves, and to form their sense of place. Broadcast media were critical in the development of the psychological maps, locating residents of East Germany and the Soviet socialist bloc aspirationally within the west: 'In the territory people know where they are because they have roots there. On the map, people know where they are by tuning into it: here we no longer have roots, we have aerials' (Wark 1990, pp. 36–7).

For many years, countries with relatively regulated and censored media have been concerned about their inability to exclude totally media produced under more liberal or dissident regimes. Sometimes the prohibitionary aim is achieved by banning satellite broadcast receiving dishes, as Singapore, Malaysia and China tried to do in the early 1990s (Atkins 1995, p. 61). On other occasions, transmitters placed close to borders enable audiences in one country to receive the media from another via terrestrial broadcasting. This is particularly an issue with countries that share the same continental landmass—such as in mainland Europe.

Leaving aside issues of media imperialism, there is a western tradition of linking free communication with the spread of democracy, such as in the cases of Panama and the fall of the Berlin Wall. Sci-fi writer Arthur C. Clarke's optimistic view of the democratic benefits of transborder information flows (quoted by William Shawcross, Rupert Murdoch's biographer) has some grounding in experience:

> The very existence of new information channels, operating in real time and across all frontiers, will be a powerful influence for civilised behaviour. If you are arranging a massacre, it will be useless to shoot the cameraman who has so inconveniently appeared on the scene. His picture will already be safe in the studio five thousand miles away and his final image may hang you (Shawcross 1992, p. 242).

Those who look for guidance in this moral maze turn sometimes to international conventions, and to the pronouncements of international bodies, such as the United Nations, and to Universal Declarations, such as that considered in the next section.

## REGULATING THE ACCESS AND DISSEMINATION OF INFORMATION

Article 19 of the Universal Declaration of Human Rights, to which most developed nations subscribe, states that 'everyone has the right to freedom of opinion and expression; this right includes the freedom to hold opinions without interference and to seek, receive and impart information and ideas through any media and regardless of frontiers'. Other documents identify responsibilities as well as freedoms. Thus, for example, The International Convention on Civil and Political Rights 1972 expands slightly upon article 19 but then goes on to say:

> The exercise of the [article 19] rights . . . carries with it special duties and responsibilities. It may therefore be subject to certain restrictions, but these shall only be such as are provided by law and are necessary:
> (a) for respect of the rights or reputations of others;
> (b) for the protection of national security or of public order . . . or of public health or morals (Johnson 1998, p. 61).

An example regarding regulation of free speech in the Singapore context, covered in Chapter 7, is one instance of the operation of these counter-balancing principles.

Regulation of free speech, the telecommunications industry, copyright issues, intellectual property rights, foreign ownership of the media, requirements for minimum provision of local content and children's programming are all hot topics which relate to a governmental desire to manage the information environment and resulting technocultures. Much of this is achieved 'at arm's length' from government itself, using Authorities, Tribunals and Codes of Practice. Some policy relating to the management of information within government is underpinned by specific legislation, however—for example, Freedom of Information and privacy. Policy statements, details of supporting legislation and outlines of relevant regulatory regimes are usually accessible via the Internet, linked through from Arts/Education/Communications/Technology areas of government Websites. National library Websites also concentrate on making information, communication and knowledge-management policies accessible, since librarians (and other information scientists) tend to see these areas as being of special professional interest.

Information beamed into and/or out of a nation via satellite dishes, or circulated via the Net, often evades the usual regulatory gatekeeping processes, and even countries that are passionate about the right to free speech attempt to regulate Internet information accessed by their citizens. Through these processes, certain technocultural forms are suppressed, and driven underground or eliminated. In the United States, the proposed *Communications Decency Act (CDA)* (1996) was scuttled by a concerted campaign built around the Constitution-enshrined right to free speech and the image of a blue ribbon. The Electronic Privacy Information Center, the Electronic Frontier Foundation (EFF) [www.eff.org] and the American Civil Liberties Union (whose Internet tools let site visitors instantly fax the US Attorney General regarding privacy issues) together sponsor the Blue Ribbon Campaign [www.eff.org/br]. The Campaign site includes hotlinks [June 2001] to national online free speech campaigns for Australia, Bulgaria, Canada, France, the People's Republic of China, Portugal and the United States.

The failure of the *Communications Decency Act* to achieve support in the US legislature meant that it was rapidly supplanted by the *Child Online Protection Act* (signed by President Clinton in 1998), dubbed CDAII. This created the crime of knowingly communicating material considered harmful to minors for commercial purposes. In a 1998 press release, Barry Steinhardt, president of the EFF, argued: 'It is the height of irony that the same Congress that plastered the salacious Starr Report [about President Bill Clinton's affair with Monica Lewinsky] all over the Internet now passes a plainly unconstitutional law to suppress a vaguely defined category of "harmful" material.' Nonetheless, the Blue Ribbon Campaign currently concentrates on opposing the use of the *Child Online Protection Act*: the fight to prevent its enactment has been lost. In Australia, the Commonwealth government's Internet censorship legislation was passed in June 1999 as an amendment to the 1992 *Broadcasting Services Act*. It came into force on 1 January 2000. Critics have argued that it does little or nothing to change the content of the Internet, but will relocate material that can be deemed offensive offshore.

Such Internet legislation indicates the existence of twin fears regarding Internet content—one internal, the other external. Externally, as discussed, is the issue of regulatory reach: Australia and the United States have no jurisdiction over the content of hardcore pornography sites located in (for example) European countries, even though this content is accessible within their national borders. Unless a citizen downloads a file, or prints an image (in which case that person may be in illegal possession of illicit material), no potential offence has been committed.

Internally, however, the regulatory fear includes concerns about managing a changing environment, and particularly the role of 'publishing'. That concern, and the ambiguities of the new situation, can be seen as constituting a 'moral panic' (see below). Further complicating these issues is a lack of agreement across countries as to what constitutes pornography (*Austin Powers*, for example?) and whether childhood ends at twelve, sixteen or eighteen.

Much western Internet legislation aims to regulate content located on Websites held on servers within the nation's geographical domain. ISPs—whose servers are the usual locations for private/small-scale commercial Websites—do not, and arguably cannot, know what is being stored on their server unless they are alerted to a potential problem. ISPs argue that to see their role as a 'publisher' is a distortion of the facts—even though they provide the technological platform through which the images/content are accessed by others. The panic over Internet content thus includes regulators' fears that the old ways of defining content creation, publishing, possession, etc. are redundant, as are the old regulatory regimes and principles. There is now uncertainty and imprecision regarding established regulatory tools controlling defamation, copyright and so on (see Chapter 5 for further discussion of copyright). The dynamic of techno-cultural change creates new problems and policy issues.

Leaving aside issues of pornography versus erotica, and which is which in different circumstances, there are images on the Net which were produced without consent, and which are exploitative, violent and repugnant. They include paedophile pornography and violent-seeming images of nonconsensual sex. Patricia Wallace's view, as the joint author of a psychology textbook (with Jeffrey Goldstein 1993), is: 'We can't really be certain whether non-violent pornography has any negative long-term effects . . . but evidence about harmful effects from the violent pornography is more compelling' (Wallace 1999, p. 165). Further, violent pornography and/or pornography involving children indicates issues involving power, fear and coercion rather than sexuality. Indeed, feminist scholars have argued that this is always the case with rape (Clark & Lewis 1977; Toner 1982). Thus harassment may be symptomatic of misogyny, but violently pornographic and power-distorted images may be evidence of hatred.

As well as containing expressions of hate, rage and fear relating to authority and sexuality, the Internet includes hate sites based on race and ethnicity, and images of death, decay and carnage. Such material may be relevant to individuals who are exploring/integrating their 'dark/shadow side' as addressed in the psychoanalytic theories of Freud, Jung and others. Nonetheless, a student of mine, with four years' experience of Internet research and VL community membership, sought professional counselling when she came across some images of atrocity accessible on the Internet. She had planned to research a tutorial topic on Tester's (1997) views of 'moral culture' (see Chapter 11), but decided to rewrite her paper and use alternative ways of addressing the issue to avoid traumatising other students in the class. The fear of what can be found on the Internet constitutes a 'moral panic'. Moral panics occur when a significant section of society responds in alarm or outrage to the potential harm of a new technology, or other challenges to the cultural *status quo*.

## MORAL PANICS

The concept of moral panics was first popularised in 1972 when Stanley Cohen wrote his influential book, *Folk Devils and Moral Panics: The Creation of the Mods and Rockers*. Mods and Rockers were a 1960s British phenomenon, but Cohen's emphasis was not on the activities of these two (mainly young adult) subcultures, but on society's reaction to them:

> Societies appear to be subject, every now and then, to periods of moral panic. A condition, episode, person or group of persons emerges to become defined as a threat to societal values and interests; its nature is presented in a stylised and stereotypical fashion by the mass media; the moral barricades are manned by editors, bishops, politicians and other right-thinking people; socially credited experts pronounce their diagnoses and solutions; ways of coping are evolved or (more often) resorted to; the condition then disappears, submerges or deteriorates . . . sometimes the panic passes over and is forgotten, except in folklore and collective memory; at other times it has more serious and long-lasting repercussions and might produce such changes as those in legal and social policy or even in the way society conceives itself (Cohen 1980, p. 9).

Moral panics are often a social response to new technocultures, and to technological innovation and to change. Indeed, Umble's case study of the Old Order Amish in Pennsylvania (1992, see Chapter 2) indicates that the Amish community experienced a moral panic around the use of the telephone. Stockwell's article (1997) on the Port Arthur massacre in Tasmania, Australia (see Chapter 1) was deliberately framed in 'moral panic' terms, with the panic relating to guns and the effects of media violence. Moral panics tend to centre around fears of what effect 'they' (the others, and the technology) are going to have on 'us', and our sense of what is right and appropriate.

Morley and Robins discuss the television 'screen' (see Chapter 11) in the sense of a screen which lets through only selected elements: 'the image of them [others] is screened in the different sense of being filtered, with only selected images getting through. At the same time, in a psychic sense, the screen is not only the medium through which the images are projected for us, but also the screen onto which we project our own fears, fantasies and desires' (1995, p. 134). It may well be this sense of 'projection' which explains many of the moral panics that surround the introduction of new communications media—including film, television, 'information' phone calls and the Internet. Commentators project on to the new medium the greatest fears they hold for themselves and their society.

Carolyn Marvin, recounting her research for *When Old Technologies Were New* (1988), recounts this century-old newspaper tale of moral panic concerning the telegraph, which was an emerging technoculture of the time:

> I especially remember a story about a young woman working as a telegrapher in her father's store, who struck up a flirtation by wire with a married railroad telegrapher. Their relationship became a romantic liaison. When her enraged father threatened her with physical harm, she had him arrested on the spot ('The dangers of wired love' 1886). I liked this story for its sensational distrust of new media, its fears of women using technology, and other typical themes all neatly collected in one paragraph . . . It finally occurred to me that this anecdote expressed the fear that new media would destroy the family group, and that a pervasive theme . . . was that of established social groups trying to make sense of how new ways of associating affected the stable social structures and amenities of life to which they were devoted (Marvin 1988, p. 194).

Old media often circulate social panics about the introduction of new media. (Thus the newspapers carried the tale about the telegraph, as television carries stories on violent videos, pornography on the Net and the perniciousness of hate sites.) It is not surprising that the Internet is feared for its ability to remove individuals psychologically from their social setting (even though the phone, the television, the book and all other media-based technocultures share this trait). Such moral panics address threats to the stability of life as society accommodates the new medium. The moral panic around cyber-porn, for example, is one of the major spurs for attempts to regulate the Internet.

One dimension of the cyber-pornography panic, according to Evans and Butkus (1997), rests in the fact that in the early years of the Internet, young people were cybercompetent while their parents (and teachers) were not. Panic reflects the fear of the powerful faced with the emerging competence of 'powerless others' in arenas where established social leaders feel threatened. Evans and Butkus quote a US senator as saying: 'We face a unique, disturbing and urgent circumstance, because it is children who are the computer experts in our nation's families' (1997, p. 68). The argument is that the cyber-porn moral panic is not (or not simply) a clash of intergenerational value systems, but a fear about the results of differential technological competence. 'Although parents still occupy the role of the initiated with regard to sexuality, if they are uninitiated technologically then they lose the power base from which to set the markers for progressive socialisation.'

The threat to established power differentials is one impetus for the traditional media to spread 'dis-information' and 'panic' about cyber-porn. The established media—television and the press—here represent a power base of the technocultural older generation. The emerging media threaten established profits, existing social structures, job security and herald the redundancy of respected skills. For some people, the effect of this negativity is a pervasive fear that can result in an avoidance of the new medium. The existence of a moral panic, however, does not mean that the fears are groundless. Evans and Butkus' research indicates that the fears of parents—if not of the mass media—may have some grounds. While it may be hard to find un-censored pornographic images 'by accident' on the Internet, it is a very simple matter to access them with a straightforward search using words like 'sex', 'pornography' and 'hardcore'. Parents can assume that most unsupervised children will use these search words at some point in their Internet experience. 'The ease with which these sites were accessed, and the volume of hardcore material available is in sharp contrast to the claims of many about the difficulty in finding pornography on the Net' (1997, pp. 65–6).

Online porn purveyors, on the other hand, use various devices to indicate their commitment to a socially responsible use of the Web. These responsible devices include demanding that users of porn sites declare that they are adult, that they realise the images might offend, and that they are not prohibited from accessing pornographic material by laws in their local area. For example:

YOU MUST BE 18 OR OLDER
to access this site!
The material on this server is adult oriented, sexually explicit and related to XXX material. This site provides access to images of nude adults possibly engaging in sexual acts, and other material of an adult nature. Access is made available only to those who accept the terms of the following agreement:
By accepting this agreement, I certify the following:
- I do not find images of nude adults, adults engaged in sexual acts, or other sexual material to be offensive or objectionable.
- I am at least 18 years of age and have the legal right to possess adult material in my community.
- I understand the standards and laws of the community, site and computer to which I am transporting this material, and am solely responsible for my actions.
- I am not a law enforcement agent.
- I will not sell and/or in any way redistribute the contents of this site.
- I will not attempt to by-pass any security and/or access feature at this site.
If I use these services in violation of the above agreement, I understand I may be in violation of local and federal laws and am solely responsible for my actions.
By logging on, I will have released and discharged the providers, owners and creators of this site from any and all liability which might arise [www.hardcorejunky.com June 2001].

Perhaps it is as well that some moral panics make some site proprietors panic! Nonetheless, with or without panic, the regulation of content (and of technoculture) remains an arena within which power dynamics are particularly visible.

## CONCLUSION

This chapter considered the regulatory process, and the inevitability of a struggle between competing interests. The regulation of telecommunications was taken as a case study, and the language of the debate was addressed in context.

Even in the West, however, some regulators feel that the Internet goes too far in providing a hard-to-regulate communication platform for those who wish to communicate dangerous, obscene, hate-ridden or degrading information and images. In the recent past, such concerns have constituted a 'moral panic'. Those who fear the new medium, and emerging technocultures, often encourage or circulate the moral panic (in this case, the press and broadcasters).

The chapter also addressed the issue of free speech as a regulatory concern, particularly in terms of post-coloniality and the struggle of nation states to regulate the media within their borders. This can be particularly relevant where the media to be regulated emanate from transnational communications companies. One reason why some countries fear the effects of unregulated media lies in the fact that the free media have been associated with the downfall of a number of totalitarian and undemocratic political regimes.

# 9

## POPULAR CULTURE IN
## TECHNOCULTURE

### POPULAR CULTURE AND THE PUBLIC SPHERE

Although Habermas identified the space between the public and the private as the public sphere, and as a place where the state can be criticised, it is also a space where popular culture can be created, personalised, recognised and enjoyed. While this is not Habermas' perspective (interested as he is in issues of citizenship and the political economy), it is a perspective of relevance to the field of cultural studies. Cultural studies is concerned, amongst other things, with the creation and circulation of popular culture—and popular culture is of critical importance both to technoculture and to commercial media. The motivation of many publishers of popular culture may be to sell the commercial audience to advertisers, but this aim does not compromise the inherent popularity of the content. Active participation in popular culture, and in early-adoption technoculture, is voluntary. Generally we become involved because we wish to be so.

Where commercial media are complemented by public service media, funded by government finance or by subscription, the justification for the public service is to provide material and programming which would be ignored or marginalised in commercial media. Thus, public service broadcasters are under an obligation to produce programming that might not get made or shown if commercial interests were the only ones operating in the mass media sphere. In practice, the public service/subscription broadcaster concentrates upon political comment and current affairs, innovative programming, alternative and highbrow culture, the analytical, the radical, the controversial/critical (which may upset advertisers) and other programming for minority interests. Public service broadcasters also operate as an independent voice, able to comment upon the affairs of corporations that own commercial media. The imperative to provide quality broadcasting for minority interests sits uneasily with the injunction to get good ratings: the mission of these publicly funded non-commercial media institutions is to make the less popular as popular as possible. Sometimes, innovation and quality win through and the public service ends up producing a blockbuster. Frequently this ends with the new idea, or the new presenter, being poached by a commercial channel. In most mixed economy broadcasting systems (with public service and commercial channels), the commercial channels win the ratings war most of the time, and gain the greater audience share.

Commercial media are integral to popular culture because they get extra kudos and audience credibility for being up with/setting the trends. The leading-edge channel becomes the topic of conversation and the springboard for new expressions of popular culture. The dynamic for this is particularly clear in children's popular culture, where the most successful programmes spawn games, toys and clothing—from Britain's *Teletubbies* to Japan's *Pokemon*. Being popular, people gain social cachet from trading ideas, opinions and information on games, shows, stars, soaps, sports, etc. The Internet is a new site for these trades—along with the playground, the pub, the workplace and the weekend barbecue.

## CONSTRUCTING POPULAR CULTURE

The everyday construction of popular culture operates as a realm of pleasure, desire, creativity and consumption. This is at odds with the early academic construction of popular culture, when 'elite' conceptions of culture (ballet, the opera) were contrasted with the culture of the masses, seen as dupes of the capitalist bourgeois. Karl Marx, for example, argued that the proletariat were bought off/distracted from their revolutionary mission by 'bread and circuses', and that religion 'was the opiate of the people'. In the first half of the twentieth century, critical scholars who shared this perspective, such as Theodor Adorno and the Frankfurt School, had little sympathy for the popular. Instead, they constructed high art as if it 'embodied a vision of an alternative to existing social relationships and, in doing so, kept alive the concept of transcendence. It was, in short, subversive' (Bennett 1982, p. 44).

The rejection of mass culture as an opiate of the people changed with the acute observation by the man known as 'the father of cultural studies', Raymond Williams, who said that: 'there are in fact no masses; there are only ways of seeing people as masses' (1966, p. 289). British scholar Tony Bennett was later to comment that: 'Popular culture was approached from a distance and gingerly, held out at arm's length by outsiders who clearly lacked any fondness for or participation in the forms they were studying. It was always the culture of "other people" that was at issue' (1981, p. 6). Culture itself, within the field of cultural studies, has worn various qualifiers in addition to that of 'popular'—for example, elite, folk, mass, people's, 'other people's' and organic, all of which have helped define it for analysis within the academy. Arguably, all these epithets can apply as appropriately to technoculture as they do to culture.

An early example of the arm's length approach to popular culture is Richard Hoggart (1958), who was interested in the mass (contemporary) culture of the 1950s: 'modern popular music, American television, the jukebox, popular crime and romance novels, and cheap magazines'. According to cultural theorist Graeme Turner (1996), Hoggart saw 1950s culture as 'displacing, but providing no substitute for, a popular culture experientially connected to the social conditions of those who produce and consume it'. To Hoggart, this dynamic indicated mass culture's 'failure to emerge from specific roots within the lived cultures of ordinary people' (Turner 1996, p. 45).

Cultural studies consequently struggled (and still struggles) with a conception of a 'fall from grace' whereby mass culture replaced an indigenous folk or organic culture created by 'the people' from their own experiences and artistic resources. The implication is that 'mass culture' and 'mass media'—in appealing to the masses and turning a profit for media proprietors and their advertisers—compromised culture's quality and value. According to Turner, 'a high-culture view of popular culture [is primarily] interested in aesthetic rather than social pleasures and meanings' (1996, p. 42). Contemporary theorists of popular culture tend to be vitally interested in social pleasures and meanings.

Hoggart's arguments against the adoption of a popular culture originating outside the community of consumption continue to be made, albeit in different guises, by those who decry cultural imperialism. For example, American scholar Herbert Schiller argues that colonial imperialism has been replaced by cultural imperialism and includes:

> the English language itself, shopping in American-styled malls
> . . . the music of internationally publicised performers, following

newsagency reports or watching the Cable News Network in scores of foreign locales, reading translations of commercial best-sellers, and eating in franchised fast food restaurants around the world . . . The domination that exists today, though still bearing a marked American imprint, is better understood as transnational corporate cultural domination (1991, p. 15).

There is little doubt here that value judgements are in operation, and that cultural imperialism—a culture transmitted into cultures other than that from which it has organically sprung—is constructed as undesirable.

Janice Radway, whose 1984 study of romance fiction readers broke new ground in cultural studies and feminist theory, explains some of the heat in this debate by differentiating between a 'folk culture' (or folklore) and a 'mass culture'. She identifies the commercial imperatives that underlie the production of mass culture, and sees such products as coming into existence to make a profit. Radway initially constructed 'profit-making' as exploitation, but found her views challenged by the women she was investigating. Her ethnographic study of romance readers established other criteria by which romance reading could be judged as a subversive and/or resistant activity (in terms of pleasure, desire and time away from the demands of the family): 'It seems clear that we must rethink our notion that all mass culture consumption perpetuates isolation and anomie and thus hinders the creation of potentially transformative contacts between people with similar interests' (1984, p. 23).

Radway's desire in the 1980s was to explain the popularity of mass culture whilst at the same time excusing the audience's willingness to participate in the creation of their subjugation and the production of profit for the producers and distributors. Nowadays, it is generally accepted that the construction and consumption of popular culture is neither passive, nor isolating. Consuming cultural products involves the production of new meanings by consumers, and the circulation of these meanings. There is no anaesthetic involved in this aesthetic.

Popular culture represents that subsection of the products of mass media which are appropriated by people in their daily lives and remodelled as the raw material through which they communicate their values and enthusiasms, and through which they connect to others—the epitome of Turner's 'individual pleasures and social meanings' (above). In fact, with the development of interactivity via the Net in MUDs, MOOs and online community (see Chapter 11), there is a new kind of folk/organic techno-culture created by Internet users from their own experiences and resources.

## TELEVISION IN POPULAR CULTURE: *THE YOUNG AND THE RESTLESS*

Given the role of the mass media in circulating raw materials for the creation of popular culture, the technocultural institution of television has been at the centre of popular culture production for the past several decades. Television integrates other elements of mass culture and is the technocultural channel through which they are embedded in the domestic sphere. It operates as a hub drawing together (and providing content for) fiction, reportage, films, images and music—and showcases style, fashion, humour and gossip. Since popular culture concerns media products circulating in discussion, debate and social discourse, it is quintessentially the new, the exploratory and the breaking story (especially gossip) which has greatest value and which is traded most readily. By its nature dynamic, popular culture is voracious in its search for the innovative angle by which stories and ideas can be revisited and recommunicated. Popular culture is up to the minute; yesterday's popular culture is no longer popular—it is passe and boring: been there, done that.

British anthropologist Daniel Miller (1992) offers a classic example of the workings of popular culture, and the local appropriation of global products, in his provocative case study of the Trinidadian consumption of an American soap opera, *The Young and the Restless*. At first glance, *The Young and the Restless* appears a million light years away from the concerns of a struggling post-colonial nation state like Trinidad. It deals with the (improbable) lives and loves of mainly white American characters who are . . . young and/or restless. Yet Miller, on fieldwork in Trinidad, was struck by the great importance this community placed on being able to watch the next episode of the drama:

> Few televisions [tuned to the programme] fail to attract a neighbour or two on a regular basis. Individuals may shout deprecations or advice to the characters during the course of the programme. Afterwards there is often collective commentary and discussion. There is a considerable concern to spread news of important events quickly. I was slightly 'shocked' in my vicarious sense of propriety, when an important Muslim festival I was watching was interrupted by three ladies who collectively announced to the assembled group some new development which we had missed by taking part in the ceremony (Miller 1992, pp. 168–9).

Miller goes on to consider why Trinidadian television, concerned as it is with the *gravitas* and affairs of an emerging nation-state, is unable to produce a programme to rival the relevance to Trinidadian culture of this fragment of imported, global (American) culture. He argues that *The Young and the Restless* 'reinforces bacchanal as the lesson of recession which insists that the domestic and the façade of stability is a flimsy construction which will be blown over in the first storm created by true nature . . . [it] colludes with the local sense of truth as exposure and scandal . . . [it] is not just Trinidadian but . . . "True True Trini"' (Miller 1992, p. 179). Using *The Young and the Restless*, the Trinidadian audience discovers, and creates a way of discussing, the surface/shadow, appearance and reality, celebration and compromise which makes sense to them in the construction and narrative of their lives.

While the mass audience is increasingly represented in global terms, popular culture can be seen as a local construction from global culture (Morley 1991). New meanings are created collaboratively through the technocultural circulation and exchange of global ideas and programme-content fragments within a local context. Viewers actively use global (and local) broadcast materials to make sense of their lives as individuals, and of their households and communities.

## POPULAR CULTURE ON THE INTERNET

The Internet is a key topic of popular culture, and much popular culture circulates technoculturally upon the Internet. Images of Websites, advertising buttons and banners, and interactive touch keys adorn traditional visual media: magazines, newspapers, television. Email, chat sites and virtual community become subjects of music, film, television, novels, short stories and documentary. Websites are featured in print, TV, radio and cinema advertising, and are made to appear seductive and accessible. Popular 'how to' magazines and books throng newsagents' shelves, and local councils run fun 'Internet access' courses and ensure that the Internet is available in public libraries. Raw materials provided by the Net have been transformed by the workings of popular culture into new ways of discussing the concerns, pleasures and meanings of our societies.

James Carey (1989) suggests a 'ritual view' of communication as 'a process through which a shared culture is created, modified and transformed . . . A ritual view . . . is directed not towards the extension of messages in space but the maintenance of society over time' (quoted by

Watson 1997, p. 103). This perspective concentrates on explaining the use of communication (and popular culture is a specific kind of communication) to strengthen a sense of community, and perpetuate its existence. Where technology is used in ritual communication, the result is a technocultural one. Popular culture can serve as a barometer for the health of the society concerned; a healthy society is constantly creating and circulating new elements of popular culture (although this may be truer of healthy consumer societies rather than all human societies). The circulation of popular culture also constitutes an index of what is important to that society. Sometimes—as with the death of Princess Diana in 1997—we are taken by surprise at the strength of the feelings we associate with these icons of popular culture.

As the Net has become a theme of popular culture, so it has also become a locale for popular culture. Popular media—and media stars—use Websites to communicate with fans. Nessim Watson, an American communications scholar, documents 'a case study of the phish.net fan community'. He demonstrates the intertextuality (see below) of the Internet's integration within commercial media by referring to the constant interaction between debates on the phish.net newsgroup, responses in the printed fan media and changes in the artistic repertoire of the band. The current incarnation of the phish.net fan home is: www.phish.net/ [June 2001].

In 1993, the Phish band responded to fan discussion about the content and meanings of some lyrics in an unprinted verse by filling three newsletters with 'multiple joke answers to fan letters about the verse'. Subsequently, on tour, 'the band changed the lyrics of that verse in performance to alternate suggested answers from the publicly answered fan letters'. Phish.netters became very excited about the in-joke and coined the term WATSIYEM as a reference to new members of phish.net and the fan community since 'What are they saying in "You enjoy myself"?' had become such a common refrain of 'newbies'.

As well as expressing popular culture and indicating dynamic technocultural interaction between artists, fans, media and topic, the term WATSIYEM came to identify insiders and outsiders. The acronym was used 'to refer to: (1) the period of debate and band response in Phish.net history, considered a successful communication with the band by Phish.net and other Phish fans; (2) the sorts of questions which now identify the asker as a newbie or outsider' (Watson 1997, p. 106). To some extent, in consumer societies, a social circle reflects and is defined by shared interests in elements of popular culture. Participation in an aspect of popular culture permits social engagement with other people who also find that element of popular culture relevant to their lives.

Although popular culture circulates by, with and on the Internet, the concept of the 'mass audience' is compromised in the Internet's technological environment, since Net-based products are typically created and consumed by individuals. Given that individuals in search of Turner's 'social pleasures and meanings' tend to access the Internet in social isolation, in idiosyncratic ways and with different access points and pathways, it is likely that no two people experience exactly the same content unless they are sharing in collaborative creative interaction on a game site or online community. This situation is at odds with the mainly domestic consumption of broadcast products, where the experience of programme viewing is comparatively stable. Thus discussion about yesterday's episode of *The Young and the Restless* has a more stable 'topic' than does discussion about a Website with multiple links and pathways. With one, the matter at issue is the interpretation and relevance of characters' words and actions. In the other, the conversation may turn around identification of what is most exciting, interesting, different and useful. These differences are technocultural.

## INTERACTIVITY AND TECHNOCULTURE

Media theorists draw upon their long experience of researching television and television consumption as a starting point for investigating the creation and consumption of Internet technoculture. Both media vehicles (broadcasting and the Internet) may be positioned as popular, leisure and domestic, and both may involve considerable resources in time and money, but there are many significant differences. The most glaringly obvious is that the consumption of popular media involves the active creation of meaning from the products involved, but does not concern creation of those products. In contrast, consumers are often the co-creators of the culture they consume in many Internet technocultural domains. This signal difference can be summed up in a number of ways. Holmes (1997), for example, sees broadcasting as representing a community of consumption, whereas the Internet represents a community of interactivity. He compares and contrasts the two communities (see Table 9.1).

**Table 9.1 Communities of broadcast versus communities of interactivity**

| Communities of broadcast | Communities of interactivity |
| --- | --- |
| The many 'speak' to the many by way of the agent of message producers ('media workers', the culture industry, etc.) | The many speak to the many by way of the computer–mediated simulation of presence |
| Centred | Decentred |
| Influences consciousness | Influences individual experience of space and time |
| High level of recognition/ identification between individuals | Low levels of recognition/ identification between individuals |
| Very low level of reciprocity | Very high level of reciprocity |
| Individual experiences strong identity/identification with figures of authority, charisma or cult movements | Individual experiences weak identification with others as figures of authority or charisma |
| Concentration spans of audiences are sold to advertisers | The need to communicate in highly urbanised settings is sold to individuals |
| Primary basis of the cellularisation of social interaction in information societies | An extension of the cellularisation of social interaction via the workstation as well as the household |

Source: Figure 1.1, 'Virtual identity: communities of broadcast, communities of interactivity' from D. Holmes (ed.), *Virtual Politics: Identity and Community in Cyberspace*, 1997, Sage Publications, p. 32

## THE IMPORTANCE OF POPULAR CULTURE
## BROADCASTING IN PEOPLE'S LIVES

Holmes argues that broadcasting cellularises social interaction into domestic groups—the groups within which the broadcasting is consumed. Far from necessarily destroying community, however, broadcasting can act as an affirmation of community, as Miller's (1992) *The Young and the Restless* case study demonstrates. It can offer a common ground upon which people explore issues of relevance and importance, and through which valuable community-construction activities take place. In particular, phone-in programmes and quiz programmes, using 'everyday people' as contestants, both literally and metaphorically, include the audience as content creators and providers. Lifestyle and shopping programmes also allow viewers and listeners to interact physically with the programme content, and conversations beginning 'I got the idea from . . .' position an audience member as more than a passive consumer of broadcast product—it identifies them as an active, multi-dimensional participant in popular culture.

Broadcasting tends to be produced at the 'core' of society in terms of location, power, influence and the elite social standing of media owners and professional media workers. Even so, commercial broadcasting—as the pre-eminent site for the circulation of popular culture—has an imperative to deliver locally relevant advertising within the community. This link to advertisers and consumers, as well as producers, anchors commercial broadcasting in the periphery, as well as at the core. The advertisers' markets have to be central to the commercial broadcaster—even when those markets are peripheral to many other social institutions. Regional commercial broadcasting, for example, is much more grounded inside its audience-area than are many other core social institutions such as finance, administration and politics.

It is arguable whether, as Holmes asserts, consumers of broadcasting identify more strongly than do users of interactivity with others 'as figures of authority or charisma'. Television (rather than broadcasting) can pack a highly emotive punch with the clever use of both audio and visual cues, as refined both by advertising and by television programme production. On the other hand (while it is a moot point as to how much charisma can be gauged by celebrity), the thousands of Websites dedicated in the mid-1990s to the Spice Girls, and to Leonardo di Caprio, demonstrate that the charismatic colonises all communication channels: print, broadcast, screened and/or interactive. The charismatic is popular, and thus an integral part of popular culture, regardless of medium. Case studies of fan culture—*Star Trek* being a pre-eminent example (Tulloch & Jenkins 1995; www.startrek.com/ [June 2001])—indicate that discussion of a shared object of interest, fascination and desire binds individuals together in a community-of-sorts. Cunningham and Turner put forward this argument in support of the mass media at the end of their first edition of *The Media in Australia*:

> The mass media are the glue that holds together much of our sense of ourselves as a society. They are also the platform on which public debate and collective sense-making in today's society takes place. Their demise is less likely to lead to enhanced democratisation, empowerment and rehumanisation than to the erosion of these fine ideals (1993, p. 350).

Arguably, Cunningham and Turner are suggesting a situation in which the mass media offer critical tools to evaluate and discuss public figures who may lay claim to authority, charisma or cult status.

My ethnographic research reinforces this idea of the mass media—especially broadcasting—operating as a site for the contexting of different elements of popular culture. As a woman living on a remote station in Australia remarked to me, before she got access to broadcast television:

> If you pick up a magazine—like when we go to town we usually pick up the usual women's magazines—and it's from them that you find big gaps in things that have happened—on the political scene or just generally on the news. And people's faces—unless you watch television, you don't know who these people are . . . There was another article earlier in the year about [a particular Australian cricket star]—and he must have had a lot of smut thrown at him or something and he was in an article in the women's magazine about he and his wife and we didn't ever know what was said (Green 1998, p. 260).

Without broadcasting (and, especially, without commercial broadcasting) much popular culture unravels into fragmented speculation and comment. Broadcasting ties the different elements together. And with only partial access to popular culture, audience members denied the wherewithal to participate are effectively disenfranchised from a major social project of consumer society.

As to Holmes' concern that people whose attention is 'sold' might

find the exchange offensive or demeaning, for some people it can constitute a recognition of the audience as desirable consumers. A different
young woman from a remote Australian town commented, about the
first-ever commercials broadcast on her local television service: 'I
remember when we first got it. The first TV ad we saw, we all rejoiced!
. . . [We were] depraved [sic] of advertising! . . . The ABC, they don't
have any at all . . . I don't mind adverts—they can be funny' (Green
1998, p. 262). This community waited until 1986 to get commercial
broadcasting. In a consumer society, to be finally counted an audience
worth advertising to involves a sense of 'recognition at last'. Attention
spans may be sold to advertisers, but advertising is increasingly being
recognised as content—and as pleasurable content to boot.

## INTERNET COMMUNITY AND POPULAR CULTURE

A categorical denial of the validity of the Internet community, implicit
within Holmes, is at odds with the experience of community members
(Palandri & Green 2000). Too great an emphasis upon traditional sociological definitions of community—which position such communities in
space, time and in face-to-face relationships—simply creates tautological
arguments to the effect that 'definitions of community which rule out
cyberspace result in there being no communities located in cyberspace'.
Such definitions say nothing about people's experiences, pleasures and
motivations and the emergence of the Internet as a technocultural site
for the participative creation of popular culture.

Concepts of community are contested academic ground. Although
the Internet does not offer an exact equivalent to accepted 'old' community, this does not mean it fails to offer community to those who want
it, or that those who believe they belong to online communities have
necessarily been duped. Holmes concentrates upon the physical person in
front of the screen, rather than the psychology of the person engaged in
communication (Wallace 1999) and, perhaps—according to *their* definition—in community. Indeed, the Internet offers the opportunity for
creative and experiential psychological interconnection with others unrivalled by traditional mass media in either the local or global context.

The point made by Holmes, it seems, is that broadcasting teaches
its audiences to recognise famous people as icons (of consumption?),
whereas the Internet involves low levels of recognition. The dynamic of
recognition and identification between individuals identified by Holmes

does not apply to 'communities of broadcasting' *per se*, but to celebrity culture which constitutes part of the content of broadcasting. A viewing member of a 'broadcasting community' is no more easily identified in face-to-face discussion than a member of a community of interactivity. Celebrities, on the other hand, are made highly visible by popular culture through broadcasting, and also through print media and the cinema. However, the Internet also encourages recognition of famous individuals, since celebrity and fan Websites are plentiful.

In addition to being another medium for the propagation of celebrity images, interactivity on the Internet does teach recognition of individual Internet users—but at the level of actors in cyberspace, rather than as cultural icons. The Internet uses a number of competency cues to recognise individual users, and their levels of exposure to Internet culture. Thus acronyms—such as LOL (laughed out loud), LMAO (laughed my ass off) LMFAO—are one way of sorting out the Internet novice from the (more) fluent Netizen. A knowledge of conventions and netiquette is another. Regular community members have no long-term trouble in identifying others in their group who may engage in the (potentially anti-social) behaviour of anonymous postings. Palandri and Green offer two examples:

> Long-term chatter Iron Filings (IF) was asked if he communicated differently in VL from his communications in RL, given that cyber presented him with an opportunity to try out different personae: 'VL communication is indeed another medium to practice another persona . . . but why? . . . I find that no matter what handle [name] I use . . . I am still recognized . . . why? Because I have the same "personality" for all of them . . . the handles just hang out in different rooms is all . . . grinning . . .'
> (Palandri & Green 2000, p. 637).

The second example is the story of Marian Palandri's attempt to be anonymous when 'passive-aggressive flaming'—verbally attacking—'those with whom I did not agree'. Palandri ultimately realised 'that I was acting anonymously out of fear of risking their disapproval. Of course, one's writing style is one's signature, and soon I was found out. I chose to stay and work through my reasons for this behavior, in the face of some hostility from those I had anonymously antagonized' (Palandri & Green 2000, p. 638). Having invested some years of interactivity within her community, Palandri realised she could not easily walk away from her technocultural social connections.

'Level of recognition' online differs from the visual cues involved in perceiving and recognising—say, Madonna—on a television screen. It is a much more complex pattern of knowing, grounded in repeated experience of communication over a period of time. The fact that people engaged in an online community may (or may not) recognise each other in RL is simply one way of identifying that the way that they do recognise each other—through personality expressed in written text—is not the major communication pattern in RL. In situations where this *is* the major communication medium—in VL—then people are recognisable to those who know them.

Much of the Internet offers little in the way of a genuinely reciprocal response. Information search usually provides access to data, but while the data accessed may have elements of interactivity structured into its display, it does not constitute a communication exchange (apart from data-level communication with the use of cookies so that Websites can recognise and clock return visits). Unlike data access, online community lies at the other end of a technocultural continuum of reciprocity relating to Internet content, since those who post on the site help create the materials consumed by them.

Email is a one-to-one reciprocal communication that can also (with listserve postings and one-many messages to entire organisations) be used as a form of narrowcasting. Thus, within the email environment, it is possible to identify a continuum of communication styles in which reciprocity is more—or less—welcomed and expected. The greater the number posted-to simultaneously, the lower the potential for genuine reciprocity, however, and at this extreme email approximates a one-way information service—the electronic message board. While email is too targeted a communication medium to be a site of large-scale popular culture creation (being essentially micro-public sphere and 'particularistic' (Dayan 1998)), it has been integrated within many current popular culture texts (such as the Hollywood movie *You've Got Mail*). It is also used by individuals to exchange views on popular culture, thus helping to construct and circulate them.

## CYBORGS AND SCIENCE FICTION

Cyborgs and science fiction form an area of popular culture which seems to have increased in importance as technology has become more integral to our cultures and our communities. This burgeoning interest in narratives about the future, and about parallel universes, may indicate a desire to understand and explore the present. In speculating about 'others' we are also speculating about ourselves.

*Star Trek* has already been mentioned as an example of fan culture, but it is also an example of popular culture in general, and of sci-fi in particular. The widespread fascination with the interface of biology and technology, and the potential for fusion between the two, is a continuing theme of contemporary narratives. Through films such as *Blade Runner* and *The Matrix*, our society tells itself stories about what it is to be human in a world where humans are increasingly influenced by, and dependent upon, technology and technocultures. Here the myths of loss and longing are played out in the context of technologically driven futures, where machines can feel feelings and have roles with more humanity in them than the 'people' characters do. A recurring theme of these narratives concerns the merging of the human with the machine, and questions of the essential nature of humanity. These are boundary issues (Douglas 1978, see Chapter 3). The fascination may, in part, be attributable to questions about how much technology compromises the essentially human: not a pacemaker, nor a bionic ear; not test-tube conception, nor cultured skin—but the suspicion is that there is a boundary somewhere beyond which it is unsafe to go. How far is too far?

The 1980s saw significant growth in the number of sci-fi films, many of which have gone on to become classics and which continue to illustrate discussions of, say (as in Chapter 4), notions of the modern (*1984*) and the postmodern (*Brazil*). Annette Kuhn, arguing that 'many would maintain that *Alien*, released in 1979, was in the vanguard of a renaissance in the genre' (Kuhn 1990, p. 11), addresses the issues raised by sci-fi films during the late 1970s and 1980s. In the introduction to her influential book, *Alien Culture*, Kuhn describes five ways in which science fiction cinema relates to RL:

> First of all, there is a notion that the overt contents of science fiction films are *reflections* of social trends and attitudes of the time, mirroring the preoccupations of the historical moment in which the films were made. In this reflectionist model, films are treated as, in a sense, sociological evidence. Secondly, there is the idea that science fiction films relate to the social order through the mediation of *ideologies*, society's representation of itself in and for itself—that films speak, enact, even produce certain ideologies, which cannot always be read directly off films' surface

contents. Third is the view that films voice cultural *repressions* in 'unconscious' textual processes which, like the dreams, associations and bodily symptoms of psychoanalytic patients, require interpretation in order to reveal the meanings hidden in them. A fourth cultural instrumentality concerns what science fiction films do to and for their *spectators*—the sorts of pleasures they evoke and the fantasies they activate. Finally, there is the view that science fiction films are actively involved in a whole network of *intertexts*, of cultural meanings and social discourses (Kuhn 1990, p. 10).

Arguably, one of the preoccupations of science fiction as social reflection concerns the issue of: 'When does the human become technological; when does the virtual become real?' Certainly, this is the major theme of *Blade Runner*, and of the novel upon which it is based: *Do Androids Dream of Electric Sheep?* (Dick 1982). Other issues—such as whether bureaucracy represents a progressive dehumanisation of society—can be seen as a concern of *Brazil*, and of *1984*. *Independence Day* can be seen as working at the level of ideologies: 'Science fiction films concerning fears of machines or of technology usually negatively affirm such social values as freedom, individualism and the family', claim Ryan and Kellner (1990, p. 58), and these are all aspects of the *Independence Day* saga.

Ryan and Kellner go on to undermine this assertion with their reading of *Blade Runner*, however: 'The film deconstructs the oppositions—human/technology, reason/feeling, culture/nature—that underwrite the conservative fear of technology by refusing to privilege one pole of the dichotomy over another and by leaving their meaning undecipherable' (Ryan & Kellner 1990, p. 63). It may be the very complexity of *Blade Runner* that has made it such a rich source for cultural studies analysis.

Regarding Kuhn's third cultural instrumentality ('repressions'), Michael O'Shaughnessy (1999) discusses the theory that science fiction offers a way in which the 'repressed' can return to be considered in a different (more acceptable) guise: 'Freud argued that anything that is repressed doesn't disappear or go away. On the contrary, it will return, but in a more disturbing or violent form' (1999, p. 152). This approach suggests that there is a potentially liberating effect to examining the 'shadow side' of contemporary society as it is projected into the cyberfutures of science fiction. Through the consideration of the (possible) future, we learn to address the here and now, and come to own those aspects of our society which cause us to fear the technological developments indicated in the present.

Analysing cinema as popular culture includes consideration of the relationship between the text and the spectator, and the pleasure of consumption: Kuhn's fourth area of interest. 'As a commodity, cinema is intangible: it is sold on the spectator's expectation of pleasure or diversion. In this sense, with cinema the exchange object is really pleasure' (1990, p. 146). Since meaning is produced through the interaction of the individual with the text, the meanings surrounding science fiction, cyborgs and biotechnology are as indicative of the hopes and fears of twenty-first century humanity as they are a function of narrative and plot. Donna Haraway's feminist cyborg may be heaven to her ('I would rather be a cyborg than a goddess'), but the post-gender denial of the female is not every woman's cup of tea:

> The cyborg is a creature in a post-gender world; it has no truck with bi-sexuality, pre-Oedipal symbiosis, unalienated labor, or other seductions to organic wholeness through a final appropriation of all the powers of the parts into a higher unity . . . the cyborg is resolutely committed to partiality, irony, intimacy and perversity. It is oppositional, utopian and completely without innocence (Haraway 1991, p. 181).

Arguably, however, science fiction audiences gain pleasure from speculating about the future (and about parallel universes) and/or a pleasurably different sense of the present. Even 'escapism' can be immensely satisfying and can alter the spectator's mood and their relationship to the everyday.

Intertextuality—Kuhn's fifth cultural instrumentality—involves 'the quotation, [an in-media-text reference to other films or cultural products] the pastiche of codes, and the parody . . . Contemporary science fiction has been hailed as a privileged cultural site for enactments of the postmodern condition—usually in its more nightmarish aspects' (Kuhn 1990, p. 178). One effect of this juxtaposition of science and technology, with nightmarish visions of the future, is to build in (and give voice to) a fear of the technocultural possible and a renewed appreciation of the present. The power of the nightmare is related to the plausibility of its vision, and the likelihood that the horror will be realised. Many sci-fi films embody a warning against a particular technology—the biotechnology of cloning has a specific role in *The Sixth Day*, for example. The film becomes an element within a popular culture discussion of the future, which feeds into social debates upon regulation, legislation and ethics.

The cogent sci-fi nightmare requires a recognisable possible genesis in a contemporary social system, or in a society that has operated in the past. Thus human sacrifice to appease the techno-gods may be related to current myths about ancient cultures; and a bureaucratic obsession with lists and categories (as in *Brazil*) may echo the techno-primitive (but genocidally effective) Nazi administration portrayed in *Schindler's List*. Science fiction could envision technutopias, but instead it concentrates more upon exploring the role of the human spirit in surviving future technohells.

## CONCLUSION

Popular culture has been recognised for 40 years as a site of pleasure, desire and creativity—much cultural studies research has centred upon television's role in the construction and circulation of popular culture. This role will increasingly be evident in technocultural uses of the Internet, which has the added dimension of involving the creation of content, as well as the creation of meaning. Internet community construction may well be a particular expression of a growing interest in community, and in the relationship of community to technoculture.

The project of the construction and circulation of popular culture is implicated within all communication technologies and—given the imperative of the new—particularly in emerging communication technologies. Popular culture can be expected to reveal to us the hopes and fears within society about the present and the future, and sci-fi may be one popular culture site for the return of the repressed, where fears for the future are played out. This is as true of the Internet specifically as it is of science fiction in general. The Internet offers a technocultural site in which individuals explore their concern for the present, as well as the future. Such concerns can lead to social action, as we have seen in the role of Internet communications in linking resistance to organisations implicated in global capitalism, such as the World Trade Organisation (see Chapter 7).

# 10

## GENDER, POWER AND TECHNOLOGY

### GENDERED COMPETENCE WITH TECHNOLOGY

There is a vision, peddled by the marketing and advertising arms of hi-tech companies, that the right technology at the right time can solve most of the difficulties of modern society. From bionic implants to replace or enhance impaired biological function through to online voting which allows full-scale participatory democracy, technological solutions promise new answers to old problems.

Technology is presented as easy to use and accessible. (Both the marketers and manufacturers persuade us to see it like that.) Any incompetence lies in a fault of the user, rather than the technology *per se*, yet technology is rarely transparent to the point where it can be used simply, and repeatedly, across a range of applications without support. Complexity of use sets up a dynamic where the many who need help to realise the potential of the technology feel somehow inadequate in wanting this help. Fear of technology is learned, and much of this learned fear of technology is constructed through gender, and through age.

A decade or so ago, Judy Wajcman wrote an influential book, *Feminism Confronts Technology,* which examines the interrelationship of gender with technology, and argues that western societies construct technological competence as a masculine culture (Wajcman 1991, pp. 137–61). Knitting, cooking and gardening, for example, all have technological elements—as do many other traditionally female skills—but these are not acceptable as 'technologies' in our culture partly because they are all feminine pursuits. (Men who develop professional gardening skills tend to see themselves as horticulturists, landscape architects, land managers and farmers.) Further, technologies that become integrated within the female realm—cars, microwaves, washing machines—are used successfully by women, but women gain no general sense of technological competence through their use. Instead, technological competence is associated with the technology's (mainly masculine) maintenance.

At the extreme, the 'latest technology' can be characterised as urban, white, middle-class, masculine and American. In the early years, this was an accurate description of Internet technoculture, although by the turn of the millennium female participation rates had risen to approximately 40 per cent (GVU 1997, and see below). Traditionally—as with cars and microwaves—the democratisation and feminisation of leading-edge technologies goes hand-in-hand with the technology becoming less leading-edge than it was. Becoming more widespread, the once-leading-edge is replaced as an object of scarcity by newer and more powerful technologies, which offer further challenges of knowledge, access and equity, and which are biased by design to support the elites who sponsor them.

Most 'pink'/'women's' technologies (see next section) are well established in the domestic realm. When competence is being gauged and discussed, however, there is a disproportionate emphasis given to *new* technology—technology which is most jealously guarded, most difficult to find out about, and hardest to get to use. Wajcman sums up her position thus: 'In our culture, to be in charge of the very latest technology signifies being involved in directing the future and so it is a highly valued and mythologised activity' (1991, p. 144). Such activity is quintessentially a masculine one, and particularly associated with young, educated, western men.

## GENDERING TECHNOLOGY

Wajcman resists the interpretation that women are inherently untechnological. Instead, she argues that women are constructed, and construct themselves, as 'other' to men. In our society, 'technical competence is central to the dominant cultural ideal of masculinity, and its absence is a key feature of stereotyped femininity' (1991, p. 159). Consequently, women's reluctance to be technological can be attributed to cultural structures which differentiate women from men. Hand in hand with this mythology of masculinity's association with new or high technology is something of a 'calculated ignorance' (Gray 1987, p. 43) on the part of individual women to comprehend the detailed workings of certain technologies. This is in spite of the many pieces of technology which women use effectively. Thus one of my female interviewees (aged 40–54) and I commiserated with each other on our (late 1980s) lack of competence with computer technology:

> See, computers. They came in and we'd never seen one up here [remote Australia]. I still can't work a computer and I feel I've missed out and I'm too bloody old to learn now. They tell me I'm not. I'm going to have to make the effort and learn it. Much as I really don't like them, I think my kids are going to, so for them to do it, I've got to know how to because they're not going to have a hope in hell with education, if they can't use a computer, are they?
> <SURE.>
> Now, you're from the civilised world . . .
> <WE'VE HAD A COMPUTER SINCE '85. I DON'T KNOW WHERE WE'D BE WITHOUT IT.>
> OK, see, our kids haven't.
> <MIND YOU, I CAN'T USE IT. MY HUSBAND HAS TO TURN IT ON [LOAD THE DOS OPERATING SYSTEM]. THEREAFTER I'M FINE.>
> Are you? Where did you learn?
> <WHERE DID HE LEARN? HE LEARNED FROM THE MANUAL BUT I JUST GET HIM TO DO IT BECAUSE HE'S ALWAYS . . .>
> OK, you're as lazy as me, aren't you?
> <THAT'S RIGHT> (Green 1998, pp. 218–19).

This interviewee gives support for her children as her rationale for learning the computer, and reinforces the gender divide by seeing that role as a service. Many 'technologies of service' are gendered as female, while technologies of power and choice are gendered as male. British researcher Ann Gray, looking at gender and technology, describes an experiment whereby different domestic technologies were coloured according to their usage in gender terms. Gray asked her female respondents to characterise domestic equipment as coloured either pink or blue to indicate female or male ownership: 'This produces almost uniformly pink irons and blue electric drills . . . but my research has shown me that we must break down the VCR into its different modes . . . "record", "rewind" and "play" modes are usually lilac, but the timer switch is nearly always blue.' Gray concludes by noting that women tend to rely upon 'their male partners or their children to set the timer for them' (1987, p. 42).

According to Gray, 'although women routinely operate extremely sophisticated pieces of domestic technology . . . they often feel alienated from operating the VCR' (1987, p. 43). Gray also rejects simplistic explanations of technological incompetence, choosing instead to address the structure of VCR programming in terms of the household service dynamic. Gray quotes Edna, one of her interviewees: 'Once I learned to put a plug on, now there's nobody else puts a plug on in this house but me', before continuing:

> It would seem that there are decisions made by women, either consciously or subconsciously, to remain in ignorance of the workings of the VCR, so that it is their husband or partner's job to set up the timer. This, of course, has the function of a 'service' for the household unit . . . the more calculatedly ignorant women had perhaps recognised this latent servicing element and resisted it in view of their already heavily committed domestic servicing roles (Gray 1992, pp. 164, 169).

This phenomenon—of women delegating the functioning of new technologies to others in the household, or declining to demonstrate competence—has received critical attention in recent years. Findings in one of my research projects resonate those of Gray. As one young (25–39) woman from a shared household in remote Australia remarked to me:

> Thursday nights we used to go to the movies. I always used to videotape [*China Beach*] and it never worked and I couldn't believe it because I never had it in my video machine. I never got it right. Well, I'd put the wrong video in . . . or I'd put a two hour video in instead of a three hour because I couldn't set the time delay on it so I'd put on a three hour video so hopefully by the time I left and got back it would have taped the whole program, because I left two hours before it started and it just never worked out. It was a great program. The few I saw, it was pretty good (Green 1998, p. 218).

There is no reason, however, to assume that a reluctance to adopt—or experiment with—a new technology is entirely one-dimensional. It may also be that, at the time that this interviewee failed to program the video, the rewards of watching *China Beach* were never quite sufficient to invest the time and mental energy required to overcome the programming block. As Todd points out: 'Costs are always involved in adopting new technology. These include the obvious, such as equipment investment, license costs and the like. Less obvious are the information and screening costs involved in seeking and assessing the alternatives, the cost of time spent . . . learning how to use the new technology efficiently' (1995, p. 206).

## FEAR OF TECHNOLOGY

Fear of technology takes two major forms—fear of using the technology itself, and fear of the effects of technology. This section addresses the fear of using technology—technological reluctance. A fear such as this may be visible in the (non-)use of a number of technologies (e.g., VCRs, computers), and is commonly identified as a female trait. People may fear technology for a variety of reasons—for example, because they feel inadequate and incompetent when faced with technology. For these technophobes, fear of technology can lead to a sense of helplessness and hopelessness. In contrast, men may be reluctant to use irons, vacuum cleaners, food processors or microwaves (Gray 1989), but they are unlikely to see this as a problem of personal inadequacy, rather as an issue of gender—such technologies are female ones.

Underlining the gendered nature of technology, Morley (1986) argues in *Family Television* that patterns of television viewing reflect existing power relationships in the home, with males (sons deputising in their father's absence) taking over the remote control, and being the deciders in any conflict over which programme to watch. Male dominance is visible in a variety of technocultural contexts. For instance, over many years, female participation rates on the Net greatly lagged behind those of males although this ratio has been changing fast recently (see Figure 10.1). Men are more likely to be at home on the Net, and have been well positioned historically to keep out unwanted visitors and interlopers. Nonetheless, as Internet technoculture becomes more pervasive in the post-industrial world, women are increasingly present on the Internet and are able to remodel some aspects of the environment to suit their uses as well as those of the men.

By the mid-1990s, estimates generally indicated that women were participating online in a ratio of male:female, 2:1 (Hearn et al. 1998, pp. 38, 41). Wallace (1999, p. 218, citing GVU 1997) reports that 'the proportion of women online shot up from 31% to 38% between 1997 and 1998, and for the 10- to 18-year-olds, the sex ratio is even closer to even (46% to 54%).' The Internet can be positioned as a site of gendered struggle—not necessarily on all occasions, for all users, but sufficiently often to tell us about ourselves, our society and about our constructions of gender and communication.

Figure 10.1 Internet users by females and males, according to skill level

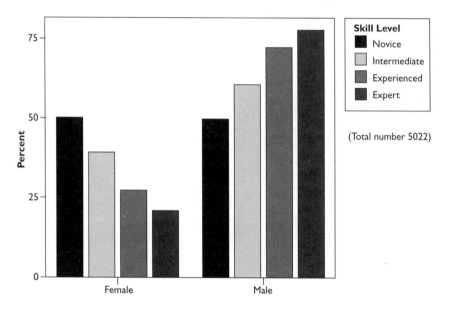

Source: most recent data from www.cc.gatech.edu/gvu/user_surveys [October 1998]. Total number of respondents: 5022.
Note: Among all users identifying as 'novice', 50.2 per cent of respondents are female

Fear of the effects of technology (rather than its use) is essentially a fear of the intentions of the elites who sponsor the development and adoption of that technology. Thus 'computers' have been constructed as a surveillance machine, as undermining the democratic system, as having the potential to cause war—through malfunction or through control—and as 'deciding wrongly'—for example where sales of shares are automatically triggered by stock falling to a specific price. Critical American scholar Theodore Roszak wears his heart plainly on his sleeve when he says: 'No doubt principled hackers, who are still with us, will continue to find valuable political applications for computers; their efforts deserve to be supported' (1994, p. 202). He goes on to sum up his concerns about computers in apocalyptic terms:

> No matter how high the promise of that age [the information age] is pitched, the price we pay for its benefits will never outweigh the costs. The violation of privacy is the loss of freedom. The degradation of electoral politics is the loss of democracy. The creation of the computerized war machine is a direct threat to the survival of our species. It would be some comfort to conclude that these liabilities result from the abuse of computer power. But these are the goals long since selected by those who invented information technology, who have guided it and financed it at every point along the way in its development. The computer is *their* machine; its mystique is *their* validation (Roszak 1994, p. 233).

Roszak here addresses the A, B and C elites identified earlier and in discussing the armed forces, bureaucracies (and political systems) and corporate power he has described a very masculine world. The 'principled hackers' praised by Roszak for continuing 'to find valuable political applications for computers' also constitute a very masculine group.

## THE MASCULINE WORLD OF THE HACKER

Hackers, as Roszak indicates, occupy a paradoxical role in technoculture and in popular culture. Hackers can be read both as 'information terrorists'—to be feared—and as evidence of the power of the individual against the system; and against the might of government, bureaucracy and international capital. For some hackers, beating the machine is the ultimate trial of human strength and ability, and they use their skills to demonstrate technological prowess, with a consequent increase in their social standing within hacker culture. This dynamic is evident in Sherry Turkle's exploration of hackers at MIT in the early 1980s.

Turkle identified the MIT culture as one in which mastery and control were seen as core values. 'Though hackers would deny that theirs is a macho culture, the preoccupation with winning and of subjecting oneself to increasingly violent tests make their world particularly male in spirit, particularly unfriendly to women' (Turkle 1984, p. 216). The kinds of tests envisioned—the modern day equivalents of the mythological trials of Hercules—included breaking into a particular corporate mainframe (beating the security system); creating a new virus; working longer and harder without a break for food, drink or toilet; living the technocultural obsession.

The physical badges of extreme computer competence and mastery are those of homelessness and social isolation: 'bright young men of disheveled appearance . . . Their rumpled clothes, their unwashed and unshaven faces, and their uncombed hair all testify that they are oblivious to their bodies and the world in which they move' (Weizenbaum 1976, p. 116). In fact, these visual cues may well signify a heightened awareness of appearance, and a desire to project a total rejection of conventional standards upon which people are judged. They do not signify social failure (as they could), but rather identification with hacker subculture, and the valuing of technological skill over social convention.

As Wajcman points out, citing Tracy Kidder (1982), the masculine world of technology development (and, by analogy, hacking) is:

A world of men working compulsively into the small hours, enjoying being stretched to the limit of their capacity, where there is no space for or compromise with life outside of work. It was 'the sexy job' to be the builder of new computers, and you had to be tough and fast; members of the group often talked of doing things 'quick and dirty', and of 'wars', 'shoot-outs', 'hired guns', and people who 'shot from the hip'. Sexual metaphors abound such that the excitement of working on the latest computer was likened to 'somebody told those guys that they would have seventy-two hours with the girl of their dreams' (Wajcman 1991, p. 141).

These kinds of case studies beg the question of how technoculture could be different, or would be different, if other perspectives and social priorities were centre stage. For example, women are remotely mothering/nurturing via cyberspace, and simultaneously participating in online/email community building and maintenance. With these priorities, over time, we can expect cyberspace to become a more nurturing environment. Eric Michaels (1994) charted the process of the reinvention of a technology and explored some of the unexpected features of television and video production that needed to be changed or adapted to fit in with Aboriginal cultural priorities (see Chapter 7). In an analogous way, we are witnessing (and many of us are actively involved in) a female reinvention of digital culture.

## POWER AND COMPULSION ON THE INTERNET

Hackers have been researched through ethnography, and explored in popular culture—in films such as *The Matrix* and *War Games*. Recently, the focus of research has changed from studying hackers and their social systems to one of studying 'addicts' whose Internet habits are out of control. The Internet has a number of addictive features: it is highly accessible (given skills, knowledge and available technology), it offers people short-term and long-term rewards, an escape from RL, an illusion of control over the environment, and is a place where the last word is always possible (provided you log off quickly enough). Arguably, the lives of hackers—even given the sense of power and mastery they experience through their prowess—offer examples of a technocultural addiction.

Patricia Wallace discusses predatory behaviour on the Internet, including the masculine-style, vigilante phenomenon of channel wars and takeovers, where some Internet activity takes on the guise of 'gang warfare'—*Web Side Story*, perhaps? 'If the owners of a chat channel annoy the wrong people—the ones who can read Websites explaining how to use programmes to flood the channel and cause the owners and operators to lose their powers of control—they may find that they have been kicked out and the guerillas own their channel' (Wallace 1999, p. 132). A counter-guerrilla vigilante group, IRCarnage, offers redress. If you tell them about your channel, lost to a raiding party, they will attempt to reclaim it for you. They publish a 'braggart's list' of all the channels they have taken over, and offer further evidence of the Internet as a technocultural site for exploring masculine solutions to issues of power, control and mastery.

Kimberley Young, who approached Internet addiction as if it shared addictive characteristics with gambling, researched users who did, and didn't, feel in control of their Internet habits. Most users who felt their Internet habit was beyond control were logged on to chat rooms and MUDs. As one of Young's contributors commented: 'MUDs are like a religion to me, and I am a god there. I am respected by all the other

MUDders. I know that I am playing against other highly intelligent people, and . . . getting stronger at the game gives me a great high' (Young 1998, p. 69). While hacking is an almost exclusively masculine culture, however, other forms of Internet addiction are more likely to affect women, particularly in the social sphere: online community, and one-to-one online relationships.

Internet addiction has spurred the development of a number of online self-/other-help resources including COLA, the Center for On-Line Addiction netaddiction.com [June 2001]. A variety of comment and resources are available at the personal website of American academic and online psychotherapist Storm King, www.webpages.charter.net /stormking [June 2001]. Further, the Website www.rider.edu/users/ suler/psycyber/cybaddict.html addresses a range of mental health issues and links to other relevant Websites (including COLA and Storm King's). Online cyberpsychology professionals actively advocate and support the healthy use of ICTs, and a balanced integration of RL/VL.

The existence of addictive behaviours online, however, does not necessarily make the Internet a dangerous place to be. As Storm King asks in an article on his Website (above): 'Is the Internet addictive, or are addicts using the Internet?' Nonetheless, the results of research studies are beginning to come in and Suler (1996) and Kraut et al. (1998) indicate that extensive Internet use is not necessarily beneficial to an individual's RL, or to their health, psyche, financial and general well-being.

## WHAT ABOUT CYBERSEX?

When I first addressed the issue of technoculture in a tertiary context, I left out specific discussion of cybersex since I thought we were unlikely to add much to the somewhat salacious debate regularly canvassed in a variety of popular media. Nonetheless, cybersex was a matter of con-siderable interest to my class—particularly the issues of 'Where does consensual cybersex fit into cyberspace?' and 'How is cybersex related to RL?' The reason for this student interest is likely to be related to age and stage rather than any technologically driven factors. As Rheingold comments: 'The single largest category of MUD'ers are college students, age seventeen to twenty-three, and the particular uses they find for this technology—identity play and sexual innuendo—reflect the preoccupa-tions of that population' (1993, online publication). Palandri and Green note, observing a group of younger chatters, that:

introductions are closely followed by requests for 'stats' (statistics: age, gender, height, weight, color of hair and eyes and physical proportions). Without much 'foreplay' the younger MUD chatters will ask/be asked for cybersex . . . it is clear that males and females . . . sense a freedom to express a side of themselves on the Net which is generally taboo in relation to their peers, their family and society in general. Even though it would be naive, and inaccurate, to argue that there is no impression management on the Net, many chatters feel liberated from the RL systems that control unacceptable language (Palandri & Green 2000, p. 637).

Possibly, the request to theorise what goes on in cybersex, and the reduction of the inhibitions of RL, addresses the sexualisation of technoculture and a desire on the part of these young adults to explain their own interests and behaviour to themselves.

As a class, we looked at cybersex in relation to phone sex, porn magazines and movies on the one hand, and in relation to RL sex on the other. Phone sex shared common features with RL and cybersex in that all had interactive elements. Phone communication predominantly involved the senses of speech and hearing. Unlike two-way RL and cybersex, however, phone sex was essentially one-way in that only one party (the client) was expecting to enjoy the experience. The designation 'client' was seen to be indicative here, since the experience is an expensive one—the fiscal investment enabled the experience to progress with minimal emotional investment. In this way, the client and sex worker are able to hold back on intimacy, since the relationship is driven by dynamics of commodity and exchange. Use of the phone for phone sex may indicate a lack of alternative options, but it may also indicate a fear of intimacy.

Sexy films—and at the extreme, blue movies—offer no interactivity with other people apart from intellectually, through empathy and identification. Nonetheless, they tend to be rich visually, and stimulating in terms of dialogue, sound effects and music. They can help create a seductive atmosphere, but the lack of interactivity (and any recognition of the individual members of the audience) lessens the viewer's identification with the movie-sex experience (unless a RL partner is involved). Porn magazines allow even less intimacy and even greater distance from interactivity, and involve only the sense of sight.

Cybersex itself was experienced by some cybersex-initiates as 'liberating'. It allowed participants to explore new behaviours in terms of verbal/sexual self-expression, and was particularly constructed as inhibition-freeing by some women (and men) whose social roles would 'normally' preclude them from uninhibited sex talk and/or the writing of erotica. The fact that the communication exchange is two-way (and the cybersex partner is fully involved in the development of the cybersex exchange) creates the potential for uncertainty and surprise and allows for the possibility of an ongoing relationship. We discussed whether sex was 'all in the mind', or whether cybersex only occurred with self-touching . . . and decided that the mind was the primary centre for activity in both RL and cybersex, and particularly with the romantic experience of both. Part of the romance of cybersex lies in the use of words and writing style to identify, signal and woo potentially compatible partners. Further, there is the sense of almost unlimited scope—nothing is impossible in cyberspace.

The cyber-romance is restricted only by the limits of expression and imagination, not by the corporeality of physical presence—however, cyber-presence *is* required. As (the submissive) sweet~fyre told Marian Palandri: 'I enjoy writing hot sex, filth, and love being the center of the action too. I have two VL lovers, Sticky K and Prince Nathaniel . . . It used to be just Sticky K but his RL was heavy, he couldn't give me enough time . . . I was lonely . . . Since Prince Nathaniel came on the scene it's been much better' (Palandri & Green 2000, p. 634). Having noted the benefits of cyber-romance, cyber-relationships might be much more quickly extinguished than in RL. There was an unreferenced recollection that cyber-romances lasted an average of six weeks.

One reason why cybersex might be particularly liberating for some participants is that it allows for the mutual exploration of 'kinky' fantasies with minimal risk of physical harm compared with an equivalent ex-perience in RL (especially with a stranger). A female student suggested that cybersex protocols may be educational for some men in that the written element slows down the exchange and foregrounds the words and emotions as an important precursor to (and accompaniment of) cybersex. Further, the lack of physical presence of the other was seen to offer more self-awareness as part of the cybersex experience. That self-awareness—of what an individual wants and what an individual wants to give—was perceived as offering benefits in VL, and potential benefits in RL.

As well as being a two-way exchange, cybersex offers an increas-ingly multi-sensory experience. Leaving aside the (rare and expensive) 'pleasure suit', webcam can communicate images of cybersexual partner(s) who have a particularly exhibitionist disposition. The involvement of the other in cybersex, and the mutual interchange of sweet~fyre's 'hot sex, filth', was seen to indicate a quintessentially consensual experience. 'Non-consensual' cybersex was consequently a theoretically troublesome construct—about as logical as the notion of self-deception. At the same time, it was clearly possible for Netizens to experience unwanted cybersexual advances, and to suffer cybersexual harassment. Such problems could usefully be referred to a moderator, if there was one, since a persistent offender could be excluded from the online group.

Compared with phone sex (and, to a lesser extent, porn and sexy movies), cybersex was inexpensive—there was no overriding financial implication beyond the wherewithal to log on. There was some suggestion, however, that maybe cybersex indicates a fear of 'real-to-real' intimacy—especially given that many RL relationships appear to last longer than cyber-relating. It was also felt that RL offered greater potential for intimacy across a wider range of self-expression, and that maybe RL intimacy was a necessary part of a continuing and deepening sexual liaison for most people. Technoculture couldn't be all things to all people, all the time.

Cybersex protagonists were keen to suggest that RL sex might be limited by physical proximity and might be 'quicker' than cybersex with less 'conversation' and exchange of thoughts and ideas. In both manifestations of sexuality, however, there was the potential for an ongoing relationship. Those who owned up to being experienced, cybersexually, claimed that individuals were vulnerable in both domains, and that the degree of vulnerability was related to the amount of individual engagement with the other, and with the sexual experience, rather than to the medium of expression (VL/RL). For this reason, it was valid to debate (hotly) the moral dimension of infidelity across partners and across media (VL/RL). Could you be unfaithful to an RL partner with a VL partner? Should you not go out with RL people when involved in a cyber-romance? These moral questions were seen to pivot upon the understandings between the parties—in essence, upon whether the VL/RL activities were open and above board.

One area in which cybersex does not match up to RL is in relationship to law and to biological procreation. (Although some cyber-partnerships involve cyber-pregnancies and cyber-kids.) No government is willing to offer nationality and residency status to a cyber-partner as a result of a cyber-relationship alone. (But, since it is a cyber-relationship, physical proximity was seen to be essentially superfluous.)

## GENDER AND HARASSMENT ON THE INTERNET

Given that the Internet began as a masculine technoculture, using masculine technology, it has traditionally seemed unfriendly—or directly intimidating—to women. For some commentators, this is no accident. Spender cites Nola Alloway's (1995) research as indicating that 'even three-year-old boys in pre-school insist that the computers are the boys' territory, and the girls are verbally and physically driven away' (Spender 1995, p. 167):

> Girls in general seemed uninterested in accessing the resource when competing for the opportunity meant entering the fray with an antagonistic group of boys and the adoption of a combative style of interaction. Within this context of aggressive competition, it seemed understandable, if not outright intelligent, to avoid the computer and to select an alternative activity that did not involve physical harassment (Alloway 1995, p. 40).

Although men took an early head start on the Internet, women could have been associated with computers from the beginning of their social biography. Computers had keyboards and, at the point of computer take-up, women were the socially designated 'typing' gender. Feminist commentator Dale Spender notes that 'just about every survey indicates that when the men have moved in, the women have moved out. In the UK [according to Cole et al. 1994] in 1978, 28 per cent of the students enrolled in computer sciences were women; by 1985–86 this figure had dropped to 13 per cent and the trend continues' (1995, p. 166). Women started off by being involved, but then it became a 'gendered' area—as computers became increasingly associated with mastery and control.

From the physical exclusion of the pre-school class to the intimidation of young adult women, this technocultural absence can be constructed as engineered by masculine activity. In western culture, sexual harassment has often been viewed as an inappropriate expression of sexuality, but it is more likely to be about issues of power and control. Given that there is a lack of physical co-presence on the Internet, it might be felt that cyber-harassment is a virtual problem, rather than an actual one. This is not the experience of those who have suffered cyber-harassment.

Judy Wajcman comments that the 'harassment of girls interested in computing continues into tertiary education. At this stage the harassment takes the form of obscene computer mail or print-outs of nude women. Women students in computer science at MIT found this problem so pervasive that they organized a special committee to deal with it' (1991, p. 153). Jacques Leslie discusses the case of a man (Sykes, who used the online female persona 'Eris') who pretended to be female online. His 'major revelation', resulting from this gendered interaction with technoculture, was the 'extent of sexual harassment of women'. After four months, Sykes abandoned his pretence 'because he could not write programmes without being constantly interrupted by male advances . . . [but] one male player who apparently had a crush on Eris became so irate that he tried to get Sykes banished from the MUD' (Leslie 1993, quoted by Danet 1997, p. 140, see www.well.com/~jacques /jacques.html and a link to the updated article in www.abacon.com/ vitanza/cyber/index.html [June 2001]).

Australian researcher Ann Willis, in her work on *Wired* and its online equivalent, *Hotwired*, 1993–97, argues that the magazine/s construct the technocultural domain as masculine frontier territory: 'One of the myriad of examples of this is an advertisement which appeared in *Wired* (1994b, p. 113) for the *Mega Race* CD-ROM game. The caption reads *"No Cops No Laws No Wimps—Are you a girlie-man or a Megaracer?"'* (2000, pp. 361–72). (Notably, there's no option to be a girlie-girl/woman.) Willis goes on to say (2000, pp. 367–8):

The film, *My Darling Clementine* is a classic example of the American frontier environment where good girls don't go until law and order are established, and bad girls who do, suffer the most dire consequences. This frontier myth operates as a convenient one for the CMC [computer mediated communication] environment because it reconfirms and justifies (particularly for men) why women shouldn't be there, and reconfirms the stereotype that (sensible, worthwhile) women themselves *shouldn't* and *wouldn't* want to participate in this environment anyway.

The frontier discourse of *shouldn't* and *wouldn't* is re-articulated in a *Wired* article called *'alt.sex.bondage'* by Richard Kadrey (1994a, p. 40). His exploration of the *alt.sex.bondage* site, provides, as it were, '. . . a novice['s] guide' to the site. Kadrey positions CMC within the masculine discourse of a cyber-frontiersville. In doing so, he reiterates the stereotype that women shouldn't really be there because it is too mad, bad and dangerous. Describing the CMC environment as an 'asylum' he states, 'while the overall tone of abs (the *alt.sex.bondage* site) is friendly and open, not everyone who visits here feels safe. Women, especially, who have posted openly about their sexual lives have reported being inundated with e-mail from guys offering to "do" them. One discouraged female user wrote, ". . . unless a woman has a strong stomach, she won't post here more than once" ' (Kadrey 1994, p. 40).

## GENDER IN INTERNET CULTURE

Although cyberspace is often constructed as a hostile environment for women, it is interesting that a significant number of men use the Internet to 'try out' a female persona. The Net is a potential laboratory for exploring gender performance—how we see ourselves in gendered roles. This is an area of considerable research interest. One project, based at the Georgia Institute of Technology, is *The Turing Game*, a:

> game to help us understand issues of online identity. In this environment . . . a panel of users all pretend to be a member of some group, such as women. Some of the users, who are women, are trying to prove that fact to their audience. Others are men, trying to masquerade as women. An audience of both genders tries to discover whom the imposters [sic] are, by asking questions and analyzing the panel members' answers. Games can cover aspects of gender, race, or any other cultural marker of the users' choice (www.cc.gatech.edu/elc/turing/ [June 2001]).

Projects like this, combined with cases analysing individual experience, help us to understand the dynamics of gender difference both within and beyond technoculture.

One famous case of gender deception occurred when a middle-aged male psychiatrist pretended to be a disabled female ('Julie') to get access to women's talk on the Net which, he felt, had 'so much more vulnerability, so much more depth and complexity' than men's talk (Stone 1991). On that occasion, some of the women 'Julie' had been talking to felt outraged and cheated, and the case raises serious ethical issues since the psychiatrist was deliberately attempting to join a women-only forum to investigate it without their consent. Elsewhere—as Eris discovered—it has been the men pretending to be women who have had the unpleasant surprises. They have found their female persona subject to harassment and innuendo, unable to carry on normal life in the technocultural realm.

The power struggle between men and women becomes more explicit when specific case studies of harassment are studied. Marj Kibby, a cultural studies theorist, charted the objectionable activities of Robert Toups' 1995 'Babes on the web' Website. Toups writes:

> 'Along with being a capitalist pig, I am a proud male chauvinist pig. As such, I have gathered all the World Wide Websites of women I could find. Instead of rating them on quality of design, I am grading them on a four Toupsie scale according to their personal pictures. My rating system is totally subjective to my personal tastes and whims . . . If this page is offensive to you then go to the National Organisation for Women (NOW) home page and cry to them. Maybe they will organise a cyber protest against my page or maybe you will find something else to bitch about. Either way, I won't care' (quoted in Kibby 1997, p. 39).

As Kibby points out, 'it may be one more factor discouraging women from participating on the Internet by limiting the choices they might make in designing their home pages' (1997, p. 39).

Joan Smith's view is that our culture is built upon 'a deep-seated hatred of women' (1989, pp. xvi–xvii). Further, 'the discrimination and denigration and violence that women suffer are no historical accident but linked manifestations of this hatred; I inhabit a culture which is not simply sexist but occasionally lethal for women . . . we live in circumstances which not only restrict our freedom but physically threaten us if we step out of line'. Whereas Smith argues that misogyny is a normal state for normal men in our society, pathological hatred is also in evidence on the Net, and will be discussed further in Chapter 11.

Lynda Davies, a (female) professor of computer science, found that it was not only the online technocultural environment but the labs themselves which were hostile to women. 'During the day, computer labs are filled with students shouting across the rooms at each other, goading each other with terms like "fuckwit", "wanker", "dickfor" being called out as terms of comradeship, seeming terms of endearment amongst the peer group. The student groups are almost exclusively male' (Spender 1995, p. 182). The absence-of-women has changed in recent years, as indicated earlier, with 38 per cent (and rising) Internet participation by women, and this is likely to affect the culture in the laboratory, as well as the technoculture of the Internet.

The growing entry by women on to the Net is partly the result of specific intervention by feminist scholars such as Dale Spender and Judy Wajcman, who have created a scenario in which women felt more empowered and seduced by technoculture. Spender, in calling her book *Nattering on the Net: Women, Power and Cyberspace*, deliberately constructs a feminised image of the Net—traditionally, men don't natter. She also analysed the centuries-long way in which women were excluded from power by illiteracy following the invention of print, and argues that the structural disadvantage of female illiteracy has deliberately been compounded by socio-political systems. In most western nations, men had the vote for decades before women, and they justified the exclusion of women on the grounds of their lower educational standard, and their inability to read and write. A competent electorate, ran the argument, is an educated one—but for many years only one of the genders was educated. Spender's concern in the 1990s was that the Internet was shaping up to replicate this privilege/discrimination dynamic.

Arguably, however, the increase in female participation is not only because the Internet has been re-engineered to make it more 'friendly', but because the men are migrating to more specialised Internet-related activities. With so many more people—including women and children—involved in the Internet, the hi-tech/leading edge area of computer use has moved from Internet access and use *per se* to Web design and security. These areas are now the 'masculinised' technocultural domain: they are the skills which command the greatest fees. (A similar movement has occurred in medical general practice: men are moving into 'specialisms', leaving women to run the less well paid, less prestigious, more demanding family practice surgeries.)

## GENDERING POSTMODERN MEDIA CONSUMPTION

Sherry Turkle, in her study of female computer students at MIT, determined that one reason behind the accessibility of computers for boys/men lies in a masculine willingness to play first, ask questions later. 'It is almost impossible to play a video game if you try to understand it first and play second. Girls are often perceived as preferring the "easier" video games. When I have looked more closely at what they really prefer, it is games where they can understand "the rules" before play begins' (1988, p. 49). This before/after male/female dynamic has also been observed in other situations. For example, John Gray's (1992) *Men are From Mars, Women are From Venus* suggests that Martians need sex to feel intimate, whereas Venusians need to feel intimacy before they want sex (www.marsvenus.com/ [June 2001]). Many commentators (Judy Wajcman, for example) remain uncomfortable, however, about sweeping statements which assert global differences between males and females unconnected with their socialisation, role modelling and upbringing (Wajcman 1991, pp. 155–9).

Technology studies in areas of ICTs other than the Internet also underline an impression that women and men differ in the ways in which they relate to their lives, their domestic spaces and the gendered technocultures within them:

> The fundamental issue concerns the differential positioning of men and women in the sphere of 'leisure' (whether as a temporal phenomenon—'time off'; or as a spatial phenomenon—'at home'). For many men, the home is principally a site of leisure and rest (in contrast to their work obligations in the public sphere); for many women (if not most) the home is a site of labour (both physical and emotional) and responsibility, at least as much, if not more, than it is a site of leisure—whether or not they also do paid work outside the home (Morley 1995, pp. 321–2).

Morley argues that television viewing styles are also differentiated, with men preferring to plan their television viewing and to watch attentively, in (other people's) silence and without interruption. Women, however, tend to watch television on a more serendipitous basis, and while carrying out domestic tasks. The rationale offered is that they can 'take it or leave it', as if conscious choice might be a harbinger of disappointment. Even when women are unambiguously watching television, such attention is often the site of further female work—those boundary ambiguities again:

> It is because of the relationship between advertising and television that watching television is work. Watching television is a leisure activity in the pursuit of which viewers are asked to lose themselves, to blur the distinctions between reality and fantasy.

They are asked to forget that watching television is also work, to see television advertisements not as a continual reminder of the work of purchasing, but as entertainment (Nightingale 1990, p. 33).

Thus television viewing reflects the distinctness of the home/work divide characteristic of men's lives, while the women's approach is more typically integrated/fragmented. These observations mirror Wajcman's view of domestic duties: that men engage in discrete, 'non-routine tasks at intervals rather than continually, and frequently the work is outdoors. This is in marked contrast to women's housework, the dominant characteristic of which is that it is never complete' (1991, p. 87). Further, although it would be overly simplistic to characterise gendered television programming as a continuum between female viewing (those daytime soaps) and male television (sports, sports, sports), such programme formats tend to reflect something of daily experience. Soap opera—women's programming of which men are (often) scornful—is a reflection of the continuing, evolving interconnectedness and fragmentation of women's lives. It is also a site in which they hone their skills in analysing 'socioemotional experience' and explore emotions and emotional situations vicariously. Men are not socialised to enjoy any equivalent practices.

(Men's) sports programming is episodic in the sense that there is order—a beginning, middle and end—and an outcome. Sports coverage is segmented, partitioned, complete in many fundamental respects. It is numerical, for those inclined to keep a mental score card, and it is 'objective'. Any ambiguity is merely in the process—was the umpire right? Was the ball (there usually is one) in or out? The drama may concern accident, injury and illness, together with the vagaries of selection and player transfer, all of which can be interpreted as having psychological components of particular relevance to the male world. This contrasts strongly with the never-ending interweaving emotional narrative of soaps, which mirrors domestic work. Uncoincidentally, as Ang points out, one of the 'structural characteristics' of soap opera is:

its lack of narrative progress. *Dallas*, like all soap operas, is a never ending story: contrary to classic narratives, which are typically structured according to the logic of order/disorder/restoration of order, soap opera narratives never reach completion. They represent progress without progression and as such do not offer the prospect of a final denouement, in which all problems are solved. Thus, soap operas are fundamentally anti-utopian: an ending, happy or unhappy, is unimaginable (1990, p. 80).

## CONCLUSION

In the past, Internet technoculture has been constructed as a hostile environment for women, although that is likely to change in some areas as female participation rates continue to climb. Examples of harassment are particularly evident from the early to mid-1990s, however, when the Internet was growing exponentially but was still grossly distorted towards masculine users. Current research into the Internet is likely to indicate masculine and feminine areas (akin to masculine and feminine audiences for films, television and books), but the Internet itself is a much less threatening environment for women than it was.

As well as being a site for gender-based harassment, anonymity on the Internet makes it an unrivalled site for gender-based research—specifically the investigation of what it means to present as female/male. These investigations have been promoted on both formal and informal levels. At the same time, women have been actively encouraged by feminist theory and practice to claim space on the Net.

# 11

## Making sense of being in cyberspace

### Getting connected to cyberspace

The Web, WWW, http, Net, Internet, information superhighway, cyber-space—how do we know what these technocultural terms mean, and how to use them? Further, when journalists coin catchy terms such as the World Wide Wait and the superhypeway, how does this alter our perceptions of what we are doing? Definitions of terms in the academic Internet literature are relatively rare and (in practice) many writers in the field use many of the terms interchangeably. Nonetheless, it is possible to tease out some nuances that are worth addressing, and which constitute a kind of anatomy of Internet technoculture.

The connection technology which 'enables' the individual computer terminal to be a player in the Internet is the modem (*modulator-demodulator*) which converts digital information into data streams suited to general telecommunications channels. Many workplace machines are 'hardwired' via fibre-optic cables, linked into local area networks, and through servers to the Internet. While the server is operational ('up'), these work-based machines have constant online access, both within the online neighbourhood and to the Internet itself.

It is comparatively rare for a domestic machine to be hardwired into a network. Most use a modem to dial-up the network connection. These modem-enabled computers communicate with the Internet via an ISP, usually on a fee-per-connection, or fee-for-service basis. Modems themselves are calibrated according to bits per second (bps) and this figure denotes their capacity. In practice, the number of bps registers in the thousands, so the unit tends to be termed Kbps, or kilobits per second. A 56 Kbps modem is thus theoretically able to transfer 56 000 bps.

This 'can theoretically download at up to 56Kbps, and upload at up to 33.6 Kbps. Unfortunately, because of phone line dynamics, you will never get to connect at the full speed' (Kennedy 1999, p. 33). The larger the K, the greater the capacity—so a 56K modem handles more data, more quickly than one which is 28K. The 'world wide wait' tends to be experienced when an older computer, with a low-capacity modem and slow processor speeds, loads a relatively large document designed by, for and with machines running the most up-to-date hardware and software. Internet technoculture, and multimedia graphics and design, are particularly unforgiving of last season's technology.

Up-to-date computer technology (hardware and software) determines effective Internet access and participation, and obsolescence is a greater issue here than in most other technology sectors. The requirement for leading edge ('bleeding-edge/cutting edge') technology fuels a dynamic of consumption and growth. New hardware comes bundled with the latest operational software to enable use of enhanced computer and communications features. Developers and manufacturers no longer support old software, beyond the provision of upgrades, and upgrades ultimately require greater computing capacity, driving the acquisition of new hardware. Thus the cycle of replacement and obsolescence dictates that few computers are generally useful for accessing Internet technoculture after about three years, and as their end-date approaches so the world wide wait becomes more tedious and frustrating. (Obsolete Internet computers may be more than adequate as unconnected games machines, typing tutors, word processors, and CD-ROM readers, but full-service interactivity demands near-current technology.)

## SOME INTERNET DEFINITIONS

Kitchin argues that cyberspace can be constructed as three different domains: 'the Internet, intranets and virtual reality. While the Internet and intranets are closely related, graphical virtual reality technologies have a different history and it is only in recent years that they have started to converge with communication media' (1998, p. 2).

The Internet is an interlocking, interweaving network of networks, interconnecting all the computers involved in each network. Insofar as there is a term for the overall network that interconnects all on-line computers, that name is 'the Internet', and the definition might be 'the interconnected computer network'. In theory, the Internet is the 'generally accessible' computer network. Thus 'the Internet' might exclude some areas of the Net that are not so accessible; these are primarily the proprietary networks—AOL, for example, or Virgin Net or Telstra Big Pond. Proprietary environments have specialised sections and services only available to subscribers. Thus the 'Net' might be the term used to refer to the totality of networks—the Internet and the proprietary services. In fact, the Net is often used as if it were 'net', a contraction of Internet. I tend to use the two terms as if they were interchangeable, and specify any particular reference to proprietary services.

'The Internet is not one networked space but consists of several separate but interconnected networked spaces (each consisting of thousands of individual networks), all linked through common communication protocols (ways of exchanging information)' (Kitchin 1998, p. 3). Using a computer, modem and a telephone, people can connect into a network (via an ISP) and through the network into the Internet. Once on the Internet, individual computers can be used as if they were the remote terminals of other distant machines—reading and copying files, for instance, and downloading information and images.

Email and bulletin boards allow some personal interactivity, sending messages in private communication (email) or posting them in comparatively public space where individuals have to choose to access the information (the bulletin board). Most mail systems allow files to be attached to the plain text message, thus enabling images and documents to be transferred from person to person. Usenet 'is a particular example of a collection of newslists that is distributed across more than one bulletin board so that people around the world can contribute' (Kitchin 1998, p. 5; and see Fabrikant case study, below).

The World Wide Web, Wallace (1999) argues, is the publishing arm of the Internet. It operates as the library, the encyclopaedia and as the display window for corporations, organisations, businesses and individuals. The WWW is that part of the Internet accessible through a browser (Netscape Navigator, Microsoft Internet Explorer) and offers multimedia data stored as hypertext—documents containing links through to other information. Javascript allows programmes to be run and downloaded across the Web—thus www.javagameplay.com is a popular site for many primary school aged boys, and has up-to-date versions of the early PacMan/Space Invader games. Higher-powered machines and greater capacity networks allow links to Web radio, Web television and other sound/image sequences.

Interactivity may (or may not) be built into WWW addresses, but many of the Websites—specific locations within the WWW, usually designated by their own URL (or uniform resource locator) and accessible using a search engine—include advertising which helps pay for/ensure a profit from hits on the site. The 'click rate', the rate of visits to the Website per hour/day/week/month, is increasingly used by advertisers to gauge the value of their Internet presence, and helps determine the advertising rate. The 'click-through rate' is the percentage of visitors to the Website who click the advertisement to go through to the next level, to access the information advertised with the button, banner, etc. The price of advertising on an individual Website may relate to (for example) a cost per thousand hits. As with other commercial media, more prestigious Websites that attract more affluent/desirable 'targets' cost more per hit than less well-known sites. The http (hypertext transfer protocol) software also enables the use of 'cookies' to keep track of visits to Websites, and allows repeat visitors to be identified through their Web browser/search engine.

Real-time interaction with other people, rather than with information or data stored on remote servers, is available through chat services—IRC. Interaction is through text and icons, called emoticons (see Table 11.1) because they allow the expression of emotion using an icon. (My computer, for example, automatically transforms colon/bracket ':)' and colon/dash/bracket ':-)' to ☺). Conversations are constructed using text and emoticons in a 'read and respond' format that allows the build-up of a reciprocal exchange.

**Table 11.1 Some common emoticons**

| :-) | smile | X= | fingers crossed |
|---|---|---|---|
| :>) | happy | {} | hugging |
| 0:-) | angel | :* | kissing |
| }:-) | devil | @}–'---,--- | a rose |
| :-D | laughing | \o/ | hallelujah |
| :-P | sticking out tongue | $-) | greedy |
| ;-) | wink, mischievous | :-I | grim |
| :-o, :O | Wow!, shock | :-II | anger |
| :8) | pig | :-( | sad |
| X-) | I see nothing | :`-( | crying |
| :-X | I'll say nothing | :>( | unhappy |
| %*@:-( | hungover | .oO | thinking |

*Source*: Adapted from Kitchin (1998, p. 7) and Kennedy (1999, p. 458)

MUDs are Multiple User Domains, textual virtual environments—
with MOOs (Multiple Object-Oriented) as a specialised MUD subset.
According to Kitchin, MUDs:

> Provide a themed context for the interactions between people
> . . . Whereas a MUD has been hard programmed to contain
> certain features, which would be textually described to a person
> entering a room, MOOs allow participants to alter and create
> environments and to assign meanings and values to objects,
> which are then stored in a large database for future use . . . The
> emergence and popularity of MUDs has led some commen-
> tators [Poster 1995] to argue that these virtual environments
> form new cultural spaces (1998, p. 7).

In comparison with the open access architecture of the Internet,
Intranets (Kitchen's (1998) second domain) are private networks—
offering equivalent features to the Internet—operated and maintained
by companies and organisations for the exclusive use of members and
authorised users. Universities will maintain an Intranet with separate
academic and student areas, using email and bulletin boards to talk across
the division. Such an Intranet might allow access to online lecture notes
and unit Websites, and searches of the library holdings, for example,
without allowing access to student records or private addresses.

Virtual reality (VR) technocultures immerse users in a computer-
generated environment that responds to their moves or actions, rather
like the 3-D gaming platforms of Nintendo, Sega and Sony Playstation.
Kitchin comments that, although at present VR 'is mainly visual, developers soon hope to be able to fully include sound and touch. The aim is
to create another world inside the computer where the experiences are
the same as in the real world [Stone 1991]; to make "cyberspace into a
place" [Lajoie 1996, p. 155]' (1998, p. 8).

## A TAXONOMY OF CYBERSPACE?

How do we relate to the Internet? This question is begged by repeated
discussions of Internet culture, Internet communications and information and Internet communities as all being 'the Internet'. Effectively,
these entities can be constructed as elements of Internet technoculture,
or as separate Internet technocultures. It is a long time since media

studies and popular culture commentators have discussed 'broadcasting' generically because concern for the specifics of genred broadcasting (both in television and radio) have rendered generalised discussion ridiculously global and oversimplified. In broadcasting, we talk about television and radio as if they were (since they are) significantly different. We recognise that the production values for soap opera, drama, sport, news and current affairs and light entertainment are dissimilar. It is simplistic to ask 'how do we relate to the Internet?' because, when we think about it, we relate differently to a range of Internet technocultures depending upon what we want to achieve, and how we wish to do that. We have varied motivations, and an array of reasons, for approaching these technocultures—including information, entertainment, business and community needs.

Faced with the cacophony which is Internet technoculture today— let alone the projected manifestation of the Internet tomorrow—we are forced to accept that this technoculture has the potential to mimic the features of all media and genres previous, and more. It operates as an information resource, as a one-to-one discrete (or niche) medium and as a mass medium. The Internet can be seen as private and/or public cultural space. Within these categories it can (or has the potential to) work in audio, video, audiovisual, text and data.

Wallace (1999, pp. 4–9) suggests a 'taxonomy' in terms of differentiating between seven different online environment 'types'. These types could also be conceived of as technocultures. These are: (1) the World Wide Web; (2) email; (3) the asynchronous discussion forum; (4) synchronous chats; (5) MUDs and MOOs; (6) metaworlds (multimedia graphical versions of MUDs—another term for VR); and, finally, (7) live interactive video and voice. Wallace's interest is in the psychology of Internet use and her view is that individual behaviour on the Net is affected by three key factors: the degree of anonymity; the presence or absence of a group moderator; and the reasons people have for their interactions in different Net environments. I find Wallace's determinants of behaviour useful and interesting, but I prefer instead to look at 'modes of interaction'.

The Internet offers a variety of degrees of interactivity within technocultural contexts from simple access (consumption) to full content creation (production) as part of the communication exchange. Arguably, the clearest distinctions occur between (1) information access and retrieval, (2) private interactive communication with individuals or small groups and (3) public interactions.

Cyberspace can be constructed as the conceptual domain within which Internet interactions take place. If the Internet is the equivalent of the physiological brain—with technological hardware equivalent to neurons, synapses, cells, neurotransmitters and the like—cyberspace is the technocultural equivalent of the mind. The sameness of and/or difference between the human 'mind' and the human 'brain' have been debated for centuries. Many issues raised in the philosophy of mind/brain are overtly canvassed in cyber-theory. The idea of the mind—as the ghost in the machine—offers a ready metaphor for the variety, complexity, ferocity and compulsiveness of cyberspace, where the effects of interactivity seem so much greater than the sum of the constituent parts. Further, cyber-culture is the new locale for society to explore the age-old concerns relating to appearance and reality. Utopia, for some, is not an answer for these questions, but an opportunity to revisit them in a different way.

The subjective perception of cyberspace raises the issue of place in a new way. Morley and Robins credit Massey as arguing: 'that places should no longer be seen as internally homogeneous, bounded areas, but as "spaces of interaction" in which local identities are constructed out of resources (both material and symbolic) which may well not be at all local in their origin, but are none the less "authentic" for all that' (1995, p. 128). If this perspective is accepted, then it is no longer the place, but the space of interaction, that is the central issue in the creation of community and culture. These spaces can be determined socially, technologically, temporally and in terms of other dimensions. However, the possibility is left open that identity within this context is constructed from materials locally available to the 'space', and that community might be similarly constructed. Watson comments that 'an individual's perceived degree of intimacy [in online community] is largely determinant of the individual's support for use of the community metaphor' (1997, p. 109). What is community for one person may simply be online chat for someone else, but this perception is likely to relate more to an individual's attitude to the interaction than to the information exchanged in the communication.

So how is communication implicated in community and in technoculture? For communication to be relevant to all parties, it has to address issues of shared interest and concern. For some, communication is the essential glue of community. Watson states the point succinctly: 'Without ongoing communication among its participants, a community dissolves. Communication is therefore vital to communities both online and off'

(1997, p. 104). Shawn Wilbur (who edits *Voices From the Net*, and who maintains Postmodern Culture MOO) cautions against the quick adoption of key terms, however: 'It is too easy to log into an online chat system and imagine that it is just like wandering into a local bar. It is too easy to log in and imagine that it is all make-believe. It is altogether too easy to enter a virtual world and imagine that this allows us to understand the "real" one' (1997, p. 20).

Howard Rheingold, whose pioneer book *The Virtual Community* mapped out a manifesto for Internet community interactivity, refers to collective knowledge and information in cyberspace as an 'online brain trust' (1993, p. 13) and as a 'computer-assisted groupmind' (1993, p. 111). Chapter 4 of Rheingold's book discusses this phenomenon in some depth, addressing 'the feeling of tapping into this multibrained organism of collective expertise' and the sense of getting 'into groupmind territory, for what you are structuring is a collective memory for many people to communicate with many others' [www.rheingold. com/vc/book/4.html]. Cyberspace offers the possibility of access to the fruits of a shared consciousness—mediated by the interests, attitudes and psychology of the individual accessing the technocultural 'groupmind'.

The prefix 'cyber', according to David Marshall 'has emerged specifically from the more general field of cybernetics. "Cybernetics" comes from the Greek, meaning a self-steering mechanism and was applied to techniques for keeping ships on course during the night watch' (1997, p. 75). These days, 'cyber' is also associated with the digital—effectively referring to digital self-regulating systems. Cyberspace can describe the physical space (related to 'place') within which the modems connect to the telecommunications channels and servers. In this case, the doorways to cyberspace are the terminal, screen and keyboard used by individual cyber-travellers. More frequently, however, cyberspace refers to a conceptual domain, indicating potential and/or temporal space—the space to think, the space to contribute an idea, or to relate to another person. Cyberspace is intellectual and emotional interactional space within a digital realm.

## SCREENING THE SENSES IN CYBERSPACE

When we make sense of cyberspace, we attempt to conceptualise technoculture in a manner that excludes logical, internal contradictions. We build a mental model that allows us to understand what is going on in cyberspace. This sense of 'sense'—the meaning of 'making sense'—is a different use of the word 'sense' from the one employed when we discuss the five senses: sight, hearing, smell, taste and touch. These five senses are the means by which we interact with the (RL) physical world and collect data. From this physical data we 'make sense', psychologically, of our environment and our emotions. Our senses are central to interactivity (and to the establishment of identity and uniqueness) in RL. According to some definitions, the use of our senses offers a key difference between VL and RL, since VL is a two-dimensional environment in comparison to RL. Nonetheless, we still need to 'make sense' of VL.

One of the difficulties in discussing issues of sense-making, perception, space and screens is that—along with feeling—these terms have a variety of meanings and uses. This variety of meanings is an indicator of nuance and complexity, and is an expression of the ambiguity that characterises concepts relating to the Internet. 'Perception' describes both the mechanics of the work done by the senses, and also the psychological processes through which we arrive at understanding. Whether we perceive ourselves as part of a community or not, whether we see ourselves as more truly 'authentic' in cyberspace or not, these perspectives relate to self-knowledge, and to ways of interacting with others. Our experience of authenticity in RL and VL locales is partly related to our willingness to be circumscribed by our physical environment of a/s/l—age, sex, location (as in RL)—and a sense of whether we have succeeded or not in genuine communication (in either locale).

The screen at the edge of cyberspace—the point at which the hardware and software interact with the warmware/wetware (you and me)—also screens the individual from the contents of cyberspace, and its other users. Baudrillard explored 'screen' theory early in the 1980s, when personal computers were available to the very few, and networked computers were not part of the story. The networks he addresses in terms of 'today the scene and the mirror no longer exist; instead, there is a screen and network' (Baudrillard 1983, p. 126) are those of television: 'the television being the ultimate and perfect object for this new era' (1983, p. 127). Many media studies theories of the screen, like Baudrillard's, apply to cyberspace as well as to film and television. Cyberspace, however, introduces new technocultures, new theories and new experiences to theorise about.

Baudrillard offers an apocalyptic vision of a 'problem' of television and the control screen, similar in many respects to moral panic concerns currently circulating about cyberspace:

> this electronic 'encephalization' and miniaturization of circuits and energy, this transistorization of the environment, relegates to total uselessness, desuetude and almost obscenity all that used to fill the scene of our lives. It is well known how the simple presence of the television changes the rest of the habitat into a kind of archaic envelope, a vestige of human relations whose very survival remains perplexing. As soon as this scene is no longer haunted by its actors and their fantasies, as soon as behaviour is crystallized on certain screens and operational terminals, what's left appears only as a large useless body, deserted and condemned (Baudrillard 1983, p. 129).

Whereas television has come to be seen by some theorists as a focus of domestic life (Morley 1986; Holmes 1997), the use of the computer and the computer game screens out the domestic, allowing the individual to be connected psychologically to people who are physically distant, while constructing a psychological distance from those who are physically present. Television—and the computer screen—can be conceptualised as technocultural media through which the dynamics of the household are communicated to its members, and to those outside. These are the dynamics of who lets whom use what, and who says what about which programme material outside the household's boundaries. Screens also provide a way in which the public sphere is introduced to the household. This dynamic is the paradoxical two-way exchange of the screen, a permeable boundary between the inside and the outside, public/private.

British academic Shaun Moores sums up postmodern screen theory from Meyrowitz (1985) onwards:

> Clearly, domestic TV consumption is a double-edged phenomenon. It involves audio-visual messages entering into the home from a distance . . . but at the same time, it is possible to conceive of television as a communications technology that 'takes us elsewhere'. Of course, we are not being transported literally. Viewers remain physically rooted in the domestic realm. Rather these 'excursions' are acts of the imagination . . . The screen brings far away settings and happenings within our sensory grasp— mediating private and public, and inviting identification with a

range of electronic image spaces. TV . . . contributes to reshaping the imaginative geography of culture and community (Moores 1996, p. 54).

Moores' insights apply equally to computer technocultures.

Baudrillard and Holmes both believe that television threatens the public sphere, and this has been discussed in Chapters 7 and 9. Nonetheless, Baudrillard argues that private space is also lost, simultaneously with the loss of public space: 'the one is no longer a spectacle, the other no longer a secret' (1983, p. 130). Baudrillard suggests here that the private has become an essential concern of the mass media while the whole world of communication has invaded the domestic realm; the screen is a conduit for anything and everything. In addition to Baudrillard's concern with the 'obscenity' of the private becoming public, is his idea of wholesale communication as the 'pornography of the universe, useless, excessive, just like the sexual close-up in a porno film' (1983, p. 130). Clearly, at the point at which these words were written, Baudrillard had yet to experience the intimacy of online technoculture!

## FEELING YOUR WAY ON THE INTERNET

Feeling, in terms of the sense of touch, is keyboard/joystick/mouse-driven at our point of access to cyberspace. Once in cyberspace, however, feelings (in the sense of experiencing emotions, or connectedness, or empathy) can be very strong. We refer to the 'feeling' components of our experience of technoculture to judge the authenticity of our interactions in cyberspace. We may feel these interactions to be genuine communication, or a genuine experience of community, or to be somehow lacking. Differences in our perceptions reflect our different characters, and emotional emphases.

Wilbur addresses the 'feeling' component of the Net when he comments: 'For those who doubt the possibility of online intimacy, I can only speak of . . . hours sitting at my keyboard with tears streaming down my face, or convulsed with laughter' (1997, p. 18). One of the many interesting things about interacting in cyberspace is that, while feelings can arise from social interactions, they are less inhibited in the technocultural setting than they may have been face to face. Wilbur may feel much more able to cry and laugh at his keyboard than in a 'normal' social exchange. The freedom to express feelings without the inhibitions of having other people present may account for some of the intensity of experience in cyberspace.

Wilbur also touches upon the conundrum of solo/connected: 'The strangely solitary work that many CMC researchers are engaged in, sitting alone at their computers, but surrounded by a global multitude' (1997, p. 6). The quality of individual participation in cyberspace is hard to define and (given that it is so individual and spatially private) is also expressive of individual difference. Students of mine who are keen members of online communities suspect that those who doubt the existence of community in VL have never invested emotionally or psychologically in online technoculture; they have allowed the screen to be a barrier rather than a conduit (Green 1999). Thus the existence of online community may be as much a function of the individual engaging in the communication as it is a function of the community with which the individual is engaged.

Cyberspace includes many disturbing, troubling, horrific and exploitative images, photographs and videos. These can sometimes make the Internet a dangerous place to be—a source of psychological threat. Troubling content on the Internet can be disturbing because it is a window upon aspects of humanity—one's own humanity—usually concealed in daily life. Apart from pornography, the Internet includes expressions of hate, rage and fear and images of death, disease, genocide and torture. Also disturbing is the unsettling knowledge that this techno-cultural content is rarely stumbled across entirely by accident; the user is implicated in triggering their own unease—what you find tends to be a reflection of what you look for. Surfers may also find themselves staying at a difficult site longer than required to register its troubling content—fascinated by the image, or by the effect of the image upon them.

It is possible to construct the widespread expression and consumption of challenging images as in some way cathartic. Wilbur suggests that 'there is some sort of attempt at self-therapy work going on "behind" the plane of the computer screen' (1997, p. 12). Psychoanalysis suggests that the 'repressed' rises to consciousness in a variety of forms and cannot be indefinitely held at bay. Cyberspace technoculture may offer one of a variety of ways—alongside psychotherapy, for instance—to deal with hidden aspects of human consciousness. Organisations such as The International Society for Mental Health Online [www.ismho.org] and journals such as *CyberPsychology and Behavior* address the relevance of cyberspace to facilitate integration of different elements of an individual's psyche.

## HATE ON THE NET

The subject of online hatred is usually addressed in terms of fascist and racist Websites; nonetheless, I am considering it in the context of a case study of individual hatred. Alan Aycock and Norman Buchignani document the obsessive tale of Valery Fabrikant, 'who murdered four persons and wounded a fifth at Concordia University in Montreal, Canada in late summer 1992' (1995, pp. 184–231). Fabrikant's hatred for his colleagues was grounded in his perception that his work was unfairly appropriated by others, that he did not get the recognition that was his due, and that he was being denied tenure because of a conspiracy between his faculty and the administration. 'It was his contention that he had been coerced by promises of tenure into permitting colleagues who had not contributed to his research to share authorship of his scientific papers.' Five days before a deadline when he might have been jailed for contempt of court, Fabrikant emailed more than 40 people the details of his failed attempt at tenure and the subsequent legal suit he had filed which (he believed) was about to land him in jail. People who responded, asking for more information, were sent a 25 000 word dossier. One of these dossiers was then posted to a Usenet newsgroup on sci.research.careers (science research careers).

Much of Aycock and Buchignani's paper documents the impact of the posting on newsgroup members in the light of its aftermath (Fabrikant's killing of four people). Although email was used by Fabrikant to express his hatred of the system he blamed for failing to promote him, there is no sense that the posting was itself connected in any way with his subsequent murderous actions. It appears to have been incidental to the escalation of Fabrikant's loss of control. In principle, Fabrikant might have been using the newsgroup simply to disperse his accusations throughout the academic community, and embarrass his superiors. Part of the paradoxical effect of the postings, however, was that, long after Fabrikant himself had been removed from the discussion, his material and his self-justifications continued to circulate and be debated. Nonetheless, extreme hatred (once identified as such) becomes almost an embarrassment, requiring defusion. As one wag remarked: 'Anyone want to guess how many slimeballs analysed the situation and decided that what all of this means is that Concordia now has several open billets for tenure track faculty?' (Aycock & Buchignani 1995, p. 223).

There are other instances of technocultural-mediated hatred. Moral panics around Internet content tend to concern the corruption of minors by pornography, but sometimes panics are triggered by the proposition that the Internet teaches users to hate. This allegation surfaced in the discussion of the horrific killings at Columbine High School (Colorado USA), in April 1999, when two senior students killed twelve of their fellows, and a teacher, before taking their own lives. Wallace analyses the circumstances:

> One of the shooters had built a Website filled with messages of hate and rage, and also instructions on bomb building . . . the media carried stories that attempted to assign blame and the Internet was mentioned frequently as a root cause . . . Their Internet access may have played some role; if they were visiting other hate sites, for example, they may have experienced some corroboration and support for their extreme views. Nevertheless, it soon became clear that the two students had a history of problems and the Internet appeared to be an outlet for their rage, rather than a cause (Wallace 1999, pp. 247–8).

Once again, Internet technoculture is located as boundary space—a frontier where (almost) anything can happen and which, as with any good moral panic, 'threatens the fabric of society as we know it'.

## PANICKING ABOUT MORALITY

Just because society is in the midst of a moral panic regarding Internet content, it is not necessarily the case that there is nothing moral to panic about. Keith Tester, a British academic specialising in social theory, has examined 'what it means to be moral in contemporary social and cultural life' (1997, back cover). His thesis makes somewhat challenging reading and he suggests we are morally culpable as 'consumer imperialists', accessing technological and information resources that most of the world will never be able to share. We are 'in touch' with events and happenings around the globe. We consume images produced for us in, and by, other national spheres. We have knowledge of all kinds of horrors, trauma and exploitation, but do we have a response? Is a response possible, and—if so—how should we respond?

To some extent, this problem was posed (in a less challenging form) by Ian Reinecke (1987, p. 21), quoting Arnoldo Ramos, who was addressing a 1984 forum of mainly American citizens when he told them that they were 'the best-educated generation in history, with access to an unprecedented amount of information. Yet their capacity for action was apparently less than almost any other group who had lived on earth' (1997, p. 21). Even the most information-rich members of Ramos' 1984 audience are unlikely to have had more access to information than do the readers of this book, yet has the exposure to more information triggered a moral response in terms of action? Reinecke's analysis of the situation was more optimistic than Tester's. He suggested that if information were produced with the 'public good' in mind, rather than simply to make a profit, then different responses might result, with different kinds of effects. Somehow, the information might be provided which would power activity.

What is our relationship with events about which we are aware, but in which we are essentially inactive? Tester (1997, pp. 3–5) suggests, using Jaspers, that there are four levels of guilt, three of which arguably apply to us:

- Criminal guilt (not usually applied to us).
- Political liability (we are liable for our acquiescence in political systems that 'allow' atrocities to be perpetrated).
- Moral guilt (this is where individual people 'went right on with their activities, undisturbed in their social life and amusements, as if nothing had happened. That is moral guilt' (Jaspers 1947, p. 73)). (The use of 'as if' indicates an acceptance that something 'momentous' has happened and a decision has been taken to go on as if it has not.)
- Metaphysical guilt arises from the knowledge that we are survivors of something which others have failed to survive; 'if I survive where the other is killed, I know from a voice within myself: I am guilty of still being alive' (Jaspers 1947, p. 71).

Further, it is 'metaphysical guilt when I propose that the victims of the genocide are of no consequence to me; when I say that neither my nation nor I have any interest in them' (Tester 1997, p. 8).

Tester offers no easy answers; in many respects, he offers no answers at all. Worse, Tester suggests (quoting Baudrillard 1994, p. 67) that genocide ('g' and 'G'), violence, depravity and chaos is raw material provided by poorer countries to be commodified by/for the rich to provide 'the moving spectacle of our own efforts to alleviate it' (1997, pp. 16–17). Tester employs Georg Simmel's (1991) classic analysis of the function of money to explain one way in which the West's response to traumatic information about atrocities is to provide cash: 'Money divides even as it connects, connects even as it divides . . . All commodified moral relationships tend to become identical in so far as they involve an emphasis upon the donation of money.' The commodification metaphor is extended further, with Tester addressing examples of horror as 'brands': 'The particularity of any given horror would be lost since it would become little more than a contingent supplier of the occasion of compassion, a supplier which would probably be replaced with an alternative, temporarily more engaging product when boredom set in with this brand' (1997, pp. 11–13).

Tester moves from discussion of individuals and their guilt to a discussion of social institutions. He suggests (1997, p. 7) that, while individuals might bear the moral conscience of the world, it is institutions that have become the moral agents (i.e., actors) in the world: 'Politics has been institutionalised so that it is now about little more than resource allocation and efficiency; thanks to the co-existence of individual moral conscience with institutionalised action, conscience ceases to be political as such and instead becomes a singular voice . . . [making] more or less incoherent personal demands.' The individual can believe themself quite guiltless, because the only true and appropriate moral force in the world is located in institutions (1997, p. 11). This perspective allows a 'myth of guiltlessness', 'a story we tell ourselves in order to be able to make sense of our lives in the world. We tell ourselves that none of it is our fault; we did nothing except keep our heads down and try to muddle through in our personal lives' (1997, p. 9).

One area problematised in Tester's discussion is the role of 'information' as opposed to 'storytelling'. Storytelling allows subjective communication of things and events 'with a certain immediacy' (1997, p. 14). Information, on the other hand, needs to be verified and quantified, so need not be immediately believed—instead it requires verification, validation, quantification. It requires a 'cynical' analysis of the who, what, when, why, where and how of the information communicated:

Perhaps then we are left indifferent because the dominance of information implies not a quest for the truth but an avoidance of the truth through the piling up of radical cynicism. In this way all the books and broadcasts which give the information might actually be undermining the very possibility that they will make any of the kind of difference that their producers undoubtedly intend that they will. Indifference emerges precisely because there is nothing that can make a difference (1997, p. 15).

Nonetheless, storytelling is a major project of Hollywood and other national cinema and television institutions. The fictionalisation of experience to create 'good stories', and the digital manipulation of images to create 'believable fiction', allow/require stories to be analysed cynically. Tester's aim in raising these issues is to ask what atrocities mean to people like us, who consume them. (He could be asking equivalent questions of the consumption of pornography; the existence of hate sites; images of natural disaster; close-ups of grief, loss, poverty and starvation.) We consume these narratives in all sorts of technocultural contexts—we read them, we see them on television, we watch them in the cinema and we access information (and stories) on the Internet. We talk about online community and the global village. What is our community relationship with those whose images, information and trauma are communicated to us; those who are communicated about, but who are often not able to communicate globally themselves?

## IS CYBERSPACE BRAIN-CHANGING?

David Porush is an American academic who has made a study of cyber-fiction, and who believes that cyber-communication and associated technocultures affect our brains. His argument, expressed in an essay on 'Telepathy: alphabetic consciousness and the age of cyborg illiteracy', is that new thoughts change the structure of our brains, and alter the potential uses for our minds. Porush suggests that 'using different alphabets (or losing the capacity to read the alphabet), even within the lifetime of an individual, is a bit like growing a new brain' (1998, p. 47). Porush's thesis is informed (as much cyber-speculation is) by reference to cyborg fiction. The other plank of his argument rests on the search for a parallel moment in the past which is akin to the introduction of the Internet—'an analogous moment in history when culture found itself in possession of an equally new and revolutionary cybernetic technology . . . for getting thoughts from one mind to another' (1998, p. 46). The technocultural moment Porush identifies is the invention of the first written alphabetic language (ancient Hebrew).

Ancient Hebrew lacks vowels. This has the effect, according to

Porush, of making the acquisition of meaning from a written text into a complex game of hide and seek. As some evidence of this, Porush asks readers to 'decode the following sentence into sensible modern English by supplying the missing vowels: TH VRL CLTR F DS MKS VR XCHNG F BD FLDS N CT F TTL FTH LV ND MRDR. SM S 'J MRT' T RGSM. DS GVS NW MNNG T THR CR' (1998, p. 51). (The answer is at the end of the chapter—one clue: two words are in French.) Whereas reading an English text is a comparatively linear process, Porush argues that deciphering Hebrew is 'a web of cross-referrals and leaps, as words at the end of the excerpt help clarify words at the beginning'. Arguably, each language is a different technoculture.

Porush's view is that, compared with the readers of later alphabets (ones with vowels), the reader of Hebrew has the following cognitive habits forced upon him/her:

1. contextualisation (continuous searching for, and checking, context);
2. interpretation (dealing with ambiguity) and tolerance of suspense (deferral);
3. right-brain processing (global, visuo-spatial, greater connection of data and emotion, ability to detect and differentiate nuances, and recognition of objects in different configurations);
4. abstraction/metaphorisation (the literal and the abstract are more linked, as are the literal and the metaphoric and symbolic);
5. multivalence/deconstruction (making sense and multiple meanings within the gaps); and
6. resistance to authority.

You may disagree with Porush that these are likely consequences of being literate in Hebrew. Even so, these may be possible consequences. Equivalent possibilities may also arise from human interaction within cyberspatial technoculture. If so, human encounters in cyberspace may eventually alter people's perceptions, and their ways of relating, as a result of reflecting new experiences and expertise gleaned from the online environment.

Porush argues that, when we compare the post-alphabetic society with that which was pre-alphabetic, the metaphysics of the new consciousness leads to cognitive, sociological, epistemological and meta-physical changes. He also goes on to link experience of the Hebrew language with experience of the postmodern. Porush sums up his excursion into a history of Hebrew by asserting that 'our culture recognises the massive reorganisation [by VL] of human relations to mind, self, others, society at large, and even transcendental questions . . . does cyberspace evolve and to which new metaphysics does it lead?' (Porush 1998, pp. 59–60).

The first world may already be moving into a post-literate phase, as indicated by the increasing use of pictographic icons (in the Windows environment, for example), the displacement of print by film, television and (computer-mediated) game-playing, and the increasing use of computer simulations for training. In the same way that the 'screen' has been identified as a two-way technology, revealing and concealing, so the possibility exists that exposure to cyberspace is two-way brain-changing. Such a perspective suggests that as we create the technoculture of cyberspace in VL, so cyberspace may change our thinking and our social and cultural organisation in RL.

The final chapter takes up this theme, examining different social and cultural dimensions to modern and postmodern societies.

## CONCLUSION

Cyberspace is essentially paradoxical—implicit in its name: a space without place accessed by a screen, which is a two-way conduit. The screen reveals the Net to the individual, but also conceals its nature from him/her. This tension indicates the complexity and ambiguity of our internal/external relationships. Our physiological experience of the outside world relates in a paradoxical way to our psychological experience of our inner world. Authenticity of experience, for example, can refer to either a physical or psychological engagement with technoculture.

Experience is not fleeting, however, in that physiological studies of the brain indicate repeated experiences have both a psychological dimension and a physiological one. The more often we do something, the more the brain is patterned to make it easier for us to perform that action, or that thought process. Before we leave this chapter, here is the solution to Porush's attempt to make English speakers think in Hebrew: 'THe ViRaL CuLTuRe oF aiDS MaKeS eVeRy eXCHaNGe oF BoDy FLuiDS aN aCT oF ToTaL FaiTH, LoVe, aND MuRDeR. SoMe Say "Je MoRT" aT oRGaSM. aiDS GiVeS NeW MeaNiNG To THeiR CRy.' Did unravelling this make your brain grow differently, or make the science, art and technoculture of reading any more complex or ambiguous?

# 12

# TECHNOCULTURE AND SOCIAL
# ORGANISATION

## WORK AND GENDER IN THE INFORMATION SOCIETY

Social discontinuities between premodern, modern and postmodern societies are reflected in their technocultures, and in gender roles available to their members. In pre-industrial societies, child-rearing post-weaning was the traditional role of grandparents (mainly grandmothers, but with grandfathers duly teaching masculine behaviours). Young mothers—carrying only their youngest baby—worked in cultivation and cottage industries, usually cooperatively, assisted by the older girls. Men typically spent their time in hunting, gambling, building and herding. Occupational divisions, although gendered, lacked the isolation, specialisation and rigidity that characterise work in the modern world.

The economic prosperity of industrialisation permitted a society in which a middle-class working man was, eventually (post-World War II), paid enough to support him and his family. A middle-class woman resigned her job upon marriage and many young females assigned themselves exclusively to unpaid home duties and socially supported 'good works'. The housewife (a late nineteenth- and early to mid-twentieth-century innovation) was socialised to espouse a house because the productive work of men, in factories and offices, would otherwise be compromised by all the messy jobs of daily life (Oakley 1974). This situation was exacerbated by social changes between the two world wars that largely ended the availability of full-time paid domestic help. At the height of the housewife era (which was also the cusp of the industrial and information ages), the 'career girl' could not also be a wife or mother, and employers were required to remove married women from the formal workforce. Social distinctions in modern society did not tolerate ambiguity. The single mother gave her child up for adoption, the unhappy marriage rarely ended in divorce: married was married, single was single. Category boundaries were only negotiable by the immensely strong, or the immensely wealthy (usually people had to be both). The dynamic disjointedness that concurs with our individual experience of contemporary community in the information age, however, is essentially postmodern. 'Fragments'—divorcees, single-parent families, de facto relationships, same-sex couples, post-menopause babies, double/triple shifts, part-time work, and employment for retirees—all speak of the postmodern condition. They also speak of telecommuting, work at home and remote parenting—much of this enabled and facilitated by good communications systems that combine to form a pervasive, postmodern technoculture.

## Is the postmodern female?

Women are arguably the group in western culture most versed in the politics of resistance and renegotiation, and the women's movement has achieved some success in the fight against the peripheralisation of women's issues. Even so, women tend to be beset by competing demands as part-time/full-time workers in both the domestic (unpaid) and the national (paid) economies. In juggling a number of different, and increasingly simultaneous, responsibilities, women are living fragmented postmodern lives—and are surviving the stresses that accompany and amplify these circumstances. Women's unpaid and undervalued labour is often the key to the effective contribution of others—especially their partners and children—but there are few external resources to support them, apart from other women friends and relatives. 'Unpaid work makes it possible for paid workers to produce and earn, and for children to grow and learn', argues Anne Else (1996), who also considers that:

> unpaid work is like a huge transparent trampoline. Without its resilience and flexibility, no-one can even get off the ground into paid work, let alone recover every time they crash back down. It's the invisible infrastructure which keeps everything else going—a vast springboard-cum-safety-net, spread beneath the formal economy (Else, cited without page numbers in Tolerton 1996, p. 66).

There are reasons to believe that women are particularly well equipped to reconcile these multiple demands, and that the very networks of responsibility in women's lives which compete for attention also offer some protection against the stresses they engender, since women enter into reciprocal obligations of support and encouragement. Each gift of unpaid work to support another can be viewed as an investment in 'social capital' (Winter 2000). In times of plenty, there are reserves of support and care available to sustain men, women and children. Ours are not times of plenty, however, and many women can no longer afford to donate their labour to unwaged causes. The slack has disappeared from the system; too many people need to draw on the social capital and there are not enough people with the time, energy and resources to make deposits to cover the withdrawals.

Circumstances facing women in paid employment at the start of the third millennium differ significantly from those in which the second-wave feminists of the 1970s demanded equal pay, affordable child care and an end to sex discrimination. For some (possibly many) of the 1970s working women, the housewife-mothers of the 1950s were able to support their working/workforce daughters with child care for their grandchildren and other assistance. These days, the support provided historically by the extended family for the working mother has tailed off—sometimes due to the geographical distance of mothers, aunts and sisters, but also because women in the extended family are increasingly in paid work themselves. The burgeoning number of childcare places, after-school and vacation programmes, and the advent of family responsibilities leave and family-friendly workplaces are the most obvious signs of the increasing lack of informal supports.

## THE FULL-TIME PART-TIME WOMAN

For some women, a possible strategy for negotiating the near-irreconcilable demands of work, home, family and self is to seek, and to settle for, part-time employment. This solution fits in well with the post-industrial, postmodern lifestyle, and the early wave of women's reintroduction to the paid workforce was marked by a decline in traditional full-time, male ('modern') employment sectors, and a huge jump in the number of casualised, part-time, fragmented jobs for women. Barry Jones offered the following analysis of the US labour market between 1970 and 1980: '13 million new jobs were created in the US and 1.5 million jobs in manufacturing were lost . . . The new jobs are largely part-time, largely non-unionized, largely for females, largely unskilled—with little prospect of advancement, little job satisfaction and poor job security' (Jones 1982, pp. 239–40).

These trends continue to predominate in some countries, especially for the core childrearing years, although the data from the United States indicate that women there may increasingly be working in full-time jobs (30 hours per week) throughout their lives (Baker, 2001).

Figure 12.1 Male/female participation in paid employment in Australia 1947–2000

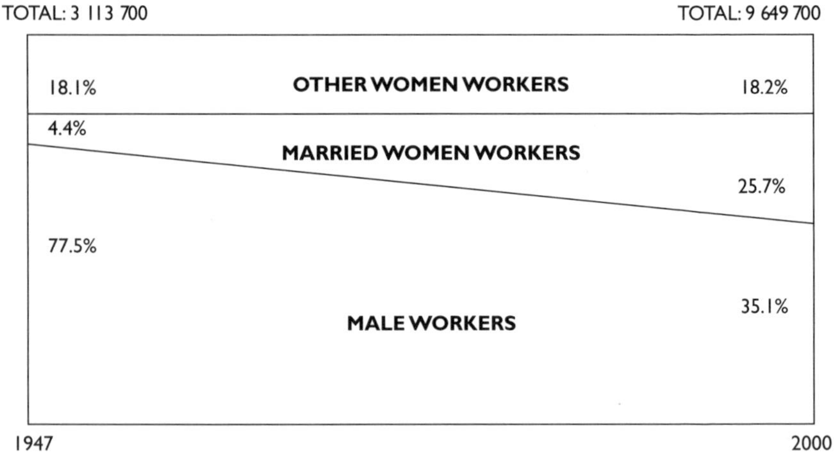

TOTAL: 3 113 700                                              TOTAL: 9 649 700

| 18.1% | OTHER WOMEN WORKERS | 18.2% |
| 4.4% | MARRIED WOMEN WORKERS | |
| | | 25.7% |
| 77.5% | | |
| | MALE WORKERS | 35.1% |

1947                                                                    2000

Source: Jones (1995, p. 134), and Australian Bureau of Statistics data (2000)

The male:female, full-time:part-time dynamic is replicated across a number of national contexts, (see Figure 12.2) although the percentage of employed women who work part time varies significantly. (Statistics in the figure are slightly skewed since 'part time' in Canada and New Zealand is fewer than 30 hours; in Australia it is fewer than 35 hours.)

Life for women in postmodern times, however, is no longer simply the traditional double shift (with Arlie Hochschild (1989) describing unpaid home duties as the second shift, added on after a day in paid work). Hochschild estimates that women work fifteen hours per week longer than men, and 'over a year they worked an extra

Figure 12.2 Part-time employment as a percentage of total employed, by gender, in Australia, New Zealand and Canada 1995

| | Part-time employment | |
| --- | --- | --- |
| | Male | Female |
| Australia | 11.1 | 42.7 |
| New Zealand | 9.3 | 36.1 |
| Canada | 10.6 | 28.2 |

Source: Table created from data sourced in O'Connor, Orloff and Shaver 1999, p. 72, contained in M. Baker 2001, p. 151 (Note: Part-time employment in Australia is less than 35 hours; in New Zealand and Canada is less than 30 hours.)

month of twenty-four hour days' (1989, p. 3). The concept of the double shift has now been expanded through ideas such as 'the parallel shift' (Rakow & Navarro 1993). The lived experience is not only of consecutive responsibilities, but also of simultaneous juggling, with technoculture playing a critical role in this. Home duties at work, work duties at home, sick children in the corner of the office, sent home by childcare or school, while the primary caregiver frantically calls every friend and neighbour they can think of. (Most agencies refuse to provide minders for sick children.) Mirroring this trend of permeable home/work boundaries, both women and men are increasingly likely to take work home in the evenings and at weekends, and middle managers are more likely to work online and off-site in their 'leisure time'.

This fragmented home/work lifestyle is not *prima facie* evidence of female masochism, although it could seem to be such. In a survey of mobile telephone use by nineteen middle-class American women, Rakow and Navarro comment:

All of the husbands work full time, many at jobs that require extensive traveling. Most of the wives who work outside the home do not work full-time or do not work all year round. Their greater responsibility for homes and children make it more likely that they will seek jobs that allow them to be closer to home and give them more time there. Then, their closer proximity to home and their greater presence in the home makes it seem natural that they should assume more responsibility for the domestic . . . [Women try] to exist in their domestic and work worlds simultaneously. They may be the harbingers of a trend for women who are trying to bridge the gap between the domestic and work worlds, women working 'parallel shifts' (Rakow and Navarro 1993, pp. 152–3, citing Rakow 1992).

In short, even in the information society, running a family requires an accessible adult to carry out the work of holding up the 'springboard-cum-safety-net, spread beneath the formal economy'. These pressures are about to worsen. The 'triple shift' is an even more recent concept, coined to describe the situation where women are responsible for their partner and self, their children and their elder family members. As the thirty-something first-time mothers give birth to their firstborn children, they find that their own mothers and fathers (the first, baby boomer, generation of thirty-something parents) are now sixty-something. The stage is set for more and more women to be juggling school and after-school care for the ten-year-old, and holding the reins of social reality for a seventy-something parent.

## THE MODERN MAN

Fortunately for their families and for society, many women are skilled in parallel shifting and never-ending work. Leaving aside theoretical considerations of whether this is nature or nurture, there is ample evidence of these dynamics woven through women's lives. Women are almost always doing at least two things simultaneously, and one of the jobs is likely to be 'never-ending' (see Chapter 10). In contrast to the cyclical and continuing domestic/work chores faced by women, a typical man's working day in urban, western society is much more likely to be compartmentalised. He is more likely to work full time, and to leave home to go to work, and leave work to come home. There are clearer delineations: home is more likely to be a site of leisure for the western man than the woman; and if the man is involved in domestic work, his is more likely to be a second (part-time) shift, rather than a parallel one. The permeable boundary is more likely to see a man take his work home, rather than take his home responsibilities to work.

It is possible to construct men's lives as more typically 'modern', while women's are more 'postmodern'. Theorists of the men's movement speculate that some men pay heavily for their compartmentalised lives, and it may be that women's work (no matter that it is undo-able) at least connects women to each other in a safety net of interdependence. The argument, in simple terms, is that although women work across more fronts and in a more fragmented way, it is the men who appear to be suffering. Evidence for this assertion includes spiralling male suicide rates, and self-destructive habits which have helped widen the gap in life expectancy between men and women: with women benefiting by three-and-a-half years a century ago, to six years now (Biddulph 1994, p. 6).

It may also be that men's mothers, wives, girlfriends, sisters—double- and triple-shifting as they are—have less time and energy to support male relatives as fully as they once did. Full-time female workers on their multiple shifts are less able to look after themselves, and others, and are more likely to need support while being less equipped to provide it. It may be that men require their own crash course in postmodernism—and in using technocultural tools to build networks of acceptance and assistance.

## METAPHOR

In the mid-1980s, Gareth Morgan wrote a ground-breaking book applying some of the principles of postmodern analysis to organisational theory. His book, *Images of Organization*, has since been reissued in a second edition (1997). The flavour of the book can be gleaned from the Contents page, outlining chapter titles from Part II, 'Some images of organization':

Mechanization takes command: organizations as machines
Nature intervenes: organizations as organisms
Learning and self-organization: organizations as brains
Creating social reality: organizations as cultures
Interests, conflicts and power: organizations as political systems
Exploring Plato's cave: organizations as psychic prisons
Unfolding logics of change: organizations as flux and
    transformation
The ugly face: organizations as instruments of domination.

In his conclusion, Morgan talks about these images being metaphors, and the role of metaphor in revealing information to us:

> Metaphors create insight.
> But they also distort.
> They have strengths.
> But they also have limitations.
> In creating ways of seeing they tend to create ways of *not* seeing
> (1997, p. 348).

Hence there can be no single theory or metaphor that gives an all-purpose point of view. There can be no 'correct theory' for structuring everything we do.

When we use metaphor to explain relationships between technology and society, and between cyberspace and technoculture, or to discuss ABC power elites and the biographies of things, these metaphors function in a similar way. They create ways of seeing, and of not seeing. Further, all theory is informed by underlying metaphors, although these metaphors may be implied, rather than stated.

The postmodern use of the metaphor-as-perspective offers multiple possible realities. It also suggests that there is no correct theory: all metaphorical perspectives have something to offer. Meaning and understanding are enriched with a variety of ways of seeing, with different perspectives and through the use of different metaphors. The remainder of this chapter looks at communication, technology and society in terms of the human construction of our daily world. It examines technoculture as refracted—metaphorically—through the lenses of communication, technology and society.

## Technocultural technology

People construct their membership of communities through conversation, and conversation increasingly is technologically mediated. In discussing technology and the construction and destruction of community (as Holmes does implicitly, see Chapter 9), it is the conversational element in the dynamic that is important. Choices are inherent in these conversations, and they reflect technological, economic, educational and gendered dimensions. These dimensions come into play both as part of the conversation, and through community formation and dissolution.

'Conversation' used in this way may be a problematic concept, but it conveys a sense of an individual or group 'speaking', literally or metaphorically, with or without words, to other individuals or groups. This concept of 'conversation' differs from 'communication' in that it involves a personal sphere of influence, and the number of participants remains small enough to allow reciprocal personal exchange.

The experiential nature of interactivity in cyberspace—and communication through the technocultures of the Internet—exposes individuals to ideas and possibilities that are capable of informing the development of new perceptions and perspectives. Tester's discussion of Ferguson (1997, p. 12) offers an image of the commodification and seduction of the Internet as perceived through exposure to numerous sites and chats. These entry points, 'rather than appearing exhaustive, offer a continuously changing point of contact, with the ideally infinite, and therefore uncontainable, commodity world beyond it' (1992, p. 34). Interactivity (rather than the technology that makes interactivity possible) changes people. Nonetheless, technology becomes implicated in interactivity, both in terms of mediated communication and in terms of face-to-face exchanges.

I have speculated previously (Green 1996) that mediated communication may have had the effect of magnifying the current crisis in western masculinity identified by men's movement commentators (e.g., Biddulph 1994). Certainly technology, the industrialisation of society and the creation of a male workforce located in factory/office spaces away from the domestic have been identified by Biddulph as contributing to the phenomenon of 'father hunger', whereby boy children hunger for one-on-one contact with adult males. Biddulph's view is that: 'Father-hunger is perhaps the most important concept in male psychology. It's the starting point for most men in their own journey to health . . . Put another way, to have a demanding job, commute to work in a city and raise sons well is an impossibility. Something has to give' (1994, pp. 26, 100). Wajcman (1991) and Spender (1995) similarly identify technology as a problematic for women. For both the men's and women's movements, then, technology raises issues. It is one of the agents which frustrates or undermines attempts to be more fully rounded and whole in the individual gendered role.

Technology is part of the conversations within communities as to what it is to be male, or female; and what it is for males and females to relate on equitable terms. This book has addressed myth and technology, the nature of technology, change and technology, power and technology and the diffusion and adoption of technology. It has considered the relationship of technology and society and technology and culture, and considered the ways in which technology is domesticated, and in which the domestic is technologised. Information technology is central to the workings of the information age, the knowledge economy, the post-industrial workforce, late capitalism and postmodern culture. While technology is implicit within technoculture, it encodes the priorities and privileges of those who sponsor, develop and market the technologies. Technoculture itself is also a reflection of, and co-created by, the people who use the technologies—as well as those who developed the technologies that make the technocultural possible.

## Technocultural policy

Most nations use some regulatory regimes—local content quotas on television, etc.—to promote the production of cultural materials expressive of that specific society, and to increase the amount of local material available for the construction of a sense of 'national identity'. Such regulation of one specific cultural vision is impossible to enforce in an uncontrolled technocultural environment like cyberspace, but individual nations attempt to monitor and influence the Internet activities of their citizens—and regulate the material held on servers physically located within their geographical jurisdiction.

'Information society' policies to make the Internet available through public libraries and through the education system drive the acquisition of information processing skills and the local production of digital media. These positive policies increase Internet consumption and hothouse the technocultural skills of installation, maintenance and product servicing and development. Even an apparently 'passive' approach, such as leaving things to market forces, is also a policy decision. Any area which involves local or national regulation includes an element of policy decision-making, although the desired policy outcomes are not necessarily produced by the regulatory regime.

A number of western countries have recently embraced the principle of competition as a way of distributing media, communication and information goods and services to the community. Yet attractive consumers are moneyed consumers, and there is a risk that the poor in the community will not be able to afford the market price. Historically, community needs have been recognised by government regulation of the telecommunications and media industries with the imposition of service obligations. Regulation is one way, therefore, of tempering the blunt instrument of market-driven commercial imperatives. Education and public access policies are others.

Information societies have identified their educational system— schools, colleges and universities—as a major locus for technology dissemination. The education system is a key technocultural environment through which students are introduced to applications of digital technology. They learn about the technology, but more importantly they have to use the technology to research the content and to produce the products assessed by teaching staff. In this way, regardless of subject, the learning environment ensures that educational achievement is synonymous with exposure to information and communication technologies. Nonetheless, an information divide still remains between the information rich and the information poor in both national and international contexts, and not all educational institutions have equal access to, or equal facility with, new technology.

People's needs and wants in terms of communications and information are rarely one-dimensional. Demand can be either service- or technology-driven and varies with the individual and their circumstances. It is in understanding these parameters that Sless' (1995) concept of 'communication ecologies within a communication environment' earns its keep. According to Sless (1995, p. 3), taking 'account of the broader communication environment within which specific media and technology are located' involves investigating a number of parameters. Individual people vary according to their:

- opportunities—the full array of communication opportunities which exist in specific ecologies;
- abilities—the abilities people have within these ecologies to use communication opportunities;
- expenditure—the amount of money available to people within particular ecologies to spend on communication; and
- time—the time available to people within specific ecologies to take part in communication activities (1995, p. 7).

The two technoculturally relevant social extremes on a communication ecology continuum are: 'time rich, cash poor' (for example, retired or unemployed people) and 'time poor, cash rich' (for example, full-time managers or professionals). These two extremes both stand to benefit greatly from access to digital information and communication, but for different reasons:

> The former group are more likely to want to access entertainment services which would offer them new ways of *spending* time on newly commodified leisure activities . . . By contrast, for the other, much smaller group of people whose occupations mean that they are exposed to the latest in information technology in their workplace (and who are therefore trained in its use), the new networks may offer new ways of *saving* time—and therefore of becoming more productive (St Clair 1995, p. 17).

Time poor, cash rich people are likely to be able to afford to purchase their own solutions to the challenge of levering their productivity through Internet access. Time rich, cash poor individuals are more likely to be able to access the Internet through libraries, adult education courses and through affordable private provision such as Internet cafes. The time poor, cash poor people are the ones least likely to be able to negotiate access on affordable terms, given the time and money requirements of Internet participation. Such a group is often too busy making ends meet, and too disparate, to mount an effective campaign to have its needs considered in terms of policy development.

Although we have been looking at policy relating to Internet access and services, there is also policy visible in the internal workings of Internet-based communities and discussion groups. For example Baym, in an analysis of an early Usenet newsgroup 'r.a.t.s.' (rec. arts. tv. soaps), discusses the mainly female computer mediated community created through discourse about daytime soap operas. She comments:

> The viewers' relationship with characters, the viewers' understanding of socioemotional experience, and soap opera's narrative structure, in which moments of maximal suspense are always followed by temporal gaps, work together to ensure that fans will use the gaps during and between shows to discuss with one another possible outcomes and possible interpretations of what has been seen (Baym 1995, pp. 142–3).

Regulation in this technocultural community, for example, included elaborate procedures to ensure that those who had seen the next episode of a soap opera under discussion (because of time differences, or differential broadcast patterns) did not spoil the narrative suspense for others who had not. Thus policy dimensions are implicit in the social culture of a group as well as in wider institutional settings.

## TECHNOCULTURAL CULTURE

'Culture' has been used in this book as a term for a socially based context constructed by families/households and wider social systems through the sharing of understandings about themselves, their lives and their communities. It is a dynamic *process*, rather than a *product*, and informs the content and the patterns of our existence. The term 'popular culture' acknowledges that some elements of life are more discretionary than others, and popular culture is what we create when we have a choice in the matter. Pleasure, power and freedom are all involved in the construction of popular culture. Although popular culture is not entirely driven by the media, it does have overtones of 'massification' in that the mass media are an important source of raw material from which popular culture (as opposed to 'folk culture') is constructed. Increasingly, technoculture is a site for popular culture activity, although interactive cyber-culture may also be a site for folk culture.

The creative element of culture makes it a project of some artistry. Although the artists of any culture distil the creative expressions of that culture, there is also a general level of creativity that pervades all areas of life. The creation of popular culture can usefully be conceptualised as an 'artistic activity' that helps develop a fluid space within which self-expression is possible. Gertsakis argues that: 'an expanding national and local heterogeneity that consumes the traditional as inheritance and the contemporary as a place for renegotiating the terms of modernity is the in-between space that carries the burden of culture' (1994, p. 39). This definition links the national/global with the local, and the past with the present. Moreover, in digital terms, it raises the issue of the locale for 'presence' and 'creation' in cyberspace.

As with other projects of popular culture—such as the uses of broadcasting—individual and household processes of Internet consumption are converted to the social process of community building in RL and in VL. Thus we can add dimensions of gender, generation and age to the cyber/space-creating dimensions of RL/VL. Individuals synthesise shared understandings for all these dimensions, constructing a cooperative expression of culture with other people. Whatever culture is experienced within cyberspace—from corporate culture on a dot.com website through to a BDSM community (bondage, discipline and sadomasochism)—it is a culture which concentrates and expresses the characteristics of the group creating the site in a way which is regulated very differently—that is, internally to the group—from cultural regulation in RL. Which is not to say that cyber-communities are unregulated; they create their own regulatory rhythms and mechanisms as part of the project of cultural creation and maintenance.

Cultural production is not a mono-dimensional process. In a world where multiculturalism, biculturalism, ethnicity, race and the cosmopolitan are such vibrant, sometimes challenging, issues, what sort of 'culturalism' does the Internet represent? Whatever the local, national, international, psychological—or maybe psycholocal?—nature of the Internet, it provides challenges of cultural coherence. New multicultural literacies are embedded in technoculture. Few RL experiences are more compelling and eye-opening than visits to other cultures 'on holiday', and the development of friendships with those from different cultural traditions. Such experiences have their equivalents online, and community construction in VL involves these dynamics, and the exploration of similarity and difference.

A small research project with a group of Australians from a variety of cultural backgrounds (Green 1997) indicates that the 'multicultural literacies' meaningful to participants appear to be 'branded' elements of popular culture. To be important components of a cross-cultural experience, the cross-cultural elements and segments had to be well-integrated and often-repeated: learning culture through cappuccinos in an Italian cafe; Thai kickboxing for recreation and fitness; obedience training with a rare breed of Egyptian dog which is traditionally associated with Egyptian deities and only ever given as a gift, never sold. For netizens, online engagement is both a well-integrated and often-repeated activity, and VL operates as an important locale for exposure to cultures which are alternatives to those experienced in RL.

Multiculturalism is never one person's or one group's cultural heritage, no matter how many cultural traditions that heritage draws upon, but necessarily incorporates or responds to multiple cultures. Stratton and Ang position multiculturalism as 'controversial precisely because of its real and perceived (in)compatibility with national unity' (1998, p. 135). Hate sites may provide a refuge for xenophobic monoculturalist nationalists, but they are also an expression of racist/nationalist/totalitarian moral panic. They indicate the potential value of the Internet as a site for cultural exchange. The value of technocultural exchange will increase as the language of the Internet becomes less Anglo-Celtic and more culturally diverse, as the technology achieves more global diffusion and as more non-western nations move online.

Stratton and Ang's article on multiculturalism compares American culture—grounded ideologically in the principles of the Constitution—and Australian culture, which (in theory, at any rate) embraces a diversity of ethnicities. Stratton and Ang argue that both the United States and Australia were 'faced with the problem of how to create a distinctive national identity without having recourse [as settler societies] to a pre-existing distinctive common culture as raw material' (1998, p. 141). America as a 'melting pot' conceptualises race and ethnicity as materials to be 'melted' into a unity:

> For Schlesinger [an American commentator] the persisting (and, alarmingly for him, strengthening) cultural and ethnic differences and divisions that characterise the American social fabric can be conceptualised only negatively, as a residue of the melting process . . . the hyphenated American [e.g. Afro-American] poses a potential danger: the danger that the particular may overwhelm the universal (Stratton & Ang 1998, p. 145).

The argument continues by asserting that, in the United States context, 'universalism and particularism, assimilation and separateness, unity and disunity are constructed as mutually exclusive, oppositional ideological forces with no in-between zone . . . the policy of multiculturalism in Australia can be constructed as an attempt to create such an in-between zone' (1998, p. 147). Stratton and Ang compare this (modern?) construction of the American national project with the (postmodern?) comparatively recent project of multicultural Australia which 'is not only un-ideological (in the sense that it is not predicated on lofty universal ideals and principles, as is American nationalism) but . . . [often boils] down to not much more than the suburban myth of "the car, the family, the garden and a uniformly middle-class"'.

Multiculturalism relates to both the culture of technoculture, and the society of technoculture. The challenge posed by requirements to construct nations from ethnically and racially diverse communities resonates in our discussion of the technoculture phenomenon. Is there an imagined community of the Internet, like that which Benedict Anderson (1991) sees as informing the construction of the nation state?

What is its foundational culture? Does technoculture represent 'the becoming' of a settler society in the virgin and uninhabited realm of cyberspace, or does it 'loom out of an immemorial past' and represent in essence the United States, online? If so, is there the potential for a multi-cultural project to negotiate a wider sense of technoculture? As well as identity *on* the Net—which we have seen as a created and creative problematic—how do we characterise the identity *of* the Net? In part, this book has represented one way in which to tackle these questions.

## TECHNOCULTURAL SOCIETY

Benedikt (1991) conceptualised cyberspace as outer space and called his landmark book *Cyberspace: First Steps*, echoing Neil Armstrong's epoch-changing 'That's one small step for [a] man, one giant leap for mankind'. Given that the first regular human incursions into cyberspace were those of information hunter-gatherers, entering to stalk and to forage, early human activity in this scenario concentrated upon mapping out the terrain. Once this was achieved, cyber-visitors planted areas with wild seed, settled nowhere specifically, took shelter in regular watering spots and moved in patterns and to places that became established over time. In this metaphor, the first settlers constructed, as did Rheingold (1993), 'homesteads on the electronic frontier'. Rheingold's image invokes a settler society, but a settler society communicating in context of comparative isolation, with homesteads separated by space.

We have yet—in general talk, at any rate—to industrialise cyber-space. Apart from science fiction and Gibson's cyberpunks, there are no cybercities—anonymous, *anomie*-ful and alienating. However, we have moved through images of comparative isolation to *CyberSociety* (Jones 1995) and *Virtual Culture* (Jones 1997) to a deep consideration of, and some sympathy towards, the idea that early settlers have made towns, villages and communities into which newbies are relatively welcomed.

The concept of community overlaps those of culture and society. Community, in etymology, derives from holding things—people, ideas, places, etc.—in common. Community is closely related, in definition at least, to communality. Yet the elements that bind people together are counterpointed by forces which drive them apart. The extended family, for example, is an explosive combination that brings together, in community, people who are related by blood and/or emotional commit-ments and/or history. It spans generations and gender, and involves relational exchanges that range from indifference to intensity, from love to murder.

Other communities, such as religious communities, may be based on same-sex selection criteria, or a shared interest, as in 'an arts community'. Most communities have an element of choice about them, but there are many—including the nuclear family (we all have a family of origin), schools and prison communities—that include unwilling members. All communities rely upon a conversation, even if it is the meditative actions of the silent religious order, to build community. This conversation can have the aim of convincing community members that the community remains a good home, and members should be active contributors—but such a conversation does not always work. Communities and conversations are dynamic entities and frequently changing, both in nature and in participants.

People invest differently in communities at different times. It may be possible to see someone as part of a community that watches public broadcasting, for example. Membership of a public broadcasting community, however, might take on greater importance at a time of cuts in funding, reduced government support and sponsorship drives. Frequent Flyer clubs, loyalty programmes and the Lexus motor car corporation attempt to persuade consumers that community membership is an important component of their product. But if home is where the heart is, then important communities in life tend to be where time is spent (mental and/or physical), or where there is intensity and anticipation. School, work, family, hobbies, neighbourhoods, religious congregations and campaign organisations are all examples of communities.

Sociologists have distinguished between communities and associations, and some social theorists would define what I term as 'communities' as 'associations'. An association has elements of choice, they argue; a community has elements of necessity. This may have been more valid as a difference in the times—centuries ago—when it was almost impossible to move communities. Nowadays, in most consumer societies, communities of residence reflect individual choice, as do communities of association. Similarly, in those pre-moving-around days, it was difficult—and usually unsatisfactory—to maintain a relationship remotely. For most residents of western societies, however, it is possible to maintain a sense of connectedness over distance.

In the interconnected globe, most people in western countries have choices as to where they live physically, and they have choices as to where they commune emotionally. For a migrant or refugee, the emotional connection with a family of origin in another country can be much stronger and deeper than any connection made with people in the new community. The distinction between community and association lies in a definition that excludes the possibility of a community being anything other than grounded in geography and locality. It does not address the possibility that the quality of interactions can create community, or that community can be forged in technocultural conversation.

Accepting that conversation is central to communities of interaction, technocultural consumption itself can be a topic of conversation —whether relating to television programmes or to a personal choice of a consumer technology. Consumption patterns structure everyday life and help create rhythms that generate the energy and the affinities for life to thrive. Consuming media, and the creation of conversation and communication, provide the raw materials that are crafted into meanings. Hodge and Tripp note, regarding television, that: 'Discourse about television is itself a social force. It is a major site of the mediation of television meanings, a site where television meanings fuse with other meanings into a new text to form a major interface with the world of action and belief' (1986, p. 143). Arguably, discourse about anything— including the Internet—is a social force and builds society. Further, discourse occurs in mediated, in multiply mediated and in unmediated (face-to-face) contexts.

The competition to attract members to communities is a life-or-death exchange. Noelle-Neumann's (1974) 'spiral of silence theory' asserts that a minority opinion is likely to be aired less and less, even if some people continue to support it, simply because the less a view is aired, the more difficult it becomes to air that view. Using a similar spiralling dynamic, the fewer the members in the community, the less rewarding it is to belong to that community, and eventually the community withers and dies. This spiral accelerates when new communities and conversations are opened up, attracting members from the old community. For the declining community, the effect can be annihilating.

It is not always the case that when a new community, or a new conversant, is added to those already existing, all existing conversations are preserved. The process is more commonly one of substitution, with a transitional period during which loyalty, and community membership, lessen. The managerial concept of the span of control, which asserts that the majority of supervisors find it difficult to manage more than about seven subordinates, appears to be generalisable. It is probable that most people have similar limits in terms of managing close relationships. Typically, there would be between five and nine significant individuals (close friends, partners, children, parents) deeply intertwined within a person's life.

Since membership of a community is likely to involve a significant individual relationship as well, a psychoemotional 'span of control' limits the number of communities to which people can realistically belong. As one community or conversation grows in relevance to an individual's life, so another becomes less important; and as one commitment becomes less important, so a space is opened for an involvement elsewhere. Certainly the features of co-evolving communities and conversations, and their waxing and waning, mimic some features of a cyclical (but generally self-sustaining) ecosystem and add credence to Sless' view that we inhabit 'communication ecologies'. Increasingly, the technocultural will be involved in humanity's communications, and in our community ecosystems. We might do well to balance our VL with our RL, but value them both for what they tell us about ourselves, about others and about our humanity.

# References

Alloway, N. 1995, *The construction of gender in early childhood*, Curriculum Corporation, Melbourne

Anderson, B. 1991, *Imagined communities*, 2nd edn, first edn 1983, Verso, London

Ang, I. 1990, Melodramatic identifications: Television fiction and women's fantasy, in *Television and women's culture: The politics of the popular*, ed. M.-E. Brown, Currency Press, Sydney, pp. 75–88

——1991a, *Desperately seeking the audience*, Routledge, London

——1991b, Global media/local meaning, *Media Information Australia*, no. 62, November, pp. 4–8

Ang, P.H. and Yeo, T.M. 1998, *Mass media laws and regulations in Singapore*, Asian Media Information and Communication Centre [AMICC], Singapore

Arendt, H. 1958, *The human condition*, University of Chicago Press, Chicago

Arens, W. 1999, *Contemporary advertising*, 7th edn, Irwin, Boston

Atkins, W. 1995, 'Friendly and useful': Rupert Murdoch and the politics of television in Southeast Asia 1993–95, *Media International Australia*, no. 77, August, pp. 54–64

Aycock, A. and Buchignani, N. 1995, The e-mail murders: reflections on 'dead' letters, in *CyberSociety: computer-mediated communication and community*, ed. S. Jones, Sage, Thousand Oaks, CA, pp. 184–231

Baker, M. 2001, *Families, labour and love*, Allen & Unwin, Sydney

Barr, T. 1994, Australia's information society, in *Framing technology: society, choice and change*, eds L. Green & R. Guinery, Allen & Unwin, Sydney, pp. 91–104

——2000, *newmedia.com.au*, Allen & Unwin, Sydney

Baudrillard, J. 1983, The ecstasy of communication, in *Postmodern culture*, ed. H. Foster, Pluto Press, London, pp. 126–34

——1994, *The illusion of the end*, Polity Press, Cambridge

Bausinger, H. 1984, Media, technology and everyday life, *Media, culture and society*, vol. 6, no. 4, pp. 343–51

Baym, N. 1995, The emergence of community in computer-mediated communication, in *CyberSociety: computer-mediated communication and community*, ed. S. Jones, Sage, Thousand Oaks, CA, pp. 138–63

Benedikt, M., ed. 1991, *Cyberspace: first steps*, MIT Press, Cambridge, MA

Beniger, J. 1986, *The control revolution: technological and economic origins of the information society*, Harvard University Press, Cambridge, MA

Bennett, T. 1982, Theories of the media, theories of society, in *Culture, society and the media*, eds M. Gurevitch, T. Bennett, J. Curran & J. Woollacott, Methuen, London, pp. 30–55

Bennett, T., Boyd-Bowman, S., Mercer, C. and Woollacott, J. 1981, *Popular television and film*, British Film Institute, London

Biddulph, S. 1994, *Manhood: A book about setting men free*, Finch Publishing, Sydney

Bryan, D. 1994, The multilocals, transnationals and communication technology, in *Framing technology: society, choice and change*, eds L. Green & R. Guinery, Allen & Unwin, Sydney, pp. 145–160

Cardiff, D. and Scannell, P. 1987, Broadcasting and national unity, in *Impacts and influences: essays on media and power in the twentieth century*, eds J. Curran, A. Smith & P. Wingate, Methuen, London, pp. 157–73

Carey, J. 1989, *Communication as culture: essays on media and society*, Unwin Hyman, London

Castoriadis, C. 1990, *Le monde morcelé*, Seuil, Paris

Clark, L. and Lewis, D. 1977, *Rape: the price of coercive sexuality*, The Women's Press, Toronto

Clarke, R. 1991, Information technology and dataveillance, in *Computerisation and controversy*, eds C. Dunlop & R. Kling, Academic Press, New York, pp. 496–522

——1994a, Dataveillance: delivering *1984*, in *Framing Technology: society, choice and change*, eds L. Green & R. Guinery, Allen & Unwin, Sydney, pp. 117–30

——1994b, The digital persona and its application to data surveillance, *The information society*, vol. 10, pp. 77–92

Cohen, S. 1980, *Folk devils and moral panics: the creation of the mods and rockers*, 2nd edn, first edn 1972, Martin Robertson, Oxford

Cole, A., Conlon, T., Jackson, S. and Welch, D. 1994, Information technology and gender: problems and proposals, *Gender and Education*, vol. 6, no. 1, p. 78

Corner, J. 1995, *Television form and public address*, Edward Arnold, London

Cunningham, S. and Turner, G. eds 1993, *The media in Australia: industries, texts, audiences*, Allen & Unwin, Sydney

Dayan, D. 1998, Particularistic media and diasporic communications, in *Media, ritual and identity*, eds T. Liebes & J. Curran, Routledge, London, pp. 103–13

Dick, P. 1982, *Do androids dream of electric sheep?* Ballantine Books, New York

Douglas, M. 1978, *Purity and danger*, first pub. 1966, Routledge and Kegan Paul, London

Druckrey, T. 1994, Introduction, in *Culture on the brink: ideologies of technology*, eds G. Bender & T. Druckrey, Bay Press, Seattle, WA, pp. 1–12

Eastwick, R. 1895, *The oracle encyclopaedia*, vol. 1, George Newnes Ltd, London

Else, A. 1996, *False economy: New Zealanders face the conflict between paid and unpaid work,* Tandem Press, North Shore City, NZ

Evans, M. and Butkus, C. 1997, Regulating the emergent: cyberporn and the traditional media, *Media International Australia*, no. 85, November, pp. 62–9

Featherstone, M. 1990, Global culture: an introduction, in *Global culture: nationalism, globalization and modernity*, ed. M. Featherstone (*Theory, culture & society*, vol. 7, special issue), pp. 1–14

Ferguson, H. 1992, Watching the world go round: atrium culture and the psychology of shopping, in *Lifestyle shopping: the subject of consumption*, ed. R. Shields, Routledge, London

Fernback, J. 1997, The individual within the collective: virtual ideology and the realization of collective principles, in *Virtual culture: identity and communication in cybersociety*, ed. S. Jones, Sage, London, pp. 35–54

Franklyn, U. 1992, *The real world of technology*, House of Anansi Press, Ontario

Galvin, M. 1994, Vectory in the Gulf: technology, communications and war, in *Framing technology: society, choice and change*, eds L. Green & R. Guinery, Allen & Unwin, Sydney, pp. 176–90

Game, A. 1991, *Undoing the social: towards a deconstructive sociology*, Open University Press, Milton Keynes

Garnham, N. 1990, *Capitalism and communication, global culture and the economics of information*, Sage, London

Gertsakis, C. 1994, An inconstant politics: thinking about the traditional and the contemporary, in *Culture, difference and the arts*, eds S. Gunew & F. Rizvi, Allen & Unwin, Sydney, pp. 35–53

Giddens, A. 1991, *The consequences of modernity*, Polity Press, Cambridge

Gillard, P., Bow, A. and Wale, K. 1994, *A major line to the outside world from the house: defining the significance of telecommunications in social contexts*, RMIT, Melbourne

Gray, A. 1987, Behind closed doors: video recorders in the home, in *Boxed in: women and television*, eds H. Baehr & G. Dyer, Routledge & Kegan Paul, London, pp. 38–54

——1992, *Video playtime: the gendering of a leisure technology*, Routledge, London

Gray, J. 1992, *Men are from Mars, women are from Venus*, HarperCollins, New York

Green, L. 1996, Technology and conversation: construction and destruction of community, *Australian Journal of Communication*, vol. 23, no. 3, pp. 54–67

——1997, *Multiculturalism and the arts—a laughing matter?*, Paper presented to the Australian and New Zealand Communication Association Conference, La Trobe University, Melbourne, July

——1998, *Communications and the construction of community: consuming the Remote Commercial Television Service in Western Australia*, unpublished PhD thesis, Murdoch University, Western Australia

——1999, The end of the virtual community, *M/C—A Journal of Media and Culture*, vol. 2, no. 8, www.api-network.com/mc/ [June 2001]

——2001, Technoculture: another of those rubbery transdisciplinary terms that means nothing and gets us nowhere?, *Media International Australia Incorporating Culture and Policy*, no. 98, February, pp. 11–25

GVU 1997, *GVU's WWW survey*, Graphics, Visualization and Usability Center, Georgia Institute of Technology. Available online: www.gvu.gatech.edu/user_surveys/ [April 2000]

Habermas, J. 1989, *Structural transformation of the public sphere: an inquiry into a category of bourgeois society*, trans. by T. Burger with the assistance of F. Lawrence, Polity Press, Cambridge

Hale, B. 2000, Amazon: the party's over, *The West Australian*, Saturday, 29 July, p. 58

Haraway, D. 1991, *Simians, cyborgs and women: the reinvention of nature*, Routledge, New York

Hawkins, D., Neal, C., Quester, P. and Best, R. 1994, *Consumer behaviour: implications for marketing strategy*, Irwin, Sydney

Hearn, G., Mandeville, T. and Anthony, D. 1998, *The communication superhighway: social and economic change in the digital age*, Allen & Unwin, Sydney

Hochschild, A. 1989, *The second shift: working parents and the revolution at home*, Viking Penguin, New York

Hodge, B. and Tripp, D. 1986, *Children and television: a semiotic approach*, Polity Press, Cambridge

Hoggart, R. 1958, *The uses of literacy*, Penguin, Harmondsworth

Holmes, D. 1997, Virtual identity: communities of broadcast, communities of interactivity, in *Virtual politics: identity and community in cyberspace*, ed. D. Holmes, Sage, London, pp. 26–45

Hughes, T. 1999, Edison and electric light, in *The social shaping of technology: how the refrigerator got its hum*, eds D. MacKenzie & J. Wajcman, 2nd edn, Open University Press, Milton Keynes, pp. 50–63

Innis, H. 1991, *The bias of communication*, first pub. 1951, University of Toronto Press, Toronto

Jameson, F. 1984, Postmodernism, or the cultural logic of late capitalism, *New Left Review*, no. 146, pp. 53–92

Jaspers, K. 1947, *The question of German guilt*, Dial Press, New York

Johnson, J. 1998, *Information policies: guide*, Edith Cowan University, Perth

Jones, B. 1982, *Sleepers, wake!*, 1st edn, Oxford University Press, Melbourne

——1995, *Sleepers, wake! Technology and the future of work*, 4th edn, Oxford University Press, Melbourne

Jones, S., ed. 1995, *CyberSociety: computer-mediated community and communication*, Sage, Thousand Oaks, CA

——ed. 1997, *Virtual culture: identity and communication in cybersociety*, Sage, London

——ed. 1998, *CyberSociety 2.0: revisiting computer-mediated communication and community*, Sage, Thousand Oaks, CA

Kadrey, R. 1994, alt.sex.bondage, *Wired*, vol. 2, no. 6, pp. 40–2

Katz, E. and Lazarsfeld, P. 1955, *Personal influence*, Free Press, New York

Kennedy, A. 1999, *The Internet: The rough guide 2000*, Rough Guides Ltd, London

Khoo, E., Trang, T., Sia, P., Songan, P., Harris, R. and Bala, P. 2000, Rural secondary school teachers' attitudes towards information technology: a study in the Kelabit Highlands of Bario, Borneo, in *Proceedings: cultural attitudes towards communication and technology 2000*, eds F. Sudweeks & C. Ess, Murdoch University, Perth, pp. 57–73

Kibby, M. 1997, Babes on the Web: sex, identity and the home page, *Media International Australia*, no. 84, May, pp. 39–45

Kidder, T. 1982, *The soul of a new machine*, Penguin, Harmondsworth

Kitchin, R. 1998, *Cyberspace: the world in the wires*, John Wiley and Sons, Chichester

Kopytoff, I. 1986, The cultural biography of things: commoditization as a process, in *The social life of things: commodities in a cultural perspective*, ed. A. Appadurai, Cambridge University Press, Cambridge, pp. 64–91

Kraut, R., Patterson, M., Lundmark, V., Kiesler, S., Mukopadhyay, T. and Scherlis, W. 1998, Internet paradox: a social technology that reduces social involvement and psychological well-being?, *American Psychologist*, vol. 53, no. 9, pp. 1017–31

Kuhn, A. ed. 1990, *Alien zone: cultural theory and contemporary science fiction cinema*, Verso, London

Kuhn, T. 1996, *The structure of scientific revolutions*, 3rd edn, first pub. 1962, University of Chicago Press, Chicago

Lajoie, M. 1996, Psychoanalysis and cyberspace, in *Cultures of Internet: virtual spaces, real histories and living bodies*, ed. R. Shields, Sage, London, pp. 153–69

Lasswell, H., Casey, R. and Smith, B. eds 1969, *Propaganda and promotional activities*, first pub. 1935, University of Chicago Press, Chicago

Lee, P.S. 1995, A case against the thesis of communication imperialism: the audience's response to foreign TV programmes in Hong Kong, *Australian Journal of Communication*, vol. 22, no. 3, pp. 63–81

Leslie, J. 1993, Technology: MUDroom, *Atlantic Monthly*, no. 272, pp. 28–34

Litchenberg, J. 1991, *Democracy and the mass media*, Cambridge University Press, Cambridge

Livingstone, S. 1992, The meaning of domestic technologies: a personal construct analysis of familial gender relations, in *Consuming technologies: media and information in domestic spaces*, eds R. Silverstone & E. Hirsch, Routledge, London, pp. 113–30

Los Angeles Times 2000, Napster's mobile music fans show inadequacy of laws, *The West Australian*, Saturday, 29 July, p. 20

MacKenzie, D. and Wajcman, J. eds 1999, *The social shaping of technology: how the refrigerator got its hum*, 2nd edn, first pub. 1985, Open University Press, Milton Keynes

Mahathir, M. 1991, *Malaysia: the way forward,* paper presented at the Malaysian Business Council, Center for Economic Research and Services, Kuala Lumpur

Makridakis, S. 1995, The forthcoming information revolution: its impacts on society and firms, *Futures*, vol. 27, no. 8, Oct., pp. 799–822

Malaysia, Ministry of Education 1997, A vision of the Malaysian Smart School [on-line]. Available: http://welcome.to/smart_school [June 2001]

Marshall, P.D. 1997, Technophobia: video games, computer hacks and cybernetics, *Media International Australia*, no. 85, November, pp. 70–8

Marshall, T. 1949, *Citizenship and social class*, Cambridge University Press, Cambridge

Marvin, C. 1988, *When old tchnologies were new*, Oxford University Press, Oxford

——1989, Experts, black boxes and artifacts: new allegories for the history of the electric media, in *Re-thinking communication*, vol. 2, eds B. Dervin et al., Sage, London, pp. 118–98

Maslow, A. 1948, 'Higher' and 'lower' needs, *Journal of Psychology*, vol. 25, pp. 433–6

Masuda, Y. 1972, *Social impact of computerization: an application of the pattern model for industrial society*, Kodansha, Tokyo

——1978, Future perspectives for information utility, in *Evolution in computer communications*, International Council for Computer Communications, Amsterdam

May, G. 2000, Worldviews, assumptions and typologies of the future, *Journal of Future Studies*, vol. 5, no. 2, November, pp. 37–51.

McArthur, C. 1985, Scotland's story, *Framework*, nos. 26–7, pp. 64–74

McLuhan, M. 1964, *Understanding media*, McGraw-Hill, New York

McLuhan, M. and Fiore, Q. 1968, *War and peace in the global village*, Bantam Books, New York

Melody, W. 1990, The information in IT: 'where lies the public interest?', *Intermedia*, vol. 18, no. 3, June/July, pp. 10–18

Meyrowitz, J. 1985, *No sense of place: the impact of electronic media on social behaviour*, Oxford University Press, New York

Michaels, E. 1994, *Bad Aboriginal art*, Allen & Unwin, Sydney

Miles, I. 1985, *Social indicators for human development*, Francis Pinter, London

Miller, D. 1992, *The Young and the Restless* in Trinidad: a case of the local and the global in mass consumption, in *Consuming technologies: media and information in domestic spaces*, eds R. Silverstone & E. Hirsch, Routledge, London, pp. 163–82

Molnar, H. 1994, *Indigenous media developments in Australia: inadequate government response to Indigenous broadcasting initiatives*, paper presented to the International Communication Association Conference, Sydney, 11–15 July

Moores, S. 1996, *Satellite television and everyday life: articulating technology*, Acamedia Research Monograph 18, University of Luton Press, Luton

Morgan, G. 1997, *Images of organization*, 2nd edn, Sage, Thousand Oaks, CA

Morley, D. 1980, *The* Nationwide *audience: structure and decoding*, BFI Television Monograph, BFI, London

——1986, *Family television: cultural power and domestic leisure*, Routledge, London

——1991, Where the global meets the local: notes from the sitting room, *Screen*, vol. 32, no. 1, Spring, pp. 1–15

——1995, Theories of consumption in media studies, in *Acknowledging consumption: a review of new studies*, ed. D. Miller, Routledge, London, pp. 296–328

Morley, D. and Robins, K. 1995, *Spaces of identity: global media, electronic landscapes and cultural boundaries*, Routledge, London

Morris, P. 1996, Newspapers and the new information media, *Media International Australia*, no. 79, February, pp. 10–21

Murdock, G. and Golding, P. 1989, Information poverty and political inequality: citizenship in the age of privatized communications, *Journal of Communication*, vol. 39, no. 3, pp. 180–95

Murdock, G., Hartmann, P. and Gray, P. 1992, Contextualising home computing: resources and practices, in *Consuming technologies: media and information in domestic spaces*, eds R. Silverstone & E. Hirsch, Routledge, London, pp. 146–60

Nightingale, V. 1990, Women as audiences, in *Television and women's culture: the politics of the popular*, ed. M.-E. Brown, Currency Press, Sydney, pp. 25–36

Noelle-Neumann, E. 1974, The spiral of silence: a theory of public opinion, *Journal of Communication*, vol. 24, pp. 43–51

Oakley, A. 1974, *Housewife*, Allen Lane, London

O'Shaughnessy, M. 1999, *Media and Society: an introduction*, Oxford University Press, Melbourne

Palandri, M. and Green, L. 2000, Image management in a virtual bondage, discipline and sadomasochist community: A cyber-ethnographic study, *CyberPsychology and behavior*, vol. 3, no. 4, August, pp. 631–41, www.liebertpub.com/CPB

Palmer, L. 1994, Regulating technology, in *Framing technology: society, choice and change*, eds L. Green & R. Guinery, Allen & Unwin, Sydney, pp. 77–90

Penley, C. and Ross, A. eds 1991, *Technoculture*, University of Minnesota Press, Minnesota

Porat, M. 1977, *The information economy, definition and measurement*, Office of Telecommunications, US Department of Commerce, Washington DC

Porush, D. 1998, Telepathy: alphabetic consciousness and the age of cyborg illiteracy, in *Virtual futures: cyberotics, technology and post-human pragmatism*, eds J. Dixon & E. Cassidy, Routledge, London, pp. 45–64

Poster, M. 1995, *The second media age*, Polity Press, Oxford

Pusey, A. 1995, *Wire journalism* [talk], Edith Cowan University, Perth, August

Radway, J. 1984, *Reading the romance*, University of North Carolina Press, Chapel Hill, NC

Rakow, L. 1992, *Gender on the line: Women, the telephone and community life*, University of Illinois Press, Urbana

Rakow, L. and Navarro, V. 1993, Remote mothering and the parallel shift: women meet the cellular telephone, in *Critical studies in mass communication*, vol. 10, pp. 144–57

Rath, C.-D. 1985, The invisible network, in *Television in transition*, eds P. Drummond & R. Paterson, British Film Institute, London, pp. 199–204

Reinecke, I. 1987, Information and the poverty of technology, in *Communications and the media in Australia*, eds T. Wheelwright & K. Buckley, Allen & Unwin, Sydney, pp. 21–39

Rheingold, H. 1993, *The virtual community: homesteading on the electronic frontier*, available online: www.rheingold.com/vc/book [June 2001]

Rimmer, M. 2001, Napster: Infinite digital jukebox or pirate bazaar?, *Media International Australia Incorporating Culture and Policy*, no. 98, February, pp. 27–38

Ritzer, G. 1996, *The McDonaldization of society: an investigation into the changing character of contemporary social life*, rev. edn, Pine Forge Press, Thousand Oaks, CA

Rogers, E. 1995, *Diffusion of innovations*, 4th edn, Free Press, New York

Rogers, E. and Larsen, J. 1984, *Silicon Valley fever: growth of high technology culture*, Basic Books, New York

Roszak, T. 1994, *The cult of information: a neo-Luddite treatise on high tech, artificial intelligence and the true art of thinking*, University of California Press, California

Rule, J., McAdam, D., Stearns, L. and Uglow, D. 1980, *The politics of privacy*, New American Library, New York

Ryan, M. and Kellner, D. 1990, Technophobia, in *Alien zone: cultural theory and contemporary science fiction cinema*, ed. A. Kuhn, Verso, London, pp. 58–65

Savage, J.G. 1989, *The politics of international telecommunication regulation*, Westview Press, Boulder, CO

Schiffman, L., Bednall, D., Watson, J. and Kanuk, L. 1997, *Consumer behaviour*, Prentice Hall, Sydney

Schiller, H. 1991, Not yet the post-imperialist era, *Critical studies in mass communication*, vol. 8, no. 1, March, pp. 13–28

Schultz, J. 1990, Media flowering under watchful eyes, *Australian Society*, vol. 9, no. 10, October, pp. 8–9

——1994, Universal suffrage? Technology and democracy, in *Framing technology: society, choice and change*, eds L. Green & R. Guinery, Allen & Unwin, Sydney, pp. 105–16

——1998, *Reviving the fourth estate: democracy, accountability and the media*, Cambridge University Press, Melbourne

——ed. 1994a, *Not just another business: journalists, citizens and the media*, Pluto Press/Monash University, Melbourne

Scruton, R. 1994, *Modern philosophy: an introduction and survey*, Sinclair-Stevenson, London

Shawcross, W. 1992, *Rupert Murdoch*, Chatto & Windus, London

Silverstone, R. 1994, *Television and everyday life*, Routledge, London

Silverstone, R., Hirsch, E. and Morley, D. 1992, Information and communication technologies in the moral economy of the household, in *Consuming technologies: media and information in domestic spaces*, eds R. Silverstone & E. Hirsch, Routledge, London, pp. 15–31

Simmel, G. 1991, Money in modern culture, *Theory, Culture & Society*, no. 8, pp. 17–31

Sinclair, J., Jacka, L. and Cunningham, S. 1996, *Global vision: revising the debate from the periphery*, Oxford University Press, Melbourne

Sless, D. 1988, Forms of control, *Australian Journal of Communication*, vol. 14, pp. 57–69

——1994, Between dreams and reality, *Communication News*, vol. 7, no. 4, Communication Research Institute of Australia, Canberra

——1995, Our communication ecologies, in *The informationless society*, ed. D. Sless, Communication Research Press, Canberra, pp. 1–13

Smith, J. 1989, *Misogynies*, Faber and Faber, London

Smith, J. and Gumbel, A. 1999, Activists of the world, unite!, *The Independent on Sunday*, 5 December, p. 16

Spender, D. 1995, *Nattering on the Net: women, power and cyberspace*, Spinifex, Melbourne

St Clair, J. 1995, Future demand for the information superhighway in the home, in *The informationless society*, ed. D. Sless, Communication Research Press, Canberra, pp. 15–18

Stockwell, S. 1997, Panic at the port, *Media International Australia*, no. 85, November, pp. 56–61

Stone A. 1991, Will the real body please stand up? Boundary stories about virtual cultures, in *Cyberspace: first steps*, ed. M. Benedikt, MIT Press, Cambridge, Mass, pp. 81–118

Stonier, T. 1990, *Information and the internal structure of the universe: an exploration into information physics*, Springer-Verlag, London

Stratton, J. and Ang, I. 1998, Multicultural imagined communities: cultural difference and national identity in the USA and Australia, in *Multicultural states: rethinking difference and identity*, ed. D. Bennett, Routledge, London, pp. 135–62

Suler, J. 1996, Computer and cyberspace addiction [online] www.rider.edu/users/suler/psycyber/cybaddict.html [June 2001]

Tester, K. 1997, *Moral culture*, Sage, London

Todd, J. 1995, *Colonial technology: science and the transfer of innovation to Australia*, Cambridge University Press, Cambridge

Tolerton, J. 1996, Balancing act, *Next*, no. 67, October, Auckland

Toner, B. 1982, *The facts of rape*, rev. edn, Arrow Books, London

Tulloch, J. and Jenkins, H. 1995, *Science fiction audiences: watching* Star Trek *and* Dr Who, Routledge, London

Turkle, S. 1984, *The second self: computers and the human spirit*, Granada, London

——1988, Computational reticence: why women fear the intimate machine, in *Technology and women's voices*, ed. C. Kramarae, Routledge & Kegan Paul, London

Turner, G. 1996, *British Cultural Studies: an introduction*, 2nd edn, Routledge, London

Turner, G. and Cunningham, S. 1993, The media in Australia today, in *The media in Australia: industries, texts, audiences*, eds S. Cunningham & G. Turner, Allen & Unwin, Sydney, pp. 3–15

Umble, D. 1992, The Amish and the telephone: resistance and reconstruction, in *Consuming technologies: media and information in domestic spaces*, eds R. Silverstone & E. Hirsch, Routledge, London, pp. 183–94

Wajcman, J. 1991, *Feminism confronts technology*, Allen & Unwin, Sydney

——1994, Technological a/genders: technology, culture and class, in *Framing Technology: society, choice and change*, eds L. Green & R. Guinery, Allen & Unwin, Sydney pp. 3–14

Wallace, P. 1999, *The psychology of the Internet*, Cambridge University Press, Cambridge

Wark, M. 1990, Europe's masked ball: East meets West at the wall, *New Formations*, no. 12, Winter, pp. 33–42

——1991, News bites: war TV in the Gulf, *Meanjin*, vol. 50, no. 2, pp. 5–17

Watson, N. 1997, Why we argue about virtual community: a case study of the phish.net fan community, in *Virtual culture: identity and communication in cybersociety*, ed. S.G. Jones, Sage, London, pp. 102–32

Weizenbaum, J. 1976, *Computer power and human reason: from judgement to calculation*, Penguin, Harmondsworth

Wheelock, J. 1992, Personal computers, gender and an institutional model of the household, in *Consuming technologies: media and information in domestic spaces*, eds. R. Silverstone & E. Hirsch, Routledge, London, pp. 97–112

Wilbur, S. 1997, An archaeology of cyberspaces: virtuality, community, identity, in *Internet culture*, ed. D. Porter, Routledge, New York, pp. 5–22

Williams, R. 1966, *Culture and society 1780–1950*, first pub. 1958, Penguin, London

Willis, A. 2000, Nerdy no more: a case study of early *Wired* (1993–96), in *Cultural attitudes towards technology and communication 2000*, eds C. Ess & F. Sudweeks, Murdoch University, Perth, pp. 361–72

Winter, I. ed. 2000, *Social capital and public policy in Australia*, Australian Institute of Family Studies, Melbourne

*Wired* 1994, No cops, no laws, no wimps—Are you a girlie-man or a megaracer?, *Wired*, vol. 2, no. 12, p. 113

Young, K. 1998, *Caught in the net: How to recognize the signs of Internet addiction and a winning strategy for recovery*, John Wiley, New York

# INDEX

goals vs needs, 56
government, 133–5, 139, 141; and
    public interest, 99
groupmind: and online community,
    199
guilt levels, 206
Gulf War 1991: media coverage of,
    67–8
gun control, 3–5

Habermas, Jurgen: idealised view of
    public sphere, 116–17, 128, 153
hackers: at MIT, 177; principled, 177;
    as subculture, 177–8, 180
hardwired, xviii–xix
hate sites, 147; as moral panics, 224
hatred online: case studies, 204–5
Hebrew, ancient, 208–10; cognitive
    habits required to learn, 209
hegemony, xix
helplessness, 8, 75, 107, 109, 175
Hemingway, Ernest, 64
high involvement decisions, 29, 38,
    42
home vs household, 44
*homo incommunicatus*, 111–12
*homo informaticus*, 111–12
homogenisation, 70–1
households, 58, 128; as audience, 48;
    and community, 59; definition of,
    44; relationship with society, 44–6;
    technologised, 43–4; technology
    choices of, 45; as unit of
    consumption, 48
hypertext transfer protocol (http), xix

identity, 130–1; of the Internet, 226;
    on the Internet, 165, 226
imperialism, xix
incorporation, 45

*Independence Day* (film), 168
indigenous culture, and broadcast
    television, 126–8; representation
    by mass media, 126
information, xix, 78; collection, 90–2;
    commercialisation, 118; as
    commodity, 79; controlled by
    elites, 79–80; definitions, 78–82;
    dissemination and regulation,
    144–5; divide maintained by First
    World, 108–9; economy, 73–6;
    equity of access to, 104; about
    individuals, 79–80, 90–1, 95, 97;
    information characteristics, 80–1;
    information loss effects, 103–4,
    106–7; overload, 75, 78, 93;
    ownership, First World notions of,
    128; policy, 140, 145; poverty, 115;
    proliferation, 80, 83; relation to
    power and control, 78; revolution,
    82; standardisation, 90; vs
    storytelling, 207–8; transfer in
    Aboriginal culture, 126; not a
    trigger to action, 206; and trust,
    92
information access, 75, 92–3, 136; as
    public good, 124; regulation,
    144–5
information and communication
    technologies (ICTs), xix; access,
    108; access by adolescents, 49–50;
    and collective identity, 58; and
    community, 47; and community
    building, 59–60; consumption,
    49–50, 53; domestication, 43–4;
    and family relationships, 50–4,
    57–8; and household dynamics,
    50–4; incorporation, 45; inherent
    pleasure, 49–50; layering of
    adoption, 73; and moral panics,